HISLAM

Corrupt Religion and the Search for Spiritual Peace

E. Douglass Brown, Ph.D.

Copyright © 2023 by E. Douglass Brown, Ph.D.

No part of this book may be reproduced, stored in a retrieval system, or transmitted by any means, electronic, mechanical, photocopying, recording, or otherwise, without written permission from the author.

ISBN: 978-1-952302-76-3 (sc)
ISBN: 978-1-952302-77-0 (hc)
ISBN: 978-1-952302-78-7 (e)

Library of Congress Control Number: 2021920368

Preface

The title of this book is *Hislam*. You may wonder if Hislam is not a soft sell title for the religion known as Islam. The word *Islam* literally means a "state or condition of submission;" i.e., submission to God. Why the title Hislam? You may have concerns that this book is simply an attempt to promote Islam as it is understood and professed by most Muslims. This is not the case. Hislam designates the *corruption* of the human worship of God and spiritual yearning. Hislam sounds similar to the word Islam. **Hislam is *not* Islam.** Not at all related to authentic Islam, Hislam encompasses *all* expressions of spiritual falsehood.

The "His" in Hislam refers to the introduction, acceptance, and practice of religious beliefs and practices never revealed and authorized by God. Someone (i.e., the "His") other than God *owns* or is the *source* of the innovations and false practices. Hislam consists of: 1) hundreds of denominations, branches, offshoots, and sects of Judaism, Christianity, Islam, and other spiritual belief systems, 2) cultural ideologies deemed as religions, 3) superstitions, and 4) secret systems. *It is God's Plan to rid Islam, Judaism, Christianity, and all other revealed religions of Hislam.* Throughout life, each individual is guided to certain crossroads that serve as opportunities for the individual to hopefully move closer to spiritual truth. What one person sees as an opportunity to advance spiritually another person perceives as an annoyance or irritant. This is the spiritual reality of freedom of choice. A reader of this book may ponder, "What relevance does this information have for me?" It is not for me to insist that readers accept the contents of this book. I can say with confidence that the proven information in this book is an aid in discovering or re-affirming the submission and peace experienced by all *sincere* spiritual seekers. This book is not an aid along the road to spiritual peace because I think it is or I wrote it. True spiritual peace cannot be attained by *clinging* to Hislam, especially after being informed about it.

With the first *intentional* distortion of Divinely-revealed spiritual truth, Hislam emerged. The first Hislamist probably shared his or her misinterpretation of the worship of God with a few people. What started out as a few individuals deviating from Divine guidance has evolved into the *most massive system of corruption, distortion, and denial in history.* The system is distorted religion. Hislam also influences people who do not believe in God and people who do not take human spirituality seriously. In the case of atheists, distorted religion has helped escort many of them away from belief in God. It has also provided fodder for many atheists' persistent disbelief. Hislam cannot forcibly push a person away from the worship of God. If a person wants to worship God in the correct manner, the person intuitively realizes, by God's will, that every movement away from Hislam is movement towards the true worship of God. The specific nature and course of such movement is uniquely tailored to each individual. Movement towards or away from Hislam is consistent with an individual's innermost spiritual intentions.

Raised in an African-American Christian family in urban middle America, I enthusiastically embraced the religion of my parents, relatives, and friends. As a child, my parents took me to Sunday school and I enjoyed listening to stories about Jesus and other prophets. I clung with fascination to narratives about miracles; church on Sunday was an opportunity to visit relatives and see neighborhood friends dressed up in their 'Sunday best.' I belonged to a small well-organized tight knit family church. Many of the ministers in the church were my great uncles. For me, church *was* family. No more than three and a half feet tall, I remember peering up at my father, grandfather, uncles, and great uncles. The men folk in my family left an indelible impression on me. They were independent, hard working, studious, honest, God-conscious men. As I grew older, my interest in Sunday school and church services waned. But, the seed of spiritual consciousness had been firmly planted. In my adolescence and high school years, I developed interests that pulled me away from weekly church attendance. In my late teens, the voices of the civil rights movement and the thrust towards self-definition in the African-American community sparked a strong curiosity in me about things "African" and in non-Western belief systems. Soon enough, I read material about false Christian doctrines. Following some inquiries of my own, I gradually divested myself of the false doctrines. I continue to believe in God, wholeheartedly identify with the truths in Christianity, and remain open to all truths about the worship of God.

Islam intrigued me. I was moved by its universality, acceptance of all people, and the Oneness of God. This was a very potent message amidst the ethnic group tensions (i.e., racism) and inequities in the U.S. at that time. The question that came to my mind was, "How could God be partial to any group of people based on skin color or anything other than righteousness?" I was tired of rhetoric from all sides about the "color" of Jesus, the "color" of God, racial and ethnic gods, and fights about religion. I moved closer to Islam. Yet, I did not make a wholehearted commitment to embrace Islam until my sophomore year in college. In that collegiate period, I met Muslim students and exchanged views with them and learned more about key tenets of Islam. The moment of truth came in my sophomore year. I was afraid and seated alone in a small cubicle in the school library. In retrospect, I fully understand how an individual finds comfort in believing that he or she is headed in the right direction, especially if the belief is embraced by a majority. The thought that I was about to step outside of the religion of my family, relatives, and friends was quite unsettling. But, my spiritual comfort zone was penetrated by truths that I could not ignore. I prayed to God to guide and strengthen me against what I anticipated would be a tide of suspicion and even rejection from some family members, friends, and others who know me. My initial fear that I was about to tread down the wrong spiritual path was overwhelming. But, the certainty that God guides and protects the sincere obliterated the fear. In such situations, one should not doubt God's Omnipotence and Mercy. Countless numbers of individuals have had and countless numbers in future generations will have similar experiences of movement from religious falsehood to religious truth in their lives. This is God's system.

The decision not to ignore the truth had less to do with me and more to do with what God knows about each soul. There is no room for me to congratulate myself for "my insight." *I could not ignore the truths because I was guided by God not to ignore them.* I prayed to God to protect me from making the wrong decision and then I decided to move closer. God answered my prayer. I thank Almighty God for the spiritual strength and vision to 'move closer' and trust Him, and for disabling any fears implanted in me to ignore the truth. By God leave, I made a commitment to separate from false doctrines of any religion.

Like committed followers of any faith who study their religion, I immersed myself in traditional canons of Islam and read some translated writings of early Islamic scholars. I wrote numerous articles about Islam and psychology. In 1972, I returned to St. Louis University in order to pursue a Doctorate degree in Psychology. When I contacted the Muslim community at St. Louis University, I met a Muslim Egyptian-American named Dr. Rashad Khalifa. I was free of the Hislam in Christianity. Unbeknown to me, my entrance into that small Muslim community jettisoned my journey towards independence from the Hislam in Islam. A person does not have to become a Muslim, in the traditional sense before divesture of Hislam. What I have shared with you are aspects of my journey, an on-going journey that, by God's grace, inspired me to write this book. Each person is on his or her spiritual journey.

Humans have an innate desire for inner peace and serenity. Many people have discovered that this serenity and peace only comes from the acceptance of God into their lives. In seeking God's presence, a person attains the highest destiny. The innate human yearning to connect with God is from God. You acknowledged your spiritual yearning and God's Plan for all creation before the beginning of time. Human birth into this time/space world is part of God's Plan. According to this Plan, you have a traveler's manual that the *real* you follows unknowingly and unerringly. The manual leads you from point to point, moment to moment, guidepost to guidepost, and insight to insight in this life. You have the precise mental, spiritual, and physical faculties that you need to tread your path in this world. Each individual has what he or she needs to tread life's path. By your beliefs and intentional deeds, you are completing your journey on a path that leads to God's Presence and Peace, or away from God.

This book is not meant to encourage you to abandon any idea, belief, or behavior that is genuinely conducive to true spiritual growth and happiness. An idea, belief or behavior is conducive to spiritual growth to the extent that it is *congruent* with God's revealed guidance and free of Hislam. This book is not a "put down" of religion. It is a candid truthful discussion of the difference between revealed Divine guidance and the distortion of religion. Submission to God and seeking God's Presence are the most important enterprises a human being can undertake. The *real you* knows that this is true. The other "you" ignores the traveler's manual. The other "you" thinks it knows what it is, knows what to believe, knows what it wants, and knows what it needs. The other "you" has been maneuvering to get the upper hand for a long time. It is part of life in this world.

When an individual converses with you, the person may refer to you by your name or just use the word "you." Depending on the nature of the information, either the *real you* or the other "you" pays attention. The other "you" will not like some truths discussed in this book. How do I know that? The "you" that I once thought was me did not take kindly to becoming aware that I had been misled and misinformed. Had I followed the other "you" in me, my *real self* could not return to God's true path.

Doctrinal distortions of religion are like thick dead underbrush with sharp thickets along a once beautiful path. To journey on the path towards submission to God alone, is to recognize and disconnect from the underbrush, the doctrinal distortions and false practices. When you follow the Creator's directives for humanity, you cannot be spiritually maimed and injured by *distortion and deceit*. Doctrinal "weeds" and "thickets" are cleared away so your soul can grow and you can move closer to God, in this life and in the Hereafter.

Some people become resentful and guarded when informed about religious distortions that have been promoted as truth for so long. Through distortion and deceit, Satan and his human compatriots have attempted to render religion and the worship of God meaningless. An inner current of intense spiritual emotions in one's heart is surrounded by an external vortex of religious deceit and distortion. Those inner spiritual feelings include the love of God, the desire to please God, and spiritual steadfastness. Your expression of the innate spiritual feelings and yearning should not be misread as proof that Hislamic beliefs and practices are true. When a person refuses to examine Hislamic doctrines, the person's spiritual feelings and yearning are degraded to love of a "god" (with a *small* "g"), the desire to please a "god," and allegiance to doctrinal distortions. The "god" is anyone, anything, any doctrine, any idea, or any belief the person believes is superior to authentic Divine guidance.

As an illustration of the degradation of spiritual yearning, imagine a person who is enraptured by the scent and color of roses. When the person thinks about the scent and color of roses, the person has very beautiful feelings. When someone presents "fake flowers" that look like roses, the person experiences some of those same feelings. The person's *belief* and *perception* that the "fake flowers" are roses kindles strong positive feelings. No longer as certain about the true shape, color, and scent of a rose, a sincere person can be temporarily led to believe that "fake flowers" are real roses. Everything that looks like a rose is not a rose. Hence, everything that appears to be the worship of God is not.

"The relief is in the belief and the grief is in the belief." Twenty-seven years ago, I heard these words spoken by a fellow Muslim and professional psychiatrist. Seared onto my consciousness and memory, the words were in response to my reactions to witnessing individuals with medical injuries and conditions go to a revered rural religious leader in their hometown and supposedly be "instantly healed." The "healed" individuals apparently had not received any medical attention prior to going to the local religious leader. Such scenarios take place daily throughout the world. Most of the scenarios are counterfeit, especially when "healers" invoke the names of individuals, dieties, and forces other than God. In many cases, the "healed" feel compelled to "feel cured," to shout and give praise to their "healers," and amplify their *belief* in false doctrines. The thought of not being "cured" is simply to devastating to contemplate. If I am not healed does it mean that I am not a true believer? What will others think about me? Will others abandon me? I again turn to the analogy about "fake flowers." For some individuals, the thought of not responding joyously to false religious doctrines, especially in the presence of others, is to devastating to contemplate. The person dismisses verifiable information that contradicts false spiritual teachings (i.e., "fake flowers").

Four factors influence how a person perceives or interprets information and experience. The factors are *constancy, selectivity, set,* and *motivation. Constancy* occurs when some information or experience is repeated the same way with little variation. *Selectivity* is present when a person tends to see what he or she *wants* to see, rather than what there is to see. *Set* means that a person tends to see what he or she *expects* to see. In this case, m*otivation* means that a person's *needs and values* influence how the person perceives and interprets information and experience.

Most people cling to false spiritual teachings because the teachings (i.e., "fake flowers") have been repeated to them for so long (constancy). People accept "fake flowers" because they *want* the "fake flowers" (selectivity). People expect you to give them "fake flowers" (set). Such persons' spiritual values and yearning have been shaped so that they become satisfied with "fake flowers" (motivation). In contrast, sincere seekers *consistently want* real roses (i.e., to be aware of spiritual truth), *expect* to see real roses, and are *motivated* to get real roses. Regardless of religious identification, sincere spiritual seekers do not dismiss proven verifiable information that contradicts false spiritual teachings. By God's grace, the real you can overcome any feeling that the truth about the worship of God is to devastating for you to contemplate.

No person who sincerely believes that a false religious doctrine or practice is true would readily abandon it without question. You may read information in this book that initially seems difficult to accept. Figuratively speaking, the exposure of cherished false spiritual doctrines is like an "iron wrecking ball" that knocks down a "belief structure" that is suppose to protect and shield individuals from assaults to their faith. Many individuals do everything they can to stop the "iron wrecking ball" from striking or shattering false religious structures. But, the brick wall starts to shatter and fall on the very people it was allegedly erected to protect. A person might exclaim, "What is happening to the wall!... It's scary...We have to keep the wall together!" *Any positive feelings you may have about false religious doctrines are not generated by the doctrines.* Independent of the false doctrines, the genuine spiritual feelings you have are a gift and guiding light from God. The feelings refresh and invigorate your yearning to please God. This is a connection that you should break. If you do not break it, it will spiritually break you. It is each person's responsibility to cultivate genuine spiritual yearning. In identifying weeds and thorns along the spiritual path, this book is a narration of *proven* facts, regardless of whether a reader accepts the facts. I did not write *Hislam* to convince a reader to join any congregation or group. Submission, the religion of creation, is for anyone anywhere who sincerely wants to worship God alone.

I frequently hear questions like: "Well, who is to say that God placed a miraculous code in any book? Do you think that your definition of right and wrong is the correct one? Do you think that your religion is better than mine? Are you trying to pressure me into believing that I am wrong?" The *fact* is that Our Creator placed a miraculous mathematical Code in the Divine revelation known as the Quran, and in other authentic scriptures. You no longer have to guess and question if the narratives about past prophets and their communities are true. You do not have to doubt that the information in the Quran is from God. You can distinguish between truth and falsehood in revealed scriptures that have been distorted. A sincere seeker's belief in God is strengthened by virtue of the existence of such a Code. Discussed in the index of this book, the purposes of the Code are stated in the Quran.

Divine guidance and the basic parameters of moral right and wrong are determined by God in His revelations to humanity. The belief that moral parameters are left up to each individual to determine, is an arbitrary social construction.

Depending on whether the *"real you"* or the other "you" has the upper hand, you choose the spiritual path you want to tread in this life.

Almighty God has granted us minds and intelligence. There is no force or coercion when it comes to the worship of God. Seek answers to your questions and examine all evidence and proof. There is no greater journey in this life than to return to the path of spiritual Truth. This book is for anyone who is interested to know the truth about the worship of God, not my truth or anyone else's truth, not my road or anyone else's road. Alongside the weeds and thorns in this perennial journey, there is tremendous awesome beauty. If you choose to seek out the beauty of submission to God alone, do not mistake the weeds and thorns of Hislam for healthy life-giving flora along the spiritual path.

E. Douglass Brown

Grateful acknowledgement is due to Abdullah Arik, Lydia Kelley, R. A. Mitchell, Lisa Spray, and Paul Thomas for their critical feedback. Michael Landwehr merits particular acknowledgement for his editorial input and assistance.

All Praise be to God.

Contents

Preface		iii
Chapter 1	Proof for the Spiritual Seeker	1
Chapter 2	Distortions of Judaism	27
Chapter 3	Distortions of Christianity	65
Chapter 4	Distortions of Islam	103
Chapter 5	Distortions in Other Religions	135
Chapter 6	Professional Clerics: A Bogus Institution	149
Chapter 7	Truth about Religion: A Matter of National Security	161
Chapter 8	A Conclusion Begins	217
Appendix		227
Index		241

One

Proof for the Spiritual Seeker

> *You shall invite to the path of your Lord with wisdom and kind enlightenment, and debate with them in the best possible manner. Your Lord knows best who has strayed from His path, and He knows best who are the guided ones. (Quran, 16:125)*[1]

With a sacred travel manual in hand and as a child of innocence, you begin a journey like millions who preceded you on a most inviting beautiful path. All that you sense, beacons you on. Moving with ease and without fear, you see animals, large green trees, and a clear creek glistening in the sunlight. Colorful insects and butterflies pollinate beautiful flowers. Your feet gently rest upon sun-warmed soil. Breathing clean fresh air, you look up into the vast blue sky. Birds of every size, shape, and color hover and soar above. Passing heavily laden fruit trees, you pluck fruit from long branches, eat some, and take some to enjoy later. Reaching another crystal-clear creek filled with fish, you swim and wash yourself. Downstream, you see calm ponds filled with beautiful lotus flowers. From every direction, there is beauty, serenity, and harmony. Walking on, your amazement continues. You joyously say, "What made this...How did I get here?"

Time passes. Eventually, the path starts to divide. One course seems to repeat all the peace and beauty you have experienced. The other course is strange but it appears safe. From afar, you see many people on the alternative course. You reflect to yourself, "Mmm....Maybe I should see what that path is like." Failing to look at the directions you were given when you started on the path, you decide to travel on the alternate course.

Almost immediately, you sense that something *is* strange. Unlike the path you started out on, the alternate course has signs on it that say, "BE CAREFUL. DANGERS AHEAD." The dangers can be overcome and avoided if you follow the directions you were given. As you journey on, you begin to notice changes. You see fewer animals and insects. Creeks are murky, narrow, and have less aquatic life in them. Large fruit-laden trees give way to dead flowerless brush and thickets of sharp weeds. You do not see any flower-laden ponds. Your steps now become heavy and exhausting. You begin to tire frequently and run out of breath after short distances. Landmarks and signs you saw when you started the journey are replaced with man-made signs pointing in directions that are not in the authentic traveler's manual. You become confused. You know that something is wrong. "Let me check my directions." You open your traveler's manual and read the passage: "For a short time, you will *choose* an alternate course." You conclude, "That's weird. I just decided to do exactly what is written in the traveler's manual."

Seemingly out of nowhere, self-indulgence guides, dressed as leaders, insist that you follow their directions. Mere travelers like you, they and their followers constantly squabble and argue about which way the best way to go is. Each group claims that its way is the best way and, if you do not join them, you will be lost. Groups carve out their own paths, write their own traveler's manuals, and give you new directions to replace the traveler's manual you were given. The changes are a combination of directions in the original traveler's manual and directions composed by the self-appointed guides. You do not realize what is going on. Your confusion and concern increase but you do not know exactly what to do.

You wonder if you should find another group of travelers, or embark on your own course. Bewildered, you exclaim, "What happened to the beautiful path I started out on... the path I thought I was on... what happened to that path!" Other sojourners overhear you and utter, "What is wrong with you? What other path are you talking about? You're going in the right direction." You reply, "This is not the path I started out on. Deep down inside of me, I know that these are not the right directions." They again respond, "What is wrong with you?" *In their eyes, something is wrong with you*. You are not behaving like most travelers on the alternate course. Even though they started out on the beautiful path and chose to take the alternate course, most of them can no longer imagine or remember the original path. They said the same things that you are saying now. But, they decided to just "go along with the program." Ironically, they chose to be convinced to go along with the crowd on the alternate course.

Because you want to get back to the original path, you start to recognize a yearning that you have always had—a yearning to return to the One who made you and all this, your Maker and Creator. You ask yourself, "Are there directions for returning to the peace, happiness, and serenity of the original path? What signs should I look for? How will I know if the directions I have are correct?" It dawns on you that you still have the original traveler's manual in your heart. If an unblemished human soul is asked to share its greatest longing, it would say, "I love God, my Creator, and want to please Him." When you sincerely follow the Creator's guidance, the Creator removes spiritual blemishes, so you can recognize and heed His commands. You can experience peace and harmony during your journey in this life.

The beautiful spiritual path is now a vast obstacle course. The obstacle course reflects the current state of religion. Religion has been so corrupted and fragmented that its original face is beyond recognition unless a person is guided to the truth. Over many generations, religion has been disfigured and fashioned into a vast spiritual obstacle course laden with:

- idolatry,
- sects, denominations, and schools of thought,
- blasphemous doctrines,
- legions of professional clergy,
- religious rules, rites, and rituals never authorized by God,

- norm troopers (spiritually blind traditionalists) who enforce man-made dogmas, and
- separatists who isolate themselves and exclude others.

Religion was never intended to be "an opiate of the people," but today's distorted, disfigured religion is clearly an opiate. Corrupt religion induces spiritual sleep. It is one thing to be physically asleep, and another thing to be spiritually asleep with your eyes wide open. Many apparently religious people, in the popular sense of religion, are asleep with their eyes wide open and content with being lost and without true direction. Amidst widespread spiritual slumber, there are individuals who have awakened and seek the original path. By God's leave, such persons are guided back in all times to the true worship of God. *They have nothing to fear nor will they grieve.*

From the Quran:

Surely, those who believe, those who are Jewish, the Christians, and the converts; anyone who (1) believes in God, and (2) believes in the Last Day, and (3) leads a righteous life, will receive their recompense from their Lord. They have nothing to fear, nor will they grieve. (2:62)[2]

In this journey, plants, animals, and other life forms are in harmony with the great divine scheme. Each life form has its purpose. Hopefully, you are endeavoring to find your purpose, and want to remain vigilant in your search for spiritual truth. All are in submission to the Creator. Others who also recognize that something has gone awry with religion echo your questions about changes on the path. What are considered normal religious practices by many are spiritually harmful and toxic to you. This imaginary journey pauses at a place where you say you want to return to the right path. It is very important for you to know what is fact and what is fiction regarding religion. Many current doctrines and practices in the three monotheist religions divert you from the right path. By placing distortions (i.e., weeds and thorns) in religion, Satan seeks to divert as many people as possible from the true worship of God. He hopes that people abandon their inborn yearning to worship God. Hundreds of other religions and beliefs systems are as distorted as the monotheist religions. There are more than four thousand religions, denominations, sects, religious bodies, faith groups, and spiritual movements in the world. But, *there is only one original spiritual path—the religion ordained by God for creation: surrender or submission to Him.*

In attempts to make true worship difficult to understand and practice, Satan distorts it with lies. Individuals react in four distinct ways to the dilution and distortion of the worship of God. Imagine a situation when four people are offered a dish of food. Their reactions mirror the four ways people react to distorted, corrupt religion. The four recipients of the food dish represent human travelers on the spiritual journey in this life. Authentic religion and the true worship of God are *foods for the soul*. The good portion on the dish is the genuine love and worship of the One God. The good portion is the right path. Someone does not want people to benefit from the good nutritious portion. Someone puts bitter substances in the food, and the someone is Satan. Satan wants humans either to throw away the entire dish or delight in the bitter (false) portions.

The first person tastes bitter portions, reacts with displeasure, and briefly pushes the dish away. But, the person intuitively believes that the dish contains good portions. The person later tastes the good portion and delights in it. The second person does not want to eat *any* of the food. The second person uses his or her displeasure with bitter portions as an excuse to reject the entire dish. The third person tastes bitter portions and develops a preference for them. When invited to taste the good nutritious portion, the third person says, "I am satisfied and I don't want to sample anything else. What I have is good enough for me." The third person sometimes complains about bitter portions and expresses a desire for "better food." When offered good portions, the person finds fault with the good portions. The fourth person takes portions from many plates – a little bit of this and a little bit of that – to make their own food dishes to suit them.

The first person is a sincere seeker who *unknowingly* follows corrupt spiritual practices and is guided back to the right path. The second person refuses to believe in God and never returns to the right path. Due to starving his or her soul, the person is spiritually dead. Although informed about distorted and false doctrines, the third person clings to distorted beliefs, and is convinced that he or she is moving in the right direction (i.e., that bitter portions are good). Discounting opportunities to embrace spiritual truths, the third person continues to say, "I am satisfied." It is psychologically comforting for some people to think that they pursue spiritual truth. Invitations to sample good portions that are departures from their long-held trodden paths (i.e., distorted view of worship) disturb them. Carving out a personal "modern" spiritual path, the fourth person discards what he or she thinks are mere remnants of an original traveler's manual. The person adopts philosophies that fit his or her lifestyle and idea of spirituality, and makes up directions as he or she goes along. The person wants to believe in something spiritual, inspiring, and esoteric, but shies away from belief in God. The person likes ideas of union and harmony but rejects the reality of One Unifier and One Harmonizer. All societies are composed of these four recipients of spiritual food or travelers.

Satan *knows* that there is no god but the one God. Satan's self-proclaimed mission is to promote idolatry and disbelief in God alone *in any form* on the vast spiritual obstacle course.

From the Bible:

*Do you still think that it is enough just to believe that there is one God? Well, even the **demons believe this, and they tremble in terror**. (James 2:19)*[3]

From the Quran:

And the devil will say, after the judgment had been issued, "God has promised you the truthful promise, and I promised you, but I broke my promise. I had no power over you; I simply invited you, and you accepted my invitation. Therefore, do not blame me, and blame only yourselves. My complaining cannot help you, nor can your complaining help me. I have disbelieved in your idolizing me. The transgressors have incurred a painful retribution." (14:22)

They are like the devil: he says to the human being, "Disbelieve," then as soon as he disbelieves, **he [devil] says, "I disown you. I fear God, Lord of the universe."** *(59:16)*[4]

Existence of God Confirmed for Believers

The existence of God and eternal life in God's Presence remain topics of debate and speculation. The debate and speculation are mainly polemics for the sake of polemics. Informed individuals who use common sense and reason do not doubt the existence of God. For some time, science has *confirmed* the existence of a Divine Designer or Supreme Being.[5] Yet, outside of religious programming on Christian cable stations and conventional stations, this scientific fact is not straightforwardly stated on network television and radio news broadcasts. For fear of sounding unscientific, many modern scientists avoid couching their confirmations of the existence of God in religious terms. However, the scientific facts are clearer than ever before. In their explorations of the physical beginning of our universe and order and design at every turn, scientists who are not beholden to anti-theistic agendas acknowledge that there is an Absolute and Eternal, a Supreme Architect, a Supreme Being, a First Cause that is uncaused.

Humans have a limited free will. A person has an inborn ability to doubt or deny the existence of God. There are those whose doubts only augment their denial of God and distortion of worship. Despite what they may fervently insist, such individuals do not attain true happiness in this life or in the Hereafter. *Their changeless doubt is their peril. There is absolutely no room for doubt in the presence of God.* As spiritual beings in the Divine Presence, we doubted God's power and authority. We ruptured our souls and we now reside in this universe. The following verses from Chapter 38 of the Quran shed light on what took place immediately before our first parents were placed in this world or dimension. All of us were in the genes of our first parents.

From the Quran:

Say, "I warn you; there is no other god beside God, the One, the Supreme. "The Lord of the heavens and the earth, and everything between them; the Almighty, the Forgiving." Say, "Here is awesome news. That you are totally oblivious to. I had no knowledge previously, about the feud in the High Society. I am inspired that my sole mission is to deliver the warnings to you." Your Lord said to the angels, "I am creating a human being from clay. Once I design him, and blow into him from My spirit, you shall fall prostrate before him." The angels fell prostrate, all of them, except Satan; he refused, and was too arrogant, unappreciative. He said, "O Satan, what prevented you from prostrating before what I created with My hands? Are you too arrogant? Have you rebelled?" He said, "I am better than he; You created me from fire, and created him from clay." He said, "Therefore, you must be exiled, you will be banished. You have incurred My condemnation until the Day of Judgment." He said, "My Lord, respite me till the Day of Resurrection." He said, "You are respited. He said, "I swear by Your Majesty, that I will send them all astray. **Except Your worshipers who are devoted absolutely to You alone.***" He said, "This is the truth, and the truth is all that I utter. I will fill Hell with you and all those who follow you." Say, "I do not ask you for any wage, and I am not an imposter. This is a reminder for the world. And you will certainly find out in awhile." (38:65-88)* [6]

The last two verses state that the disclosure about what occurred in the Presence of God is a *reminder* for this world and we humans *will certainly find out in a while.*

Now, look at the first eight verses of Chapter 38, cited below. The first verse contains the initial "S" ("Saad" in Arabic), and specifically refers to the Quran containing a *proof* that it is a divine revelation. The next seven verses describe persons who do not believe that the Quran is a divine revelation or that the Quran beacons humanity to worship God alone. Verse eight indicates that disbelievers are *"doubtful of My [God's] proof."*

From the Quran:

S. (Saad), and the Quran that contains the proof. Those who disbelieve have plunged into arrogance and defiance. Many a generation before them we annihilated. They called for help, in vain. They wondered that a warner should come to them, from among them. The disbelievers said, "A magician, a liar. Did he make the gods into one god? This is really strange." The leaders announced, "Go and steadfastly persevere in worshiping your gods. This is what is desired. We never heard of this from the religion of our fathers. This is a lie. Why did the proof come down to him, instead of us?" <u>*Indeed, they are doubtful of My proof.*</u> *Indeed, they have not yet tasted My retribution. (38:1-8)*[7]

This Temporary Station on the Path

We reside in the innermost of seven universes. Created by God, the seven universes are like a "buffer" between God's Divine Presence and hundreds of billions of beings that cannot withstand His Divine Presence. God's Presence *is* Heaven or Paradise. We humans followed a doubting minority that was relegated to this dimension. Once thrust into this world, our souls were assigned to physical forms (man and woman). The repentant spiritual beings that entered this world took the forms of all aquatic and land animals, birds, insects, trees, stars, planetary bodies, the sun, the moon, and countless other animate creatures. Only God knows the expanse and vastness of the universes. Placed in the middle of seven universes, this world called "earth" is only a temporary abode for us.

From the Quran:

He is the One who created for you everything on earth, then turned to the sky and perfected seven universes therein, and He is fully aware of all things. (2:29)

Do you not realize that to God prostrates everyone in the heavens and the earth, and the sun, and the moon, and the stars, and the mountains, and the trees, and the animals, and many people? Many others among the people are committed to doom. Whomever God shames, none will honor him. Everything is in accordance with God's will. (22:18)

The stars and the trees prostrate. (55:6)[8]

Satan cannot mislead the hundreds of billions of once doubting creatures that repented prior to entering this dimension. Instead, Satan uses distortion and doubt to convince humans to remain on a vast spiritual obstacle course. Doubt coupled with a genuine spiritual yearning leads, God willing, to dissolving the doubt about the way to worship the Almighty. There is no coercion in religious belief and practice. There are those who have distorted and defaced the manner we should acknowledge and remember our Creator. This book is about the corruption of that manner—the corruption of the human worship of God.

The terrorist attacks of September 11, 2001 in New York City, Washington, D.C., and in the sky above northern Pennsylvania were three examples of a countless number of horrific acts committed throughout history in the name of God and religion. The evil of so-called "God-inspired" physical aggression by anyone towards innocents anywhere can never be justified in the authentic scriptures. More harmful in the spiritual sense than physical weapons of mass destruction, corrupted religions are weapons of mass distortion and deceit deployed against millions of souls throughout the ages. In Paradise, Satan first used spiritual distortion and deceit on our first parents, Adam and Eve. Satan encouraged them to doubt that only God possesses the majesty and ability to be a god. Satan continues to use such weapons on human souls in this world. In every age, he uses the weapon of corrupt religion to convince millions of people to accept false doctrines and practice idolatry. Almighty God protects the sincere from succumbing to Satan and his forces. In God's system, proofs that unequivocally expose false religious beliefs and practices defuse Satan's spiritual distortion and deceit.

From the Quran:

He [Satan] said, "My Lord, since You have willed that I go astray, I will surely entice them on earth; I will send them all astray. Except those among Your worshipers who are devoted absolutely to You alone." He [God] said, "This is a law that is inviolable. You have no power over My servants. You only have power over the strayers who follow you." And Hell awaits them all. (15:39-43)

[Satan said,] "I will come to them from before them, and from behind them, and from their right, and from their left, and You will find that most of them are unappreciative." (7:17)[9]

The Meaning of Hislam

The "His" in "Hislam" refers to the introduction, acceptance, and practice of religious beliefs and practices never revealed and authorized by God. Someone other than God (i.e., the "His" in Hislam) *owns* or is the *source* of the innovations and false practices. Hislam also consists of: 1) hundreds of denominations, branches, offshoots, and sects of Judaism, Christianity, Islam, and other spiritual belief systems; 2) cultural ideologies deemed as religions; 3) superstitions, and 4) secret systems. Like their deceased counterparts, contemporary custodians of Hislam:

1. alter the text of revealed scriptures or refuse to acknowledge that the texts have been altered;

2. invent and promote bogus rulings, laws, and practices as valid elements of religion;

3. revere and obey their religious leaders and saints instead of God;

4. dismiss any person or groups who challenge them to discard false practices and teachings;

5. regard themselves as the only persons "worthy" of the truth;

6. attempt to disseminate and enforce their rulings and beliefs on others;

7. maintain elitist groups comprised of individuals sworn to uphold false institutions and secret allegiances.

The truth about Hislam gives rise to relief in some, and gives rise to suspicion and anger in others. Relief comes when a sincere person discovers that a religious belief or practice violates God's commands. The person has a greater opportunity to learn the *confirmed* truth about the worship of God. Negative reactions to the same *confirmed* truth are either a blessing or a curse. It is a blessing when suspicious reactions are short-lived because the person wants to please God by correcting his or her behavior. It is a curse when a person further commits him or her self to false spiritual beliefs and practices. The person is permanently cut off from the right path after making the choice to discard and ignore proofs about the worship of God. The person never intended to be on the right path and fails to heed directions provided by our Creator, The True Guide.

From the Quran:

I will divert from My revelations those who are arrogant on earth, without justification. Consequently, when they see every kind of proof they will not believe. And when they see the path of guidance they will not adopt it as their path, but when they see the path of straying they will adopt it as their path. This is the consequence of their rejecting our proofs, and being totally heedless thereof. (7:146)

"We have given you the truth, but most of you hate the truth." (43:78)[10]

Negative reactions are directed at those who expose distortions of religion. Many people are primed by their religious leaders to reject information that exposes false doctrines. A person should not accept any information without examining the information and sources of the information. If the information does not make sense, if it sounds irrational, you should not accept it. Genuine faith and belief in God are never based on irrational, unreasonable doctrines, beliefs, and practices. God endowed us with brains, senses, and intelligence. We should use these faculties in the search for spiritual truth. Many individuals blindly accept (i.e., blind faith) false religious doctrines and practices of their parents, their tribe or ethnic group, their religious leaders, and groups in their societies. Modern custodians of Judaism, Christianity, and Islam have lost, discarded, or failed to follow the authentic scriptures revealed to the prophets.

From the Quran:

<u>Judaism</u>

The example of those who were given the Torah, then failed to uphold it, is like the donkey carrying great works of literature. Miserable indeed is the example of people who rejected God's revelations. God does not guide the wicked people. (62:5)

<u>Christianity</u>

Subsequent to them, we sent Jesus, the son of Mary, confirming the previous scripture, the Torah. We gave him the Gospel, containing guidance and light, and confirming the previous scriptures, the Torah, and augmenting its guidance and light, and to enlighten the righteous. The people of the Gospel shall rule in accordance with God's revelations therein. Those who do not rule in accordance with God's revelations are the wicked. (5:46-47)

Islam

Have you considered the watering of the pilgrims and caring for the Sacred Masjid a substitute for believing in God and the Last Day, and striving in the cause of God? They are not equal in the sight of God. God does not guide the wicked people. (9:19)

Those who have rejected the Quran's proof when it came to them have also rejected an Honorable book. (41:41)

This is because those who disbelieved are rejecting (the Quran). (84:22)[11]

Submission, the Only Alternative to Hislam

God approved the authentic religion of creation as *Peace* or *Submission* ("Islam" in Arabic). People who genuinely embrace the religion of creation and worship God alone are "Submitters," regardless of what they may call themselves or where they reside.

From the Quran:

*O you who believe, you shall embrace **total submission**; do not follow the steps of Satan, for he is your most ardent enemy. 2:208)*

The only religion approved by God is "Submission." *Ironically, those who have received the scripture are the ones who dispute this fact, despite the knowledge they have received, due to jealousy. For such rejecters of God's revelations, God is most strict in reckoning. (3:19)*

*You shall strive for the cause of God as you should strive for His cause. He has chosen you and has placed no hardship on you in practicing your religion—the religion of your father Abraham. **He is the one who named you "Submitters" originally**. Thus, the messenger shall serve as a witness among you, and you shall serve as witnesses among the people. Therefore, you shall observe the Contact Prayers*

(Salat) and give the obligatory charity (Zakat), and hold fast to God; He is your Lord, the best Lord and the best Supporter. (22:78)[12]

Miraculous Code Confirms Divine Scriptures and Rites of Submission

The first hint that there could be a mathematical Code in Divine scriptures was made by Rabbi Judah the Pious in the 12th century AD. Joseph Dan and Frank Talmage[13], authors of *Studies in Jewish Mysticism*, quoted Rabbi Judah regarding how some Jews in France were altering their morning prayers. Rabbi Judah was certain that God incorporated a mathematical code or system in divinely revealed scripture. He was aware of many details of the "great and hidden secret" mathematical system.

> The people [Jews] in France made it a custom to add [in the Morning Prayer] the words: Ashrei temimei derekh [blessed are those who walk the righteous way], and our Rabbi, the Pious, of blessed memory, wrote that they were completely and utterly wrong. It is all gross falsehood, because there are **only nineteen times that the Holy Name is mentioned** [in that portion of the morning prayer] ...and similarly you find **the word 'Elohim nineteen times in the pericope of Ve-'elleh shemot**.... Similarly, you find that **Israel is called "sons" nineteen times**, and there are many other examples. **All these sets of nineteen are intricately intertwined, and they contain many secrets and esoteric meanings, which are contained in more than eight large volumes.** Therefore, anyone who has the fear of God in him will not listen to the words of the Frenchmen who add the verse "Ashrei temimei derekh," and blessed are the righteous who walk in the paths of God's Torah, for according to their additions, the Holy Name is mentioned twenty times...and this is a great mistake. Furthermore, in this section there are 152 words (152 = 19 x 8) but if you add "'Ashrei temimei derekh" there are 158 words. This is nonsense, for it is a great and hidden secret why there should be 152 words...but it cannot be explained in a short treatise. ...In order to understand this religious phenomenon, we have to take the basic contention of this treatise exactly as it is stated: every addition or omission of a word, or even of a single letter, from the sacred text of the prayers destroys the religious meaning of the prayer as a whole and is to be regarded as a grave sin, a sin which could result in eternal exile for those who commit it....[14]

Seven centuries later, in his classical book, *The Two Babylons* written in the early nineteenth century, Alexander Hislop[15] reflected:

> The commandments of God, to our corrupt and perverse minds, may sometimes seem to be hard. They may require to do what is painful, they may require us to forego what is pleasing to flesh and blood. But, whether we know the reasons of these commandments [of God] or not, if *we only know that they come from "the only wise God, our Savior, we may be sure that in the keeping of them there is great reward;* we may go blindfold wherever the Word of God may lead us, and rest in the firm conviction that, in so doing, we are pursuing the very best of safety and peace. Human wisdom at the best is but a blind guide; human policy is a meteor that dazzles and leads astray; and they who follow it walk in darkness, and know not whither they are going; but he "that walketh uprightly," that walks by the rule of God's infallible Word, will ever find that "he walketh surely," and that whatever duty he has to perform, whatever danger he has to face, "great peace have all they that love God's law, and nothing shall offend them."[16]

Alexander Hislop sought a means of distinguishing between "God's infallible Word," and man-made innovations presented as revealed commands. Now unveiled in our age according to God's Plan, the "great and hidden secret" recognized by Rabbi Judah is the answer to Alexander Hislop's prayerful yearning for an irrefutable standard to recognize authentic Divine guidance. Spiritual corruption is exposed by a miraculous, incontrovertible, mathematical Code in the revealed scripture known as the Quran. Sincere seekers who examine the Code know for sure that: 1) the Quran and authentic portions of earlier scriptures *are* the revealed Word of God, 2) a great and unimaginable reward awaits all people who submit to God alone, and 3) the course or path of obedience to our Lord and Creator is the only ultimate safety and peace in this life and the Hereafter. God has unveiled a tangible *miraculous scientific proof* to humanity that the text of the Quran is wholly intact. It is the *Quran's Proof* mentioned above in verse 41:41. Based on the number 19 and its multiples, the Code is a scientific confirmation that: 1) the Quran "could not possibly be authored by other than God;" 2) it is the *final divinely revealed* scripture to humanity, and 3) it confirms previous revelations. The Code also confirms the Divine origin, wording, and letter-sequence of the Jewish Morning Prayer that Rabbi Judah spoke about nine centuries ago. The 19-based Code is also found throughout the universe and in our bodies. For example, the number of bones in the human body (209, 19x11) and the number of days of the average full-term pregnancy (266 days, 19 x 14) are multiples of 19. Halley's comet returns to earth every 19 years.

By scientific verification of the authenticity and text position of every letter in the Quran, the Quran's verses emerge as indisputable truth. The Code cannot be manipulated in any way to distort or obscure its miraculous properties. The Code does not accommodate a single exception to its basic grounding in multiples of 19. Code-based verses fully unmask the corruption of Judaism, Christianity, Islam, and all other religions. The Code echoes the unifying message that *there is no god but the One God. Worship God alone.* The Code is so vast that people the world over *continue* to discover components of it. The probability of such a code being embedded in *any* written work by chance is nonexistent. Even with the aid of the most sophisticated computers, the Code cannot be duplicated in any document in any language at any time. *The Code is tamperproof because the slightest alteration in the authentic text of the Quran is immediately exposed.* Embedded in the count of letters and words in the Quran, the Code remained hidden from human awareness for fourteen hundred years. Almighty God forewarned humanity about the enduring miracle of the Code in Chapter (Sura) 74, verses 30-37.

From the Quran:

Over it is nineteen. *We appointed angels to be guardians of Hell, and we assigned their number (19) to: (1) disturb the disbelievers, (2) to convince the Christians and Jews (that this is a divine scripture), (3) to strengthen the faith of the faithful, (4) to remove all traces of doubt from the hearts of Christians, Jews, as well as the believers, and (5) to expose those who harbor doubt in their hearts, and the disbelievers; they will say, "What did God mean by this allegory?"*

God thus sends astray whomever He wills, and guides whomever He wills. None knows the soldiers of your Lord except He. This is a reminder for the people. Absolutely, (I swear) by the moon. And the night as it passes. And the morning as it shines. **This is one of the great miracles.** *A warning to the human race. For those among you who wish to advance, or regress. (74:30-37)*[17]

According to God's Plan, access to the Code in the Quran would occur after the invention of the computer.

From the Quran:

At the right time, we will produce for them a creature, made of earthly materials, declaring that the people are not certain about our revelations. (27:82)[18]

The creature mentioned in verse 27:82 is the computer. The use of a computer was essential for the initial discovery of the elements of the miraculous Code-related counts, alphabet combinations and patterns, specific words, the sequence and placement of letters, and placement of verses in the Quran. In addition, a computer declares i.e., shows (visual), speaks about (audio), or communicates a vast array of information that otherwise would be inaccessible to many people. An outlet for all views and opinions, the Internet hosts many websites that minimize, distort, and deny the truth in the revealed scriptures. Since the unveiling of the Code, people now have the opportunity to exam the Code directly on the Internet. Despite immediate access to verification of the Quran, many informed individuals remain doubtful and uncertain about the veracity of the Quran. Some individuals *do not wish* to see the *Quran's Proof.* In verse 27:82, the Arabic word *ak'raj'naa* (denotes producing, making or manufacturing) is used instead of the word *khalaq'naa* (denotes the act of creating). Like a car, a computer is not created. It is made or manufactured of earthly materials. A critical component of a computer is the silicone chip. Silicate minerals make up ninety-five percent of the earth's crust and upper mantle. Silicate minerals are found in rocks and rock dust.[19]

Discovered in 1974[20] by Dr. Rashad Khalifa (1935-1990), the miraculous mathematical Code was initially embraced then rejected by Muslim, Christian, and Jewish leaders who were informed about it. When they realized that the Code exposes false religious doctrines and practices, Muslim religious leaders stopped endorsing and disseminating knowledge about the Code. They began to wage a public relations campaign to cast misgivings in the minds of thousands in the Muslim world who had heard about the Code and who were awaiting an opportunity to review it. Books and articles about the Code were confiscated and destroyed. Jewish and Christian religious leaders who know about the miraculous Code have kept silent. When Dr. Khalifa discovered the Code, he was heralded as a hero and great Muslim scholar by the same groups in Muslim countries that later claimed that he was an apostate from Islam. Paradoxically, the groups now claim that only God knows the meaning of the letters atop twenty- nine chapters of the Quran, and erroneously say that God intends to keep it secret (see Chapter 4, Distortions of Islam). Three decades ago, while visiting an executive member of one of the largest Muslim organizations in America, I asked him why they no longer would accept Dr. Khalifa. The leader replied, "He is not one of us." I concluded that his phrase, "one of us," meant that the leader and his cohorts believe that only individuals like themselves (i.e., who embrace prevailing distortions of Islam) can understand Islam and the Quran. Apparently, some of them view themselves as the only ones worthy of receiving such a great blessing (i.e., discovery of the Code) from God.

As part of his duties as God's Messenger of the Covenant,[21] Dr. Khalifa specifically challenged religious leaders in Muslim countries and religious leaders the world over to return to the authentic worship of God alone. In 1990, Dr. Khalifa was assassinated. U.S. government investigations and documents reveal that Dr. Khalifa was murdered by home-grown elements of the same terrorist groups who committed the terrorist acts in New York City, Washington, D.C., and in the sky over Pennsylvania on September 11, 2001. Mentioned in the 9/11 Commission Report, Dr. Khalifa was possibly the first U.S. citizen and religious leader murdered by domestic operatives of international Hislamic terrorists.

The assassins and their supporters demonized Dr. Khalifa as a "devil" attempting to: 1) misguide Muslim masses, 2) alter the Quran, and 3) violate Islamic law. Of course, these accusations are false. Efforts to malign Dr. Khalifa and fabricate lies about the miraculous Code continue in many Muslim communities, domestic and abroad, and on the Internet.

Do not describe such persons as "fundamentalist Muslims." *This is misleading, and inaccurate. Such persons do not reflect the teachings of the Quran or Islam.* Regardless of their faith or country of origin, "fundamentalists" of this type are "fundamental" with respect to their myopic vision of what constitutes religion and righteousness. These so-called fundamentalists are far adrift from the authentic teachings in the revealed scriptures.

The information in this book is *confirmed* by verses from the Quran. The phrase **"From the Quran"** is written atop the verses. My observations and analysis of the state of religion reflect the truth in the Quran. The Quran verses cited in this book are from the translation written by Dr. Khalifa. The verses cited are not the only verses in the Quran that pertain to the topics discussed. I also cite some supportive verses from the Bible. It is not I or anyone else who proves these truths. *God proves the truth and elevates it above falsehood.*

From the Quran:

This is the truth from your Lord; do not harbor any doubts. (3:60)

Proclaim: "O people, the truth has come to you herein from your Lord. Whoever is guided is guided for his own good. And whoever goes astray, goes astray to his own detriment. I am not a guardian over you." (10:108)

Had your Lord willed, all the people would have been one congregation (of believers). But they will always dispute (the truth). (11:118)[22]

Irrefutable divinely-revealed truth is the best way to clear away pervasive distortions (i.e., "weeds") along the path of the worship of God.

Nevertheless, the Quran can be verbally disputed by individuals who: 1) never examine the Proof, 2) who examine the Proof then delude themselves into believing it is not true, and 3) concoct schemes to divert others from examining the Proof. As stated in verse 11:118, there will always be individuals on the beautiful path we all started out on, who dispute and distort God's revealed directions. A physical miracle embedded in the entire text of a divine scripture eliminates room for doubt or speculation. After sufficiently examining it, a person either eventually accepts or rejects it. Persistent maneuvers to avoid accepting the Miraculous Code and the Quran serve to uncover informed individuals' intentions not to pursue the right path. Such individuals' evasive behavior may stem from a desire to continue their lives as if the mathematical Proof/Code did not exist. The miraculous Code does not debunk distortions about the worship of God for those who find comfort in the distortions. The Code exposes the deluded ones and grants certainty to the rightly guided ones. Almighty God has willed that all corruption of worship shall be ultimately exposed so that the right path that we all started out on is restored to its pristine beauty and purity.

A seeker who *unknowingly* adopts false religious teachings drifts temporarily off the path. When the sincere seeker realizes that he or she is headed in the wrong direction, the seeker proceeds to return to the right path. We all wonder off the right path innumerable times during this life. This is one reason why God is Most Merciful. The sincerity of a seeker is tested when a seeker has opportunities to examine *proofs* of the true alternative, changes direction, and again moves on the right path. The truly lost are those who do not desire to or fear contemplating return to the right path.

From the Quran:

Anyone who commits evil, or wrongs his soul, then implores God for forgiveness, will find God Forgiving, Most Merciful. (4:110)

Your Lord is fully aware of those who stray off His path, and He is fully aware of those who are guided. (6:117)

> A.L.R. *A scripture that we revealed to you, in order to lead the people out of darkness into the light—in accordance with the will of their Lord—to the path of the Almighty, the Praiseworthy. …The path of God; the One who possesses everything in the heavens and everything on earth. Woe to the disbelievers; they have incurred a terrible retribution. (14:1-:2)*
>
> *Say, "Everyone works in accordance with his belief, and your Lord knows best which ones are guided in the right path." (17:84)*

Messenger of God and Prophet of God: Is There A Difference?

All prophets of God taught the same message—worship the One God (i.e., worship God alone). A prophet of God is an individual to whom a divine revelation is revealed from God, via the angel Gabriel. Following directions from God, a prophet writes and instructs his followers to write the revelation in the form of scripture *exactly according to God's instructions.* In the case of Moses, he received the laws on tablets. The process of original revelation and recording of divine scripture may transpire for many years of a prophet's life. The prophet Muhammad is the last prophet and the Quran is the Final Testament or revelation to humanity. These facts are confirmed by the Miraculous Mathematical Code. *Only prophets received divine revelation.* The designation "prophet of God" has nearly lost its true meaning in some societies. Many religions and sects claim to be initiated by prophets *after the time of Muhammad and revelation of the Quran.* Anyone who proclaims that he or she is a *prophet* of God after the Final Testament is a charlatan, possibly deluded, and undoubtedly confused. Some groups and sects claim to be waiting for their *prophet* to redeem them.

By the fact that they taught and lived spiritual truth, prophets were also messengers of God. However, *a messenger of God is not a prophet of God, because messengers of God did not receive divine revelation or scriptures.* There will continue to be messengers of God among all communities until the Last Day. A messenger of God is *any* individual who promotes the worship of God alone and lives a righteous life. Anytime a righteous person enjoins submission to God alone, the person is a messenger of God. Some messengers have greater functions and much more responsibility than others. For example, as the Messenger of the Covenant, Dr. Khalifa discovered the Miraculous Code, invited all people back to the true unadulterated worship of God, and reiterated important information about the purpose of life. Like all authentic divine scriptures, the Quran is a messenger of God in book form to humanity. The Quran guides to the best path on the spiritual journey.

From the Quran

This Quran guides to the best path and brings good news to the believers who lead a righteous life, that they have deserved a great recompense. (17:9)[23]

I humbly beseech you to reflect on these facts as you travel on your spiritual journey: Satan would never admit in this life to distorting religion and using it as a tool to encourage people to practice idolatry. Satan is the expert when it comes to weapons of mass spiritual distortion and deceit. Satan never comes in true form. If he did, you would immediately recognize him. Satan and his compatriots come in the guise of someone you trust and admire, someone who steps forward and presents prevailing religious falsehoods as truth, someone who tells you that he or she would never mislead you, someone who is accepted by people, someone who reads your discomfort and uses humor to make you feel at ease when you question the truthfulness of false doctrines, someone who knows how to make you feel that you are on the right path and you are in the right group, someone who comes across as informed and intelligent, and someone who knows that a person tends to feel better when the person is with others who believe the same way, even when the beliefs are false. As an individual soul in this life you are on your own. Short of a sincere yearning for untainted spiritual truth, religious affiliation and identification mean nothing. It is God's Plan that revealed truth about the worship of God be confirmed at this time in a physical, objective, verifiable, miraculous form, independent of the words of men.

Nevertheless, enemies of the spiritual truth continue to criticize, dismiss, and create doubt about the miraculous Proof-Code. None have succeeded (nor can they succeed) in debunking it. Sincere seekers of every age recognize God's proofs in themselves and in creation.

Satan hates humans and blames us for his eternal damnation. Satan advises humans to worship anything and anyone beside God, including prophets of God. A sincere seeker would never ask others, in the name of religion, for any money to do anything, especially to support him or herself. A sincere person learns that God provides for his sincere servants. A sincere seeker learns that God's truth is free and not for sale. God knows all things and the truth will prevail.

From the Quran:

*Thus, **the truth prevailed**, and what they did was nullified. (7:118)*

*For He has decreed that **the truth shall prevail**, and the falsehood shall vanish, in spite of the evildoers. (8:8)*

*They sought to spread confusion among you in the past, and confounded the matters for you. However, **the truth ultimately prevails**, and God's Plan is carried out, in spite of them. (9:48)*

*Say, "My Lord causes **the truth to prevail**. He is the Knower of all secrets." (34:48)*

*He is the One who sent His messenger with the guidance and **the religion of truth, to make it prevail over all other religions.** God suffices as a witness. (48:28)*

Notes

[1] Rashad Khalifa, Quran: *The Final Testament: Authorized English Version.* (Freemont, CA: Universal Unity Press, 2000). Quran verses cited in this book are from the Divinely-authorized translation of the Quran written by Dr. Khalifa. This translation can be read on-line at <http://www.submission.org.>.

[2] Ibid, 2:62.

[3] D.A Stoop. and S.F. Arterburn, *The Life Recovery Bible: New Living Translation* (Wheaton, Ill.: Tyndale House Publishers, 1998), James: 2:19.

[4] Khalifa, *Quran*, 14:22 and 59:16.

[5] You can go to a public library or search the Internet for information about scientific discoveries that point directly to the existence of a Supreme Intelligence or Designer. The latest research has led to what scientists currently deem "Intelligent Design Theory."

[6] Quran: The Final Testament, 38: 65-88, Chapter 38. "Saad," is an initialed chapter. It has one initial, the letter "Saad" or "S." The letter "S" also occurs atop two additional chapters and totals 152 in the chapters, 152 = 19 x 8.

[7] Khalifa, *Quran*, 38: 1- 8.

[8] Ibid, 2:29, 22:18, and 55:6

[9] Ibid, 15:39-43, and 7:17

[10] Ibid, 7:146 and 43:78

[11] Ibid, 62:5, 5:46-47, 9:19, 41:41, and 84:22.

[12] Ibid, 2:208, 3:19, and 22:78

[13] Joseph Dan and Frank Talmage, *Studies in Jewish Mysticism.* (New Jersey: KTAV Publishing House, 1996).

[14] Ibid, 88 - 89.

[15] Alexander Hislop, *The Two Babylons* (Ontario, CA.: Chick Publications, 1984-2005).

[16] Ibid, 290.

[17] Khalifa, *Quran*, 74:30-37.

[18] Ibid, 27:82.

[19] *"Silicate Mineral."* Britannica Concise Encyclopedia. 2004. Encyclopedia Premium Service. <http://www.britannica.com/ebc/article?=eu 403979 > May 18, 2004. Hundreds of products are made from silicate minerals. As pointed out,

silicate minerals comprise 95 percent of the earth's crust and upper mantle. The number 95 is a multiple of 19 (19 x 5).

[20] The year of the discovery (1974) of the Code corresponds to chapter 74 of the Quran where the number 19 is mentioned in the Quran. This is no coincidence.

[21] Dr. Khalifa was a messenger of God whose mission was to discover the Miraculous Code and purify Islam, the religion of creation, from all pollutants. The modern organized religion of Islam is so corrupt that it is almost a totally different system from what is decreed in the Quran. Dr. Khalifa was directed to remind us that all humans made a Covenant with God before the creation of this world to worship God alone and uphold His commands. His mission also involved clarifying other important matters. For more information about Dr. Khalifa, the miraculous Code, and Islam as clarified in the Quran, visit <www.submission,org> and <www.masjidtucson.org.>.

[22] Khalifa, *Quran*, 3:60, 8:8, 10:108, and 11:118.

[23] Ibid, 4:110, 6:117, 14:1-2, 17:84, and 17:9.

Two

Distortions of Judaism

The return to the original path begins by clearing away distortions (i.e., weeds and thorns) associated with the community of the ancient Hebrews and the Prophet Abraham. Our journey begins with specific words and names that have served as identifiers on the path. Like signs along a physical road, words and names associated with early sojourners' spiritual travels are meant to point us in the right direction. Yet, when the original meaning of some words and names are distorted and lost, so too are we until we are once again guided in the right path. Some important signs on the spiritual path have been distorted. I remember when some childhood peers turned street signs in the wrong direction such that unknowing travelers would go in the wrong direction. Some travelers realized that they were headed in the wrong direction. The street signs were eventually re-aligned parallel to the proper streets. It is time to reconnect certain spiritual themes, names, and words to their authentic meanings.

Let us start correcting the signs on the path with the word, *Judaism*. According to the Oxford American Desk Dictionary, the word *Judaism* denotes the *"religion of the Hebrews."* The term *"Jew"* is defined as *"a person of Hebrew descent* or *whose religion is Judaism."*[1] Contradicting fact, these definitions suggest that a Hebrew is Jewish and that one should adopt the Hebrew culture and language in order to practice Judaism. Put another way, it is roughly parallel to the simplistic notion that a non-Hebrew person who embraces Judaism suddenly is of Hebrew descent or the simplistic notion that a non-Arab person who embraces Islam suddenly is of Arab descent. The definitions unite two concepts that do not normally fit together -- ethnicity and religion. The concepts of ethnicity and religion have been weaved together via the construction of histories, indoctrination, and what I designate as arbitrary ethnic assignment. Arbitrary ethnic assignment refers to the practice of defining oneself as *genetically* related to a people or tribe to which one has no blood ties. In the broadest sense, science has confirmed that all individuals are genetically related to each other. Throughout history, some members of groups that inhabit the same geographic lands and share close cultural traditions have come to practice common religions. There is no inherent relationship between ethnic identity and religious belief. For example, Prophet Jesus was a Hebrew, but the message revealed to Jesus was not limited to Hebrews. People who refer to themselves as Jews do not constitute a single ethnic group.[2] A person can convert to Judaism by learning and embracing the tenets of the Jewish religion and joining a synagogue or temple.

In the authentic scriptures, Hebrews are called "the children or descendants of Israel" and "the people of the Book." The term "Israel" is a title of honor that God bestowed on Jacob, the son of Isaac. The phrase, "people of the Book," refers to the ancient Jewish and Christian communities who received Divine revelation through their Prophets prior to the revelation of the Quran to Prophet Muhammad. The revealed scriptures of each community constitute parts of one revealed message referred to in the scriptures as the "mother of the Book." Analogous to siblings being born from the same mother, all revealed scriptures are derived from a single origin, fountain, or source in God's Presence. In all authentic revelations, the primary message is one and the same: worship *God alone and obey His commands.*

The word "Hebrew" refers to the tribal descendants of the twelve sons of Jacob, the son of Isaac. Isaac was the *second* son of Abraham. The firstborn son of Abraham, Ishmael, is the forefather of the *non-Hebrew* Semitic tribes. Contrary to distorted Jewish and Christian doctrine, it was Ishmael who was offered up for sacrifice by his father Abraham. During those times, the birthright was routinely given to the firstborn son. Thinking that he received a command from God, Abraham was willing to sacrifice his firstborn son. Because of their unswerving submission to God, God blessed Abraham, Ishmael, and their righteous descendants. God *also* blessed Isaac and his righteous descendents. The denial of the birthright to Ishmael and dismissal of his mother Hagar in doctored Jewish and Christian scriptures are acts of prejudice that initially took place hundreds of years ago. At the time the distortion occurred, it was an effort to prop up the descendants of Isaac as superior and more worthy of God's blessings than the descendants of Ishmael. Upon re-examination, it becomes clear to any serious reader of Genesis 16:11 and 15 that Ishmael was the firstborn son of Abraham.

From the Bible:

And the angel also said, "You are now pregnant and will give birth to a son. You are to name him Ishmael, for the Lord has heard about your misery.... So Hagar gave Abram [Abraham] a son, and Abram named him Ishmael. Abram was eighty-six years old at that time. (Genesis 16:11, 15)[3] [Translation A]

And the angel of thy Lord said unto her, "Behold, thou art with child, and shall bear a son, and shall call his name Ish-ma-el; because thy Lord hath heard thy affliction...and Hagar bare Abram a son: and Abram called his son's name, which Hagar bare, Ishmael. And Abram was fourscore and six years old when Hagar bore Ish-ma-el to Abram. (Genesis 16:11, 15)[4] [Translation B]

Yet, the *same two Bible translations quoted above* contain verses (e.g., Hebrew 11:17) that erroneously state that Isaac was the only son of Abraham. Such contradictions are not found in an intact unaltered revealed scripture.

It was by faith that Abraham offered Isaac as a sacrifice when God was testing him...Abraham was ready to sacrifice his only son, Isaac... [Translation A]

By faith of Abraham, when he was tried, offered up Isaac; and he that had received the promises offered up his only begotten son. [Translation B]

In Genesis 21: 11, God reassured Abraham that Hagar and Ishmael are blessed. Nevertheless, in doctored scripture, only the descendents of Isaac are presented as worthy of special merit.

> ...do not be upset over the boy and your servant wife. Do just as Sarah says, for Isaac is the son through whom your descendents will be counted. But I will make a nation of the descendents of Hagar's son because he also is your son.[5]

From the Quran:

As Abraham raised the foundations of the shrine, together with Ishmael (they prayed): "Our Lord, accept this from us. You are the Hearer, the Omniscient." (2:127)

Had you witnessed Jacob on his death bed; he said to his children, "What will you worship after I die?" They said, "We will worship your god; the god of your fathers Abraham, Ishmael, and Isaac; the one god. To Him we are submitters." (2:133)

"Praise be to God for granting me, despite my old age, Ishmael and Isaac. My Lord answers the prayers." (14:39)[6]

Verses 2:133 and 14:39 clearly indicate the correct sequence of the birth of Abraham's sons. Isaac was also known as Is-ra-el, a title of honor that God bestowed on Isaac. Isaac was the father of Jacob, who in turn had twelve sons. Each son of Jacob (Israel) was the forbear of a family clan or tribe. "Judah" is the name of *one* of the twelve Hebrew tribes. Derived from Christian writings, the word "Judaism" was expanded to include all twelve tribes. *There are Hebrew Muslims and Hebrew Christians. There are Arab Jews and Arab Christians.* The designation "Jewish" was gradually changed from a religious identification into an ethnic designation. The *ethnic* characterization of the descriptor "Jewish" is not supported by fact. God has never given authority to any prophet to cavalierly "name a religion." Inspired by God, Prophet Abraham was the first person to name true worshippers of God alone *"Submitters"* ("Muslim" in Arabic). God approved of the religion for the entire creation, *"Peace" or "Submission"* ("Islam" in Arabic).

From the Quran:

The only religion approved by God is "Submission." Ironically, those who have received the scripture are the ones who dispute this fact, despite the knowledge they have received, due to jealousy. For such rejectors of God's revelations, God is most strict in reckoning. (3: 19)

Anyone who accepts other than Submission as his religion, it will not be accepted from him, and in the Hereafter, he will be with the losers. (3:85)

The word, *Judaism*, has come to be regarded as synonymous with the *religion* of the ancient Hebrews. The word is used in this book with the understanding that its current meaning is an acquired one. The word "Arab" is an ethno-linguistic designation whereas the word "Jew" refers to a religious affiliation. The late Dr. Alfred Lilienthal said:

> The Jewish racial myth flows from the fact that the words Hebrew, 'Israelite', Jew, Judaism, and the Jewish people have been used synonymously to suggest a historic continuity. But this is a misuse. These words refer to different groups of people with varying ways of life in different periods in history. Hebrew is a term correctly applied to the period from the beginning of Biblical history to the settling in Canaan. 'Israelite' refers correctly to the members of the twelve tribes of 'Israel'. The name Yehudi or Jew is used in the Old Testament to designate members of the tribe of Judah, descendants of the fourth son of Jacob, as well as to denote citizens of the Kingdom of Judah, particularly at the time of Jeremiah and under the Persian occupation. Centuries later, the same word came to be applied to anyone, no matter of what origin, whose religion was Judaism...The descriptive name Judaism was never heard by the Hebrews or 'Israelites'; it appears only with Christianity. [7]

To be *anti-Semitic* means to be against or hostile towards people who are native inhabitants of the Middle East and their descendants. The word "Semite" refers to a language and a cultural group made up of ancient and modern people: Akkadians, Canaanites, Phoenicians, Hebrews, and Arabs. According to the *Oxford English Dictionary*, the first usage of the term "anti-Semitic" for a person who discriminates against Jews was in the 1880s. In his on-line paper, William Martin points out that the 2003 edition of the *World Book* restricts the word "Semite" to people who speak Hebrew, Arabic, and related languages, and have lived in regions inhabited by Semitic peoples for generations.

> The **World Book** [emphasis added by author of quote] omits any reference to the Jews, but under the word Semite it states: "Semite... Semites are those who speak Semitic languages. In this sense the ancient Hebrews, Assyrians, Phoenicians, and Cartaginians were Semites. The Arabs and some Ethiopians are modern Semitic-speaking people. Modern Jews are often called Semites, but this name properly applies only to those who use the Hebrew Language. The Jews were once a sub-type of the Mediterranean race, but they have mixed with other peoples until the name 'Jew' has lost all racial meaning."[8]

In 1954, prominent New Yorker, Benjamin Freedman, disturbed by the dissolution and abandonment of original Old Testament teachings (Torah Law) and the confusion about the meaning of Jewish identity, wrote a booklet expounding on the popular "secondary meaning" of the word, "Jew." The following is an excerpt from his booklet, *Facts Are Facts*.[9]

> ...Well-planned and well-financed world-wide publicity through every available media by well-organized groups of so-called or self-styled "Jews" for three centuries has created a "secondary meaning" for the word "Jew" which has completely "blacked out" the original and correct meaning of the word "Jew". There can be no doubt about that. There is not a person in the whole English-speaking world today who regards a "Jew" as a "Judean" in the literal sense of the word. That was the correct and only meaning in the 18th century. The generally accepted "secondary meaning" of the word "Jew" today with practically no exceptions is made up of four almost universally-believed theories. These four theories are that a so-called or self-styled "Jew" is (1) a person who today professes the form of religious worship known as "Judaism", (2) a person who claims to belong to a racial

group associated with the ancient Semites, (3) a person directly the descendant of an ancient nation which thrived in Palestine in Bible history, (4) a person blessed by Divine intentional design with certain superior cultural characteristics denied to other racial, religious or national groups, all rolled into one.[10]

In the final analysis, the common understanding of the designations "Jew" and "Jewish" are unrelated to the original Hebrew peoples who inhabited the Middle East. At least in the West, the designations have become widespread and are accepted as descriptions of anyone who professes Judaism.

Who are the Khazars?

For centuries, the geographical origin of Western and European Jewry has been enshrouded in mystery and folklore. Most people are unaware of the historical accounts about the emergence of the larger old Jewish communities in the Western world. In his article, *Most Jews are Khazars*, J. Richard Niemela [11] said:

> Ninety percent of today's people who claim to be "Jews" and thus descendants of Judah (1/12th of ancient Israel) are simply not, that they are a Turkish-Mongol people called Khazars who moved into central Russia several centuries before the time of Christ ... this fairly large tribe who was known to be animists and phallic worshipers were induced to convert to Babylonian Talmudic Judaism in 740 A.D. by proselytizing Jews from the Babylonian area.... They brought their Talmud, the "oral traditions of the elders that made the law of non effect" (Jesus' words) back to Babylon with them and expanded its content there.... Because they let the Rabbis do their thinking and research for them and assume that these Rabbis tell the Truth! (pg. 1-2)[12]

In his book, *What Price Israel?* Dr. Alfred Lilienthal[13] noted the link between the Russian Khazars and Eastern European Jewish communities. This link is related to the subsequent redefinition of the meaning of Anti-Semitism.

That the Khazars are the lineal ancestors of Eastern European Jewry is a historical fact. Jewish historians and religious text books acknowledge the fact, though the propagandists of Jewish nationalism belittle it as pro-Arab propaganda. Somewhat ironically, Volume IV of the Jewish Encyclopedia—because this publication spells Khazars with a "C" instead of a "K"—is titled "Chazars to Dreyfus;" and it was the Dreyfus trial, as interpreted by Theodor Herzl, that made the modern Jewish Khazars of Russia forget their descent from *converts* [italics added] to Judaism and accept anti-Semitism as proof of their Palestinian origin.[14]

The early Khazars who *converted* to a distorted form of Judaism did not adopt the Torah or the Gospel.[15] The Khazars followed tenets of Talmudic Babylonian Judaism. Many among their posterity later immigrated to Eastern Europe, the West, and other locations. Today, many Jews living in the West maintain family names other than names that directly connect them with their Khazar Talmudic roots. It was the ancient *Hebrew*s enslaved in Egypt, the followers of Moses and Aaron, who were prevented from entering a land promised to them by God. Their failure to follow God's commands and proceed into the Promised Land was met with a Divine consequence. Almighty God did not allow that disobedient Hebrew generation to settle in a land of their own after their Exodus from Egypt. Subsequent to that disobedient generation, righteous Hebrews entered the land promised to them by God.

> One now simply has to review just where most of the world's Jews come from to see the truth in these historical facts...all disguised to distort the truth about themselves...much like always changing their names to hide their identity...both in Russia and in the West...[16]

From the Quran:

He said, 'My Lord, I can only control myself and my brother. So, allow us to part company with the wicked people.' He said, 'Henceforth, it is forbidden them for forty years, during which they will roam the earth aimlessly. Do not grieve over such wicked people.' (5:25-26)

Almighty God chose the ancient Hebrews for *greater blessings and tests* unlike any other people. God designated the descendants of Israel who worship Him alone as chosen above pagans and idol worshipers.

From the Quran:

Among the followers of Moses there are those who guide in accordance with the truth, and the truth renders them righteous. (7:159)

We have chosen them from among all the people knowingly. We showed them so many proofs, which constituted a great test. (44:31-32)

We have given the Children of Israel the scripture, wisdom, and prophethood, and provided them with good provisions; we bestowed upon them more blessing than any other people. We have given them clear commandments. Ironically, they did not dispute this until the knowledge had come to them. This is due to jealousy on their part. Surely, your Lord will judge them on the Day of Resurrection regarding everything they have disputed. (45:16-17)[17]

Individuals who subscribe to authentic Judaism realize that the special blessings, scripture, and proofs they received necessitate that they uphold the truth and God's commands. They do not dispute God's guidance. They recognize that God will call all humans to account on the Day of Resurrection. Proofs bring with them greater responsibilities to obey God and to resist urges to abandon submission to God alone. Submitter Jews realize that anyone who insists on a path of opposition to God's guidance and commands (i.e., fails the tests) forfeits the blessing of being among the chosen (i.e., righteous). The Creator bestows prosperity and blessings on any community that follows His guidance and obeys His commands.

Submitter Jews exhibit a tenacious identification with their spiritual predecessors' Exodus from Egypt. They perceive themselves as custodians of monotheism, and the recipients of the Torah (which includes the Ten Commandments). On the other hand, followers of distorted Judaism do not adhere as close to revealed Divine laws. They approach the early spiritual history of the Hebrews as "stories, metaphors, and tales" rather than factual accounts of Hebrew prophets and their communities. For example, few adherents of distorted Judaism believe in the events of the Exodus (e.g., division of the Red Sea, God speaking to Prophet Moses, a mountain moved from its base) as the events are depicted in the Old Testament of the Bible.

Many Jews do not acknowledge Jesus as a Prophet and the Messiah to the Jewish community of his time. *This position is incorrect.* Now we have scientifically-confirmed verses in the Quran that verify that Jesus was a Prophet of God and Messiah to the Hebrews. The Injil (Gospels) was revealed to Jesus.

From the Quran:

Pagans indeed are those who say that God is the Messiah, son of Mary. The Messiah himself said, "O Children of Israel, you shall worship God; my Lord and your Lord." Anyone who sets up any idol beside God, God has forbidden Paradise for him, and his destiny is Hell. The wicked have no helpers. (5:72)

Jews do not accept the idea of Jesus as a Divine being. *This position is correct.* I present more details about this *fact* in the chapter, "Distortions of Christianity." As expected, this "pill" of confirmed truth is very difficult for most Christians to swallow.

Pagans indeed are those who say that God is the Messiah, the son of Mary. Say, "Who could oppose God if He willed to annihilate the Messiah, son of Mary, and his mother, and everyone on earth?" To God belongs the sovereignty of the heavens and the earth, and everything between them. He creates whatever He wills. God is Omnipotent. (5:17)

The Messiah, son of Mary, is no more than a messenger like the messengers before him, and his mother was a saint. Both of them used to eat the food. Note how we explain the revelations for them, and note how they still deviate! (5:75)[18]

In keeping with the correct position, the Jewish calendar is not based on the markers "B.C." (before Christ) and "A.D." (after Christ's death). The Menorah Ministries[19] indicate that:

> "B.C., meaning "before Christ," & A.D., meaning "in the year of our Lord," are abbreviations primarily used/developed by Christians. Their use implies the acceptance of Jesus Christ as divine, a concept rejected by traditional rabbinic Judaism. Hence, in Jewish scholarship, B.C.E., meaning "before the Common Era," & C.E., meaning "the Common Era," were introduced to draw a distinction between Christian and Jewish belief." [20]

In distorted Judaism, the correct position about Jesus' human nature is used to justify the incorrect position of dismissing Jesus as a prophet of God. Put simply, a truth is used to justify falsehood. Misinformed adherents of all religions mix truth with falsehood.

From the Quran:

These messengers; we blessed some of them more than others. For example, God spoke to one, and we raised some of them to higher ranks. And we gave Jesus, son of Mary, profound miracles and supported him with the Holy Spirit. Had God willed, their followers would not have fought with each other, after the clear proofs had come to them. Instead, they disputed among themselves; some of them believed, and some disbelieved. Had God willed, they would not have fought. Everything is in accordance with God's will. (2:253)

God will say, "O Jesus, son of Mary, remember My blessings upon you and your mother. I supported you with the Holy Spirit, to enable you to speak to the people from the crib, as well as an adult. I taught you the scripture, wisdom, the Torah, and the Gospel. Recall that you created from clay the shape of a bird by My leave, then blew into it, and it became a live bird by My leave. You healed the blind and the leprous by My leave, and revived the dead by My leave. Recall that I protected you from the Children of Israel who wanted to hurt you, despite the profound miracles you had shown them. The disbelievers among them said, 'This is obviously magic.'" (5:110)[21]

Many misguided Jews do not regard the miracles reported in the Old and New Testaments (including the miracles associated with Moses) as facts. In matters regarding the significance of this life in relation to the Hereafter, modern distorted Judaism places an excessive emphasis on wealth and material fortune. Some followers of distorted Judaism believe that one's worst day in this life is preferred to any heavenly reward. In his book, *What Is A Jew,* Rabbis Morris Kertzer[22] noted that:

> "Jews have always been more concerned with this world than the next and have concentrated their religious efforts on building an ideal world for the living . . . the twelfth-century (Jewish) philosopher Maimonides maintained that only the immature are motivated by hopes of reward and fear of punishment. The reward for virtuous living is the good life itself."[23]

> "Jews sanctify not just time but space...."[24]

People who ascribe to these beliefs "put all their eggs in the "basket" of this temporary life. They engage in a relentless effort to constantly accrue prestige and possessions only to discover in the Hereafter that true honor and wealth is in submission to God alone. The Quran confirms the authentic contents of previous scriptures, including the miracles, the events of the Exodus, Moses receiving the Commandments on Mount Sinai, Jesus as the Messiah, spiritual preparation in this life for the Hereafter, and the histories of earlier prophets and messengers of God. Misguided Jews do not believe in Satan (i.e., the devil) as an actual being nor do they believe that failing to follow Divine commands and prohibitions merits negative spiritual consequences for them.

From the Quran:

When we said to the angels, "Fall prostrate before Adam," they fell prostrate, except Satan; he refused, was too arrogant, and a disbeliever. (2:34)

"I will mislead them, I will entice them, I will command them to (forbid the eating of certain meats by) marking the ears of livestock, and I will command them to distort the creation of God." Anyone who accepts the devil as a lord, instead of God, has incurred a profound loss. (4:119)

Anyone who seeks the materials of this world should know that God possesses both the materials of this world and the Hereafter. God is Hearer, Seer. (4:134)

We delivered the Children of Israel across the sea. Pharaoh and his troops pursued them, aggressively and sinfully. When drowning became a reality for him, he said, "I believe that there is no god except the One in whom the Children of Israel have believed; I am a submitter." (10:90)

Your god is one god. As for those who do not believe in the Hereafter, their hearts are denying, and they are arrogant. (16:22)

We have given Moses the scripture—do not harbor any doubt about meeting Him—and we made it a guide for the Children of Israel. (32:23)[25]

God Is Not Limited in Any Way

In distorted Judaism, an individual's purpose in life is "tikkun olum"— "repairing the world." Followers of distorted Judaism believe that they have been tasked with setting affairs right in this world based on their vision of human happiness, law, and justice.[26] Followers of distorted Judaism dismiss the fact that *self-repair is impossible if an individual does not heed God's guidance. Heeding God's guidance is required before a person can make any legitimate claims to teach or show others how to repair their lives.* No one can guide others in spiritual matters. No individual or group has a legitimate claim to a privileged exclusive appreciation of God's plan for human order on earth. This idea of "repairing the world" rests on a short-sighted notion that the Creator is incapable of controlling His creation and needs human agents to help set affairs aright. In his book entitled *When Bad Things Happen to Good People*, Rabbi Harold Kushner[27] wrote:

> God can't do everything, but he can do some important things.... I recognize His limitations. He is limited in what He can do by the law of nature, by the evolution of human nature and human moral freedom.[28]

An author, psychiatrist, and substance abuse counselor, Rabbi Abraham Twerski recognizes that the opinion that God cannot do everything is illogical and false. In his book, *The Spiritual Self: Reflections on Recovery and God*, Rabbi Twerski[29] said:

> Some people have solved the dilemma [idea that misfortunes and bad things just happen] by postulating that God has simply abandoned the world or has lost control of it. If this were so, it would be meaningless to turn our lives over to the will of God or to pray for Divine guidance. Assuming that God has not abandoned the world and does maintain control over everything except for the area of free moral choice, which He has delegated to mankind, leaves us with the only conclusion. We do not understand.[30]

If God cannot do everything and is limited to the evolution of human nature and moral freedom, why *is* God The Omnipotent, Omnipresent, and The Almighty? The answer lies in the question. One cannot be Omnipotent, Omnipresent, and Almighty, and be limited *in any way*. God certainly is not limited by a law or condition He created. An individual who claims that misfortunes occur in this life because God is constrained or limited (i.e., "hands are tied") does not appreciate or choose to acknowledge the fact that God knows and controls all things. Regardless of whether an individual acknowledges this truth, some misfortunes an individual experiences are a result of his or her own action or inaction.

From the Quran:

To God belongs everything in the heavens and everything on earth, and all matters are controlled by God. (3:109)

Wherever you are, death will catch up with you, even if you live in formidable castles. When something good happens to them, they say, "This is from God," and when something bad afflicts them, they blame you. Say, "Everything comes from God." Why do these people misunderstand almost everything? (4:78)

The Jews even said, "God's hand is tied down!" It is their hands that are tied down. They are condemned for uttering such a blasphemy. Instead, His hands are wide open, spending as He wills. For certain, your Lord's revelations to you will cause many of them to plunge deeper into transgression and disbelief. Consequently, we have committed them to animosity and hatred among themselves until the Day of Resurrection. Whenever they ignite the flames of war, God puts them out. They roam the earth wickedly, and God dislikes the evildoers. (5:64)

Anything bad that happens to you is a consequence of your own deeds, and He overlooks many (of your sins). (42:30)

Nothing happens to you except in accordance with God's will. Anyone who believes in God, He will guide his heart. God is fully aware of all things. (64:11)

Most exalted is the One in whose hands is all kingship, and He is Omnipotent. (67:1)[31]

In distorted Judaism, an individual's relationship with God is not reflected in "keeping old traditions and commands." The relationship is in seeking new meaning and application of commands, and even composing new commands to allegedly fit modern circumstances. Misguided Jews are encouraged by their religious leaders to select philosophies of life or "devices for living"[32] that best suit their individual desires and needs. Adherence to Divine commands is not viewed as essential to one's psychological or spiritual development. This revised attitude towards obeying God's commands is inconsistent with proven truth in the Quran and authentic portions of the Old Testament (Torah) and the New Testament (Gospel).

From the Quran:

If only they would uphold the Torah and the Gospel, and what is sent down to them herein from their Lord, they would be showered with blessings from above them and from beneath their feet. Some of them are righteous, but many of them are evildoers. (5:66)

Any approach to Divine scripture and guidance merely to debate, conjecture, attempt to outwit text writers, compose stories, and write new laws is certainly not the worship of God. Such behavior is an encouraged tradition in distorted Judaism. When posed with the question of what rules to keep, some followers of distorted Judaism adhere to the Babylonian Talmud authored by a group of ancient rabbis known as *Amora'im Rabbis*. Not a revealed scripture, the Talmud was compiled from the third to the seventh century and consists of two parts—the *Mishnah* and the *Gemara*. The Mishna contains recorded teachings, sayings, interpretations, and explanations *by Rabbis*. The Gemara contains records of actions and recommendations *by Rabbis*. The words of Rabbis became the preferred substitutes for revealed guidance. According to distorted Judaism, the Jewish motivation to study sacred text lies in opportunities to debate and conjecture about the meaning of certain injunctions, outwit the text writers, and debunk undesirable directives.

From the Quran:

They have set up their religious leaders and scholars as lords, instead of God. Others deified the Messiah, son of Mary. They were all commanded to worship only one god. There is no god except He. Be He glorified, high above having any partners. (9:31)

They will also say, "Our Lord, we have obeyed our masters and leaders, but they led us astray. (33:67)

Despite the fact that the ancient Hebrews received the *Torah*, distorted Judaism opines that the first book of Jewish law is the human-authored Mishnah.

From the Quran:

The example of those who were given the Torah, then failed to uphold it, is like the donkey carrying great works of literature. Miserable indeed is the example of people who rejected God's revelations. God does not guide the wicked people. (62:5)[33]

The human-authored "books of law" were written at least two hundred years after the death of Prophet Jesus. Kertzer described the Babylonian Talmud as:

> A giant compendium of law and lore... the major textbook of Jewish schools for centuries. Study of its contents constitutes, even today, the largest block of time in the training of Orthodox and Conservative rabbis. Orthodox Jewish law is based largely on the decisions already found in the Talmud.... People enjoy the Talmud for its contents and for the mere fun of figuring out the rabbinic argument, a sort of Jewish puzzle in logic. The Talmud is interlaced with thousands of parables, anecdotes, and epigrams that provide a glimpse into Jewish life and lore.... To study a page of the Talmud is therefore to study great masses of interpretation that preceded us.[34]

In response to the question, "Do Jews still follow all the biblical laws, even the harsh ones like "an eye for an eye?" the authors wrote:

> No. In fact, many of the laws laid down in the Bible were never kept, even in biblical times. Frequently, the last writers of the Torah (living in the fifth century B.C.E.) wrote accounts of events that had occurred years or even centuries earlier, in which they imagined stories of people keeping the laws and customs that could not have existed at that time.[35]

Unlike tenets of authentic Judaism, distorted Judaism's perspective on Divine revelation, disobedience to God's commands and historical accounts of early prophets indicates a long-held reluctance to submit to Divine guidance. An objective observer notes a practice of dissecting Divine commands only to ignore them or grudgingly obey the commands when they are interpreted in a self-serving manner.

From the Quran:

Moses said to his people, "God commands you to sacrifice a heifer." They said, "Are you mocking us?" He said, "God forbid, that I should behave like the ignorant ones." They said, "Call upon your Lord to show us which one." He said, "He says that she is a heifer that is neither too old, nor too young; of an intermediate age. Now, carry out what you are commanded to do." They said, "Call upon your Lord to show us her color." He said, "He says that she is a yellow heifer, bright colored, pleases the beholders." They said, "Call upon your Lord to show us which one. The heifers look alike to us and, God willing, we will be guided." He said, "He says that she is a heifer that was never humiliated in plowing the land or watering the crops; free from any blemish." They said, "Now you have brought the truth." They finally sacrificed her, after this lengthy reluctance. (2:67-71)

Disingenuous rabbinical judges' practice of not revealing the sinfulness of a behavior so as to ease the guilt and anxiety of individuals is essentially granting individuals a license to commit sin. The willful non-disclosure of Divine prohibitions is nothing less than hiding the truth from others. Spiritual leaders of distorted Judaism condone and promote this behavior. The concealment of the truth also occurs in distorted Christianity and Islam.

From the Quran:

We made a covenant with you, as we raised Mount Sinai above you, saying, "You shall uphold the commandments we have given you, strongly, and listen." They said, "We hear, but we disobey." Their hearts became filled with adoration for the calf, due to their disbelief. Say, "Miserable indeed is what your faith dictates upon you, if you do have any faith." (2:93)

Those who received the scripture recognize the truth herein, as they recognize their own children. Yet, some of them conceal the truth, knowingly. (2:146)

Those who are not expecting to meet us, and are preoccupied with this worldly life, and are content with it, and refuse to heed our proofs; these have incurred Hell as their ultimate abode, as a consequence of their own works. (10:7)[36]

Distorted Judaism and Freudian Psychoanalytic Theory

During the nineteenth century in Vienna, Austria, distorted Judaism served as the most influential context for Psychiatrist Dr. Sigmund Freud to author classical psychoanalytic theory. Freud composed a psychology of living with the *specific objective* to help its adherents maintain a sense of mental well-being in the absence of acknowledgment and adherence to Divine guidance. Since the introduction of psychoanalytic theory, not a small number of individuals (Jewish and non-Jewish) have accommodated tenets of the theory as a substitute for religion. In his book, *Freudian Fraud*, Dr. E. Fuller Torrey[37] expounds on the extent that Freud regarded his new method of psychotherapy and personality development as a substitute "religion." Dr. Torrey noted:

> The similarities of Freudian theory and therapy to religion have been noted and commented upon from its earliest inception in Vienna. Indeed, the very first psychoanalytic patient, Bertha Pappehheim, who was treated by Freud's mentor, Dr. Josef Breur, noted that "psychoanalysis in the hands of the physician is what confession is in the hands of the Catholic priest." This parallel was also clearly drawn by Max Graf, one of the original members of Freud's Wednesday Society …Graf recalled:
>
> *There was an atmosphere of the foundation of a religion in that room. Freud was its new prophet who made the therefore prevailing methods of psychological investigation appear superficial. Freud's pupils, all inspired and convinced, were his apostles.*[38]

A staunch Theist, Dr. Alfred Adler soon became disenchanted with Freud, Freud's theory of personality development, and Freud's method of psychotherapy. Dr. Adler believed that Freud exaggerated the importance of sex, justified self indulgence, and diminished the important of spiritual belief in personality development. The break between Adler and Freud was inevitable. Dr. Torrey writes:

> When Freud excluded Alfred Adler because he minimized the importance of sex and thus deviated from Freudian theory, Graf observed: "Freud, as head of a Church, banished Adler; he ejected him from the official church. Within the space of a few years, I lived through the whole development of a church history. ..."[39]

Anti-religious elements of psychoanalytic theory have had a widespread deleterious impact on the society's view of human nature. Many misguided individuals who seek alternatives to a *psycho-spiritual explanation* of mental well-being subscribe to anti-religious elements of traditional Freudian theory. Some people in the West erroneously regard traditional psychoanalytic theory as the origin of psychotherapy. Freud's opinions and observations about personality development and mental illness are even equated in importance with Dr. Albert Einstein's discovery of the Law of Irrelativity.[40] A poster-size photograph depicting both men smoking pipes was very popular among college students and when I was an undergraduate student. The poster could be found in many college dormitories, college bookstores, library shops, and bookstores. The message was simple: always admire these two great thinkers of the twentieth century, whose ideas and discoveries changed our view of reality in many ways. It was politically correct and intellectually appropriate to view both men as equal in stature and equal in their discoveries: one about the outer universe and the other about the inner universe. Composed of arbitrary assumptions about human mental health and psychopathology, Freud's psychoanalytic theory is not remotely equivalent to the scientific discoveries made by Einstein. Psychoanalytic theory is *not* an example of disciplined scientific inquiry. In contrast to Freud's purported "psychic liberation of the self," Einstein's discovery about the nature of time and space set the stage for numerous incredible discoveries about the physical universe. Some of these discoveries include the Big Bang Law (it has been scientifically proven and no longer should be regarded as a theory) and Intelligent Design Theory.

Nevertheless, many individuals, especially in the intellectual and arts communities, believe that Freud's opinions about unconscious dynamics that impact on personality development and mental health are perennial truths. Over time, concepts of Psychoanalytic Theory have been absorbed into the language of popular culture, slang, and the arts in the West. In the on-line article, *The Psychoanalytic Stream of Psychology*[41], its authors wrote:

> Moreover, Freudian concepts and terms have so permeated our society that they are generally treated as facts about human nature. For instance, numerous people refer to the id, ego, and superego as if these entities truly exist, as if they are well-defined components of the personality....Freud taught that religious doctrines are illusions and that religion is the "universal obsessional neurosis of humanity." He viewed religion as the source of mankind's problems and thus formed all of his notions from a godless position.[42]

In his much-acclaimed book, *Civilization and Its Discontents*, Freud [43] wrote:

> Thus, religion would be a universal obsessive neurosis of mankind. Just like the obsessive neurosis in children, it springs from the Oedipus complex, the relationship with the father. Should this concept be correct, distancing from religion should be as inevitable as the process of growing, and we are in this junction, the middle of this junction, in the middle of this developmental phase.[44]

Freud viewed religion and moral sanctions as "the source of mankind's mental problems." His explanations of neurotic guilt and anxiety contribute to the distortion of religion in human life. Traditional psychoanalytic theory is described as a *"device of living"* that provides its proponents with a means of distancing and liberating themselves from *moral* guilt and anxiety after violating God's commands. In his book, *Rational-Irrational Man and Torah Psychology*, Avrohom Amsel[45] concluded that Freudian psychoanalysis weighs in heavily as a psychology of personality that fostered a lack of moral conscientiousness and spiritual yearning in the twentieth century. Amsel viewed Freudian methods as simply a way of absolving the sinner by diagnosing him or her as being psychologically ill.

In addition to acknowledging positive contributions that Freud made to our understanding of the human mind, Dr. Torrey pointed out significant liabilities of Freudian thought. Dr. Torrey said:

> The core of Freud's theory and therapy are both fundamentally narcissistic in assuming that one's happiness is the greatest good…The formulation is a license for unremitting self-indulgence, since the quest for self-love is never finished and since the obligation to love others must be deferred while the search continues.
>
> A second major liability of Freud's theory has been its promotion of irresponsibility.…In the Freudian schema, mother, father, family, social circumstances, and culture become the causal agents for whatever is wrong. The ripple of personal irresponsibility spreads slowly outward to cover ever-greater areas until the terms "good" and "bad" seem to no longer have meaning.[46]

In *Jewish Origins of the Psychoanalytic Movement,* Dr. Dennis B. Klein[47] postulated that there is a connection between Freud's ideas and Jewish Talmudic traditions. Note that this tradition is born from the Babylonian Talmud and Rabbinical writings and edicts, not from the Torah or any other revealed scripture. Klein stated that there was:

> …an interpenetration of the Jewish redemptive vision with the psychoanalytic movement's hope for the eradication of neurosis.[48]

Writing about the plight of modern man in rejecting authentic spirituality, Dr. Paul Brunton[49] identified Freud as an example of a scientist who suppressed his spirituality in his efforts to advance beyond a need to rely on an unseen power or force. Dr. Brunton wrote:

> The scientist who regards religion as another word for superstition, and who thinks of himself as nothing more than a body, is in a sorry state. He has lost four valuable characteristics which elevate and, among others, distinguish the human form from the animal creatures: faith in an unseen power, humility and reverence at the thought of it, and

the capacity for prayer to it. Freud, for example, denounced religious belief as an illusion to be rid of in a more evolved society, yet himself harboured the illusion that science alone could provide all the guidance in life which a man needed. How many men who once thought as Freud, continue to think so now. ...[50]

In his classic work, *Sigmund Freud and The Jewish Mystical Tradition*, Dr. David Bakan[51] explains the social and religious factors that influenced Freud when he authored psychoanalysis. Predating the reformist movement among Western Jews, an early sect of western Judaism known as Sabbatianism promoted: 1) the "holiness of participating in all things, evil and non-evil," 2) "concern for the forbidden areas of human experience," and 3) "the doctrine of the necessity of the descent into evil in order to attain spiritual liberation." According to Bakan, Sabbatianism lent itself as a "rationalization of apostacy" (i.e., violation of the command to worship one God, and other commands). Underlying this rationalization of apostacy is the supposition that a contract has been broken—a contract between the self and God as the Provider and Protector. One does not have to honor a contract with another party who has broken the contract. The implication is that God broke the contract between Himself and the Jewish people.

From the Quran:

(They incurred condemnation) for violating their covenant, rejecting God's revelations, killing the prophets unjustly, and for saying, "Our minds are made up!" In fact, God is the One who sealed their minds, due to their disbelief, and this is why they fail to believe, except rarely. (4:155)

Remember God's blessing upon you, and His covenant that He covenanted with you: you said, "We hear and we obey." You shall observe God; God is fully aware of the innermost thoughts. (5:7)

In truth, God's covenant with the children of Israel was contingent on their obeying His commands and supporting His messengers and prophets. God never breaks His promise. It is we humans who do not keep our 'end' of the covenant with our Creator. Succumbing to self-centered desires and Satan's prompts, individuals' recurrent intentional disobedience removes them from God's protection.

> *God had taken a covenant from the Children of Israel, and we raised among them twelve patriarchs. And God said, "I am with you, so long as you observe the Contact Prayers (Salat), give the obligatory charity (Zakat), and believe in My messengers and respect them, and continue to lend God a loan of righteousness. I will then remit your sins, and admit you into gardens with flowing streams. Anyone who disbelieves after this, has indeed strayed off the right path." (5:12)* [52]

Deluded in his thinking that God is harsh and oppressive, Freud dismissed the moral conscience as merely an outcome of socialization. Freud invented the "superego". The inborn spiritual compass was relegated to a "superego" that reflects dictates of parents, authority figures, religion, and society.

> From a psychological point of view, we envisage, on the basis of what Freud has taught us, the individual, in his development, as entering into a social contract, in which the individual agrees to abide by the demands of society in return for certain satisfactions and protections. When one's life situation grows too bad, the question arises as to whether the other party is abiding by his part of the contract. If this doubt crosses the line and becomes a conclusion, that the other party has broken the contract, then the individual feels free to do as he pleases....The notion of the Covenant is psychologically the idea of the social contract, that the Jews would accept the yoke of the Law in return for God's favor. [53]

In identifying debris on this portion of the now vast spiritual obstacle course, it is important to clarify the religious underpinnings of the social contract embraced in distorted Judaism. So-called "demands of society" originally were references to commands of God and the "yoke of the Law." In this contract, submission or obedience to God is conditional. Obedience is only obligatory when God "holds His end of the contract by giving me what I want and deserve." This conditional worship rests upon the patently false notion that God is limited, too harsh, and oblivious to human travails. With these premises as his foundation, Freud literally made a pact with the devil to author a psychotherapy that would ease the guilt of his clients who violated the Mosaic Law and embraced "conditional worship." It is not uncommon to meet chronic cocaine and heroin abusers who disclose that they have communicated with and made pacts with Satan, the "demon world," and unseen forces.

Bakan comments about Freud's belief in the "curative power inherent in the Devil" and Freud's pact with the Devil.

> The idea of the contract with the Devil is of course consistent with the contractual feature of both the Covenant and the social contract, but a new one in details...The Devil is then a cure for despair. He is called upon as an assertive act when all hope is gone...The Devil presents new hope, and supports his promise by immediate tokens of his favor.[54]

In Freud's own words:

> Do you know that I am the Devil? All my life I have had to play the Devil, in order that others would be able to build the most beautiful cathedral with the materials I produced."[55]

From the Quran:

If only they implored when our test afflicted them! Instead, their hearts were hardened, and the devil adorned their works in their eyes. (6:43)

And the devil will say, after the judgment had been issued, "God has promised you the truthful promise, and I promised you, but I broke my promise. I had no power over you; I simply invited you, and you accepted my invitation. Therefore, do not blame me, and blame only yourselves. My complaining cannot help you, nor can your complaining help me. I have disbelieved in your idolizing me. The transgressors have incurred a painful retribution." (14:22)

> *Among the people there is the one who worships God conditionally. If things go his way, he is content. But if some adversity befalls him, he makes an about face. Thus, he loses both this life and the Hereafter. Such is the real loss. (22:11)*
>
> *Anyone who disregards the message of the Most Gracious, we appoint a devil to be his constant companion. Such companions will divert them from the path, yet make them believe that they are guided. (43:36-37)*[56]

Freud clearly acknowledged his "church" and his pact with the devil. Freud promoted his method of psychoanalysis as a means for others to build an alternative psycho-spiritual reality that enables them to practice any desired immoral behavior without guilt. The individual is encouraged to ignore and discard moral restraint as a means of overcoming what is deemed as "neurotic guilt."

> The disease of the neurotic is his guilt. The guilt is, in itself, an evil and its removal is good. However, within the neurosis, the guilt is a punishment for evil. Within the neurosis a counterforce to the punishing imago is required. Hence there is an alliance with such a counter-imago as will allow all to become open, accessible to consciousness. If God is the guilt-producing imago, then the Devil is the counterforce.[57]

Reflecting on his childhood, Freud said he revolted against his father's harsh imposition of religious law. As an expression of that revolt in adulthood, Freud said that he collected statuettes in his study "in open defiance of the Mosaic Law against idol worship." Freud's behavior was strikingly similar to the practices of Sabbatians who intentionally and openly violated the first commandment by worshipping a wooden image of the movement's founder, Sabbatai Zevi.

> In his room, Freud surrounded himself with every heathen God he could find. As if in sheer spite [Yiddish expression *meshamed uf tselochos*, "an apostate out of spite."], he pursued "idols" and their associated trappings with a deep fascination. His study and consulting room bulged with them.[58]

His resistance to law and his tendency towards violation of the commandment against idolatry, as manifested in his jocular yet passionate having of other gods before the Mosaic God, expressed his rebellion against orthodox Jewish religion. The "grubby old gods" lessened Moses' magic power.[59]

Bakan quotes Susan Bernfeld in her interpretation of Freud's fetish for small statues:

> He fell in love with archeology and therefore gained the strength to live in mental security without religion.[60]

In Freud's own words:

> My grubby old gods, of whom you think so little, take part in my work as paper-weights.[61]

Several major contributors to the psychology of personality development who were colleagues of Freud, broke away from his school of psychoanalysis. Dr. Carl Jung, Dr. Alfred Adler, and Dr. Karen Horney recognized the spurious nature of critical components of psychoanalytic theory. They composed alternative explanations of human personality development. In his widely read classic on the meaning of love, *The Art of Loving*, Dr. Eric Fromm[62] commented on Freud's perception of a healthy personality. Fromm wrote:

> ...for Freud love is an irrational phenomenon. The difference between irrational love, and love as an expression of the mature personality does not exists for him.... According to Freud, the full and uninhibited satisfaction of all instinctual desires would create mental health and happiness. But the obvious clinical facts demonstrate that men—and women—who devote their lives to unrestricted sexual satisfaction do not attain happiness, and very often suffer from severe neurotic conflicts or symptoms. The complete satisfaction of all instinctual needs is not only not a basis for happiness, it does not even guarantee sanity.[63]

Whatever insights that some concepts of psychoanalytic theory and therapy have contributed to the understanding of the human psyche,

Freud's methods or "alternative religion" were originally meant for people attempting to escape the reality of the spiritual Absolute (i.e., God). The escape may be conscious or suppressed. The escape may be expressed in the adoption of life views that run counter to *Divinely-revealed* moral principles. Once morality is defined as "whatever one defines it as" or as merely an "outcome of socialization," it becomes easier to dismiss restrictions on behavior deemed immoral or prohibited in authentic scripture. Within the confines of radical schools of distorted Judaism, a Jewish person's behavior is *never* deemed morally wrong or evil. Instead, the individual's actions are viewed by peers as exempt from codes of morality. Freud felt that he could at least earn a sizable income by promoting his new therapeutic method among an eager following who wanted to overcome moral guilt without having to embrace the Law revealed to the Hebrew prophets.

> Furthermore, this new set of methods which he was producing held out the promise of bringing patients to him and so solving at least the problem of making a living. That he conceived of psychoanalysis as a means of economic support is indicated by a remark he made in Sach's presence. Sachs says, "But Freud's expectation did not include any martyrdom: 'I (Freud) would probably succeed in making a living with the help of the therapeutic success of the new technique.'"[64]

Divine Commands Deemed Outdated

The notion that a Divine command could be "unrealistic" and unsuitable for "modern sensitivities" implies that God is limited and man knows better than the Creator what is best for man. Couching the defiance of Divine laws in the old rabbinical language of "Pharisaic intellectual reexamination," distorted Judaism places greater value on a deluded sense of intellectual examination than on submission to the Creator. The phrase, "Pharisaic intellectual reexamination," refers to the Pharisees' practice of scrutinizing, re-interpreting, and even re-writing Divine laws to suit their needs. Prophet Jesus informed and warned his Hebrew contemporaries against ignoring or changing Divine laws.

From the Bible:

Do not misunderstand why I have come. I did not come to abolish the law of Moses or the writings of the prophets. No, I came to fulfill them. I assure you, until heaven and earth disappear, even the smallest detail of God's law will remain until its purpose is achieved. So if you break the smallest commandment and teach others to do the same, you will be the least in the Kingdom of Heaven. But anyone who obeys God's laws and teaches them will be great in the Kingdom of Heaven. But I warn you – unless you obey God better than the teachers of religious law and the Pharisees do, you cannot enter the Kingdom of Heaven at all. (Matthew 5:17-20)[65]

Followers of distorted Judaism prefer to read volumes of *man-made* interpretations, rulings, tales and stories, and hypothetical life scenarios as sources of religious guidance. This custom is evident in the study of the *responsa*. The *responsa* are commentaries on sacred law that often take preeminence over simple application of the laws. The *responsa* are similar to volumes of case law and legal technicalities that underpin secular law in many Western societies. In distorted Judaism, Jews have the "right" to make *Midrash* or write and collect lengthy commentaries as sources of legal and religious guidance. The phrase, "until its purpose is achieved," in verse 18 above (third sentence) does not grant Jewish religious leaders the authority to dismiss Divine commands as no longer valid or suitable. It is unclear who or what granted the right to constituents of distorted Judaism, Islam and Christianity to reinterpret, redefine, and even discard Divine laws and commands.

From the Quran:

Among those who are Jewish, some distort the words beyond the truth, and they say, "We hear, but we disobey," and "Your words are falling on deaf ears," and "Raa'ena (be our shepherd)," as they twist their tongues to mock the religion. Had they said, "We hear, and we obey," and "We hear you," and "Unzurna (watch over us)," it would have been better for them, and more righteous. Instead, they have incurred condemnation from God due to their disbelief. Consequently, the majority of them cannot believe. (4:46)

It was a consequence of their violating the covenant that we condemned them, and we caused their hearts to become hardened. Consequently, they took the words out of context, and disregarded some of the commandments given to them. You will continue to witness betrayal from them, excepting a few of them. You shall pardon them, and disregard them. God loves those who are benevolent. (5:13)

Say, "Does any of your idols guide to the truth?" Say, "God guides to the truth. Is one who guides to the truth more worthy of being followed, or one who does not guide, and needs guidance for himself? What is wrong with your judgment? Most of them follow nothing but conjecture, and conjecture is no substitute for the truth. God is fully aware of everything they do. (10:35-36)[66]

Rather than discard a culture's practices that run counter to Divine guidance, followers of distorted Judaism are encouraged by their leaders and scholars of religion to either "follow the customs of the place," or "not follow the practices of the host." Conformity to local customs and practices is emphasized when to do otherwise is perceived as a serious threat to one's Jewish identity. An important question is: *What counts as Jewish identity in distorted Judaism?* Hopefully, the identity that a Jewish person embraces is as close as possible to the authentic teachings of the Jewish Prophets. If the identity is based on: 1) reverence of this material world, 2) discarding Divine commands under the guise of so-called modern thinking, 3) arbitrarily deciding what is correct for oneself without reference to revealed scripture, and 4) clinging to a *distorted* status of privilege, the identity is a pathologic one. Similar to other distorted religions, involvement in distorted Judaism serves to *maintain* a confounded religious identity. A Jewish Submitter does not dismiss any truth deemed "unacceptable" or "outdated" by someone with a distorted Jewish identity. This rule of thumb holds true for sincere seekers in all religions.

From the Quran:

Have you seen the one whose god is his own ego? Will you be his advocate? (25:43)

Have you noted the one whose god is his ego? Consequently, God sends him astray, despite his knowledge, seals his hearing and his mind, and places a veil on his eyes. Who then can guide him, after such a decision by God? Would you not take heed? (45:23)[67]

Official Symbol: Star of David?

A symbol can be anything that typifies, represents, or aids in recalling something else. Symbols can be mental and physical. Physical symbols serve as marks, signs, logos and representations of ideas or things. The letters of any alphabet are symbols. The letters prompt speakers and readers to make specific sounds and recognize different words. An obvious example is your reading of the words on this page. Humans are symbolic creatures. There is one arena where symbols, especially physical ones, are expressly forbidden. The arena is the worship of God. God has commanded us not to make or conceptualize any "graven image." God never authorized prophets and messengers to adopt any symbols of the messages revealed to them or symbols of the *religious* communities that received the messages. Nevertheless, communities have adopted icons and symbols to represent their specific religious beliefs. Soon enough, one is surrounded and swamped with religious symbols that take on meanings of their own. People worship their religious symbols and some come to believe that the symbols are sacred and have power.

Like other organized religions, distorted Judaism adopted a symbol central to its community—a six-point star that is now commonly referred to as the "Star of David." The Star of David is a basic hexagram considered to be a magical sign, amulet, and astrological symbol among the ancient Greeks, Babylonians, and Romans. The hexagram has been associated with witchcraft and free masonry. In the Jewish tradition, it has symbolized a *shield* among some Jewish communities against evil and adversaries. In his article entitled *"Star of David,"* Rabbi Scheinnerman[68] points out that:

> ...It further appears that the hexagram and pentagram were used interchangeably until this period, and then the six-point star gained favor, as it was associated with the notion of a "shield" of God and taken to have magical powers when used as an amulet. From the 14th century through the 18th century, the terms "shield of David" and "seal of Solomon" were used in magical texts indiscriminately though the hexagram ascended in popularity as the pentagram diminished in popularity. [69]

Jews adopted the hexagram and began to decorate buildings with it, and use it as a magical deterrent against demons and as protection of unborn children. The geometric symbol is also found in modern literature about Judaism. In his book, *What Is A Jew?*, Kertzer said,

> Surprisingly, however, the star did not arise within Judaism, and until recently, it has had no particularly Jewish religious meaning . . . the fiction arose that it must be an ancient and revered Jewish symbol. Whatever its origin, the Star of David really is distinctively Jewish now. [70]

Jewish Submitters

Many adherents of distorted Judaism retain a nominal identification with the Hebrews of the scriptures. Adherents of distorted Judaism embrace lifestyles and author philosophies and psychologies of life that serve as substitutes for Divine guidance. Distorted Judaism promotes a sense of intellectual elitism that grants preeminence to self-centered reasoning and behavior over submission to God. Even Aristotle would say that reason devoid of spiritual guidance ceases to be reasonable. In contrast to distorted Judaism, Jewish Submitters know that God's commands are not "dead," "obsolete," or "inappropriate." Jewish Submitters recognize that people place excessive hardships and burdens on themselves by rejecting revealed guidance. Jewish Submitters know that God knows and controls all things. Jewish Submitters reject the man-composed Talmud, so-called mysteries and mystical systems that "unite good and evil," and rabbinical innovations and inventions. Jewish Submitters follow the Torah and authentic teaching of Jesus as revealed in the Injil. Like other Submitters, Jewish Submitters are humble, follow God's guidance and commands, and are among the righteous.

From the Quran:

Surely, those who believe, those who are Jewish, the Christians, and the converts; anyone who **(1) believes in God, and (2) believes in the Last Day, and (3) leads a righteous life,** *will receive their recompense from their Lord. They have nothing to fear, nor will they grieve. (2:62)*

They are not all the same; among the followers of the scripture, there are those who are righteous. They recite God's revelations through the night, and they fall prostrate. They believe in God and the Last Day, they advocate righteousness and forbid evil, and they hasten to do righteous works. These are the righteous. Any good they do will not go unrewarded. God is fully aware of the righteous. (3:113-115)

Moses said, "O my people, if you have really believed in God, then put your trust in Him, **if you are really submitters.***" (10:84)*

Among the followers of Moses there are those who guide in accordance with the truth and the truth renders them righteous. (7:159) [71]

Notes

[1] F. Abate, *Oxford English Dictionary* (New York: Oxford University Press, 1998).

[2] Many people from Eastern Europe, Russia, Spain, America, Latin America, Portugal, and other parts of the world have adopted Judaism, but they are not *genetic* descendants of Semites (e.g., Hebrews, Arabs) from Palestine and the Middle East.

[3] D.A. Stoop, and S.E. Arterburn, *Life Recovery Bible: New Living Translation* (Wheaton, Illinois: Tyndale House Publishers, Inc., 1998).

[4] *A Reader's Guide to the Holy Bible.* (New York: Thomas Nelson, Inc.1972).

[5] Stoop and Arterburn, *Recovery Bible*, 29.

[6] Khalifa, *Quran*, 2:127, 133; 14:39.

[7] Alfred Lilienthal, *"Judaism: religion or race,"* <http://www.theodernreligion.com/comparative/jew/race-rel.html> (May 4, 2003).

[8] William Martin, *"Publications Showing the Jews to be Khazars and Not Israelites,"* <http://www.biblebelievers.org.au/jews.htlm> (May 4, 2003).

[9] Benjamin Freedman, *"Facts are Facts"*. (1954) In: "The Truth About the Khazars," <http://geocities.com/athens/olympus/9567/facts.htlm> (May 4, 2003)

[10] Ibid, Chapter 2.

[11] J. Richard Niemela, *"Most Jews are Khazars,"* <http://christianparty.net/jewskhazars.htm >(May 4, 2003)

[12] Ibid, 1.

[13] Alfred Lilienthal, *What Price Israel* (first published in 1953), <http://alfredlilienthal.com/what_price_israel.htm.> (May 4, 2003).

[14] Ibid, Chapter 12.

[15] The Khazars did not embrace the authentic scriptures and commands revealed to the Hebrew Prophets and practiced by Submitters among the Children of Israel.

[16] Lilienthal, *What Price Israel*, Chapter 12.

[17] Khalifa, *Quran*, 5:25-26; 7:159, 44:31-32, and 45:16-17.

[18] Ibid, 5:72, 5:17, and 5:75.

[19] Menorah Ministries, *What does B.C.E. & C.E. mean and why does the Jewish community use them rather than B.C. and A.D.* <http://www.menorah.org/askpr6.html > (January 1, 2003).

[20] Ibid, 1.

21 Khalifa, *Quran*, 2:253 and 5:110.

22 M. Kertzer, *What is a Jew?* (New York: Collier Books, 1993).

23 Ibid, 118.

24 Ibid, 126.

25 Khalifa, *Quran*, 2:34, 4:119, 134; 10:90, 16:22, and 32:23.

26 Most members of each one of the distorted monotheistic religions believe that its own vision of world order is the right vision. None of the distorted religions adhere to God's revealed guidance and directives for world order.

27 Harold Kushner, *When Bad Things Happen to Good People*, (New York: Schocken Books, 1987).

28 Ibid, 113 and 125.

29 Abraham Twerski , *The Spiritual Self: Reflections on Recovery and God*, (Center City, Minnesota: 2000)

30 Ibid, 93.

31 Khalifa, *Quran*, 3:109, 4:78, 5:64, 42:30, 64:11, and 67:1.

32 In this context, devices for living are strategies devoid of any spiritual accountability that a person uses to promote their interests and psychological well being.

33 Khalifa, *Quran*, 5:66, 9:31, 33:67, and 62:5.

34 The Mishna and Gemara are not revealed scriptures.

35 Kertzer, *What is a Jew?*, 47-48, and 50.

36 Khalifa, *Quran*, 2:67-71, 93, 146 and 10:7.

37 E. Fuller Torrey, *Freudian Fraud: The Malignant Affect of Freud's Theory on American Culture and Thought*. (New York, N.Y.: Harper-Collins Publishers, 1992).

38 Ibid, 253-254.

39 Ibid, 254.

40 Albert Einstein, *Cosmic Religion* (New York: Covoci-Freide Publishers, 1931). Dr. Einstein did not name his famous discovery about the nature of energy and matter ($E = MC^2$) the "law of relativity." He named it "Irrelativity" because he realized that there is as an Absolute to which everything else is relative. That Absolute is not relative to anything (i.e., Irrelativity).

41 PsychoHeresy Awareness Ministries, *The Psychoanalytic Stream of Psychology*,

Distortions of Judaism

http://psychoheresy-aware.org/freud136.html (20 April 2003).

[42] It is not a coincidence that this view is remarkably similar to the view that "religion is the opiate of the people" espoused in the *Communist Manifesto* written by Karl Marx and Vladimir Lenin.

[43] Sigmund Freud, *Civilization and Its Discontents*, (New York: W. W. Norton & Company, 1984).

[44] Ibid, 57. In reviewing several re-publications of this book, I noticed that the original words of Freud cited in this quote have been changed so as not to portray Freud as so brazenly anti-religious.

[45] Avrohom Amsel, *Rational-Irrational Man, and Torah Psychology*, (New York: Feldheim Publishers, 1976).

[46] Torrey, *Freudian Fraud*, 248-249.

[47] Dennis B. Klein, *Jewish Origins of the Psychoanalytic Movement*, (Chicago: University of Chicago Press, 1981). [quotation cited in Torrey, 255]

[48] Ibid.

[49] Paul Brunton, *The Spiritual Crisis of Man* (Ann Arbor, MI.: Mitchell-Shear, Inc., 1984).

[50] Ibid, 37.

[51] David Bakan, *Freud and The Jewish Mystical Tradition* (New York: Schocken Books, 1969).

[52] Khalifa, *Quran*, 4:155 and 5:7, 12.

[53] Bakan, *Jewish Mystical Tradition*, 235.

[54] Ibid, 134.

[55] Ibid, 136.

[56] Khalifa, *Quran*, 6:43, 14:22, 22:11, and 43:36-37.

[57] Bakan, *Jewish Mystical Tradition*, 135-136.

[58] Ibid, 235-236.

[59] Ibid, 181.

[60] Ibid, 233.

[61] Ibid, 135.

[62] Eric Fromm, *The Art of Loving* (New York: Harper & Row Publishers, 1956).

[63] Ibid, 90 and 92.

[64] Bakan, *Jewish Mystical Tradition*, 236-237.

[65] Stoop and Arterburn, *Recovery Bible*, 1120.

[66] Khalifa, *Quran*, 4:46, 5:13, 10:35-36.

[67] Ibid, 25:43 and 45:23.

[68] Scheinerman, Rabbi. *"Star of David,"* <http://www.Scheinerman.net/judaism/rituals/star.html> (22 December 2002)

[69] Ibid, 1.

[70] Kertzer, *What is a Jew?*, 174-175.

[71] Khalifa, *Quran*, 3:113-115, and 7:159.

Three

Distortions of Christianity

The Truth About the Trinity

As we move through "weeds and thickets" on the vast spiritual obstacle course, our journey takes us to a period *after* Jesus of Nazareth received the Injil or Gospel, delivered his message, and returned to the Presence of God. Jesus was *not* the "founder of Christianity." The term, *Christianity*, was never authorized by God as a "name" of the teachings revealed to Prophet Jesus. The early followers of Jesus were called "Nazarenes" (Acts, 24:5). The term Christianity is retained in this book because the term refers to current communities that claim to embrace the teachings of Jesus. Modern Christianity reflects the *distortion* of the teachings revealed to Jesus and combines the distorted teachings with ancient pagan beliefs and practices. The teachings and beliefs were codified into the canons of a new state-sanctioned religion of the Roman Empire, the Roman Catholic Church. In the dictionary, the word "catholic" has multiple meanings. In addition to meaning "universal," and "broadminded," the word "catholic" also means "official" or "orthodox." In the context of the history of the Roman Catholic Church, it is important to understand how both meanings (universal and orthodox) have been entwined. In the 1964 edition of the *American College Dictionary*,[1] the words "catholic" and "orthodox" are defined as:

Catholic *adj.* **1.** *Theol.*
"a. (among Roman Catholics) claiming to possess exclusively the notes or characteristics of the one only true and universal church…with these qualifications, only by the Church of Rome, as applicable to itself and its adherents… b. (among Anglicans) noting or pertaining to the conception of the Church as the body representing the ancient undivided Christian witness, comprising all the orthodox churches which have kept the apostolic succession of bishops, and including the Anglican Church, the Roman Catholic Church, the Eastern

Orthodox Church, Church of Sweden, the Old Catholic Church (in the Netherlands and elsewhere).²

Orthodox *adj.*
2. conforming to the Christian faith as represented in the ecumenical creeds. **3.** *(cap.)* **a.** designating the Eastern or Greek Church. **b.** of or pertaining to the Greek Church. **4.** approved; conventional.³

Thus, a more accurate rendering of the meaning of "catholic" as it specifically applies to the Roman Catholic Church is: "the universal orthodox church of Rome, the only true, universal church." In that context, the approved, conventional Roman Catholic Church was to be universally accepted as the official church of the Roman Empire, and not any other church or religion.

The official church of the Roman Empire is considered to be the "mother" or origin of all Christian denominations. Protestant churches and denominations first appeared after Dr. Martin Luther, a theologian, nailed Ninety-Five Theses or declarations on the church door of Wittenberg, Germany in 1517. Dr. Luther's declarations called to question the "infallibility" of the Catholic Pope, the Roman Church, and Church officials' practice of selling indulgences and letters of spiritual pardon. In short, the Church led people to believe that they could purchase forgiveness for their sins. The greater the sin, the more money was necessary to get a letter of pardon and merit forgiveness.

The canons of distorted Christianity rest on a very grave and widespread spiritual blasphemy—*the teaching that Jesus is God or "the son of God."* This blasphemy is also known as a "Great Lie," but it is not the only belief deemed as a "Great Lie." It is certainly one of the most dangerous destructive ones. Few people in the Christian world are aware of this *fact*. In his on-line article, *Light of Israel: The Great Lie Rejected*, Mordeci Alfandari quotes the Hebrew Scriptures regarding this blasphemy. He exposes contradictions between the worship of the one God (YHVH in Hebrew) and the myth of the Trinity. Alfandari describes Jesus as a "mythological Savior" but fails to point out that Jesus was a Prophet of God. The verses Alfandari cites from the Hebrew

Scriptures stand on their own. What follows are unmodified excerpts from his article:

'Shall a man make for himself gods which are no-gods?' Jeremiah 16:20

The hundreds of bickering, basically divided sects and churches of Christianity theoretically agree on one fundamental issue; while each sect denies all of its sister sects their claim to 'spiritual light', they will all admit that the original Hebrew Scriptures are true, and the doctrines contained therein cannot be contradicted!

The Hebrew Scriptures are very explicit about the identity of the True Deity and Creator:

Thus shall you Say to the children of Israel! YHVH, the God of your fathers; the God of Abraham, the God of Isaac, and the God of Jacob has sent me to you! THIS is MY NAME FOREVER...!' Exodus 3:15.

'You are My witness, says YHVH, and My servant whom I have chosen; that you may know and believe ME and understand that I AM HE! Before ME there was NO god formed, neither shall ANY BE AFTER ME! I, YES I, AM YHVH, AND BESIDE ME THERE IS NO SAVIOUR!' Isaiah 43:10-11.

'I AM YHVH, THAT is My Name; and My glory will I NOT GIVE TO ANOTHER! (ANY OTHER!)' Isaiah 42:8.

'Israel is SAVED IN YHVH WITH AN EVERLASTING SALVATION!' Isaiah 45:17.

'Look to ME (YHVH) and BE SAVED, ALL THE ENDS OF THE EARTH; for I AM GOD, and there is NONE ELSE! I have sworn by Myself... that unto ME (YHVH) EVERY KNEE SHALL BOW, EVERY TONGUE shall swear! ONLY IN YHVH, shall it be said of Me, is victory and strength!' Isaiah 45:24

THUS THE HEBREW SCRIPTURES!!

And along comes a little book of doubtful origin, written by unknown authors; a book rife with fundamental contradictions and strange doctrines; a book Christians call the 'New Testament', which claims that only the name of 'Jesus' offers salvation; that unto 'Jesus' every knee shall bow; that 'Jesus' is THE saviour of mankind; that 'Jesus' and the father(?) are 'one', etc. etc. All the sects of Christendom disagree about WHAT the 'New Testament' is talking about, WHAT its doctrines really are! Some find in it a trinity, some a duality, some find two 'gods', 'god almighty' and a 'mighty god'! Some believe 'Jesus' to be a manifestation of the father (?) etc. ALL HAVE TAKEN THE GLORY AWAY FROM YHVH, the ONLY TRUE SAVIOUR, and given it to a HUMAN BEING (now deceased) who had 'evolved' into a deity (at the various church councils!)!....[4]

[Capitalization is part of original quoted text]

Most Christians probably gasp with rage and anger when these truths are uttered, and outright reject this information. As a young Christian, I initially reacted with confusion and indignation towards anyone who suggested that the Trinity is false. As I grew older, the truth about the Trinity seemed to jar me from taking *any* belief for granted simply because a majority accepted the belief. People, who state that Jesus is not God or not God's son, are labeled as part of an "Antichrist."[5] I was counseled that people who do not know "The Word," disbelievers, and persons possessed by the devil make unwavering statements that Jesus is not the son of God. I was cautioned that when such thoughts entered my mind, I should seek protection in God from the devil. My fellows in faith were sincerely concerned that I not thread down the wrong spiritual path. Nevertheless, in my heart, I felt that something was wrong with the Trinity path. I never accepted the "hush-hush" response to doubts about the Trinity doctrine. My doubts did not reflect a disbelief in God or disdain for Jesus. I have always believed that there is a Most High God to whom all Praises are due. I have never doubted that Jesus was a Prophet of God. God guided me to the truth about the Trinity.

From the Quran:

O people of the scripture, do not transgress the limits of your religion, and do not say about God except the truth. The Messiah, Jesus, the son of Mary, was a messenger of God, and His word that He had sent to Mary, and a revelation from Him. Therefore, you shall believe in God and His messengers. You shall not say, "TRINITY." You shall refrain from this for your own good. God is only one god. Be He glorified; He is much too glorious to have a son. To Him belongs everything in the heavens and everything on earth. God suffices as Lord and Master. (4:171)

Pagans indeed are those who say that God is a third of a TRINITY. There is no god except the one god. Unless they refrain from saying this, those who disbelieve among them will incur a painful retribution. (5:73)

The Jews said, "Ezra is the son of God," while the Christians said, "Jesus is the son of God!" These are blasphemies uttered by their mouths. They thus match the blasphemies of those who have disbelieved in the past. God condemns them. They have surely deviated. (9:30) [6]

From the Bible:

Hear O Israel: The Lord our God is one Lord. (Deuteronomy: 6:4)

Thus said the Lord, the King of Israel, and his redeemer the Lord of hosts: I am the first, and I am the last; and besides me there is no God. (Isaiah:44:6)

Thus said Jesus unto him Get thee hence, Satan: for it is written: Thou shall worship the Lord thy God, and Him only shall thou serve. (Matthew: 4:10)[7]

The present day Bible contains many spiritual truths and reflects important teachings in the original Gospels. But, the current Bible is not the intact authentic scripture revealed to Prophet Jesus. Throughout the Quran, Jesus is cited as a prophet of God born of virgin birth. Jesus spoke as a newborn infant and performed many miracles by the power of God. His virgin birth, speaking as a neonate, and performing miracles were all proofs that he was a Prophet and messenger of God. The Gospels or *Injil* is a Divine scripture revealed to him.

Distortions of Christianity

From the Quran:

The birth process came to her by the trunk of a palm tree. She said, "(I am so ashamed;) I wish I were dead before this happened, and completely forgotten." (The infant) called her from beneath her, saying, "Do not grieve. Your Lord has provided you with a stream. (19:23-24)

She pointed to him. They said, "How can we talk with an infant in the crib?" (The infant spoke and) said, "I am a servant of God. He has given me the scripture, and has appointed me a prophet. "He made me blessed wherever I go, and enjoined me to observe the Contact Prayers (Salat) and the obligatory charity (Zakat) for as long as I live. "I am to honor my mother; He did not make me a disobedient rebel. And peace be upon me the day I was born, the day I die, and the day I get resurrected." That was Jesus, the son of Mary, and this is the truth of this matter, about which they continue to doubt. It does not befit God that He begets a son, be He glorified. To have anything done, He simply says to it, "Be," and it is. He also proclaimed, "God is my Lord and your Lord; you shall worship Him alone. This is the right path." The various parties disputed among themselves (regarding the identity of Jesus). Therefore, woe to those who disbelieve from the sight of a terrible day. (19:29-37)[8]

In ancient Hebrew, the term "christ" means "anointed," or "messiah." The title "christ"[9] was given to many pious people and was related to the expectation of a messiah who would come and 1) liberate the Hebrews from oppression by the Romans, and 2) relieve them of what many of them regarded as "old harsh laws and prohibitions" revealed to earlier Hebrew prophets. Most Jewish and Roman contemporaries of Jesus foolishly rejected him as the Messiah and a prophet of God. *The title "Christ" or "Messiah" was bestowed upon Jesus by God.* Jesus was the Messiah (with a capital M) to the community that God sent him to enlighten. Jesus was not the only messiah (with a small m). At no time in human history did a prophet or messenger of God name the religious community that heeded his message in his own namesake. The Prophet Jesus said that his mission was a *continuation* of the message revealed to the Hebrew prophets and messengers who preceded him.

From the Quran:

The angels said, "O Mary, God gives you good news: a Word from Him whose name is 'The Messiah, Jesus the son of Mary. He will be prominent in this life and in the Hereafter, and one of those closest to Me. (3:45)[10]

From the Bible:

Do not misunderstand why I have come. I did not come to abolish the law of Moses or the writings of the prophets. No, I came to fulfill them. I assure you, until heaven and earth disappear, even the smallest detail of God's law will remain until its purpose is achieved. So if you break the smallest commandment and teach others to do the same, you will be the least in the Kingdom of Heaven. But anyone who obeys God's laws and teaches them will be great in the Kingdom of Heaven. (Matthew 5:17-19)[11]

When I was a college student, I met non-Christians from all over the world who shared their religious beliefs with me. I recognized that Christianity was not as widespread throughout the world as I was led to believe. More important, I heard non-Christian beliefs rooted in the worship of one God. The beliefs renewed ongoing doubts about the Trinity doctrine that I harbored for years. I read published accounts by Church and lay authors about how the concept of the Trinity was introduced into Church doctrine long after the end of Jesus' earthly life. There are Christian clergy who know that the Trinity is false. A few choose to share this truth with others. In 1977, the eminent Christian scholar John Hicks [12] authored the book entitled *The Myth of God Incarnate*. Hicks presented historical detailed facts that the Trinity doctrine was contrived at the Nicene Conferences of the Roman Catholic Church in 325 A.D. His book is currently out of print. The book can be secured from some used booksellers and on the Internet. Although some Christian leaders discouraged individuals from reading the book, many copies of the book were sold.

After reading *The Myth of God Incarnate* and several similar books, the light of truth inside me amplified rapidly. The light started exposing and clearing away spiritual weeds and thorns on the path. I learned that Jesus never said he was the son of God. He enjoined his followers to worship the God of Abraham and Moses. In the Bible, the phrase "son of God" is mentioned 83 times in reference to 38 individuals. Many righteous people were (and are) referred to as "sons of God."

From the Bible:

All who are led by the Spirit of God are sons of God. (Romans 8:14)

When the morning stars sang together, and all the sons of God shouted for joy? (Job: 38:7)

This was the son of Enos, which was the son of Seth, which was the son of Adam, which was the son of God. (Luke: 3:38)[13]

Whenever he performed miracles, Jesus declared that he was temporarily invested with such power by his heavenly Father (i.e., God), the Lord of the universe. In Hebrew, the word "rab" means master, lord, and father. The head of a Jewish household or family is commonly referred to as "rab." The term "rabbi" refers to a member of the Jewish clergy and the spiritual head of a temple or synagogue. By virtue of being a Hebrew prophet of God, the title "rabbi" also fits Jesus. In all revealed scriptures, God reveals that He is the Lord (i.e., Rab with a capital R) of the universe.

From the Quran:

Pagans indeed are those who say that God is the Messiah, son of Mary. The Messiah himself said, "O Children of Israel, you shall worship God; my Lord and your Lord." Anyone who sets up any idol beside God, God has forbidden Paradise for him, and his destiny is Hell. The wicked have no helpers. (5:17-19)[14]

After Jesus' departure from this world, some writers and translators of the Gospel manipulated the meanings of the Hebrew word "rabbi" so as to present the idea that Jesus was acknowledging the Lord-Creator in a father/son relationship. Today, when many Christians read Bible passages suggesting that Jesus referred to God as his own father, they do not know that this is a corruption of the original text. Many Christians do not realize that a Divine scripture that is rewritten and revised by many authors does not retain the pristine quality of the original scripture. A Divine scripture is not a collection of narratives, opinions, and interpretations by followers or disciples of a prophet of God. Within the Christian community, there are individuals who do not accept the doctrine that Jesus is the "son of God" or God. The individuals acknowledge that Jesus was a prophet of God, he received Divine scripture, he performed miracles by God's leave, and he was born of virgin birth. As is the case in any Divinely-inspired religion, there are thousands of Christians who, despite false doctrines, truly believe in the One God. Such persons are *Submitter Christians*.

Bible Codes Examined

Since the discovery of the miraculous Code in the Quran, there has been an increase in purported discoveries of codes in all kinds of books (e.g., dictionaries, religious texts, and literary works). Some authors claim to have discovered and examined Bible codes. This is interesting given that only a few people, including major religious leaders, know about the discovery of the Code in the Quran. Could this be a strategy by Satan's human forces to suppress knowledge about the proven Code in the Quran, and simultaneously inundate an uninformed public with bogus scriptural codes? Eventually, some people will tire of reading and hearing about so-called Divine codes and possibly dismiss opportunities to learn about the miraculous Code. Is the publication of books about alleged apocalyptic events and Divine signs related to the belief that the end of the world and "Armageddon" are near? Is the dissemination of such disinformation a matter of financially capitalizing on a yearning for miracles and signs from God? The answers to these questions will become clear as events unfold according to God's Plan.

Authors of so-called Bible codes search for any mathematical correspondence between letters, words, and phrases in Hebrew copies of the doctored Bible. The discourse about Bible codes is embellished with subjective inference, opinion, and talk about unsolvable esoteric "mysteries." It is puzzling that Bible codes are said to corroborate false teachings that: 1) the Bible is sufficiently intact, 2) Prophet Jesus is God or the "son of God," and 3) Jesus shall return as a world Messiah. Not one of the reported Bible codes has withstood the test of scientific scrutiny. It is interesting that not one of the Bible codes reaffirms the oneness of God and the worship of God alone.

Regardless of their religions, sincere seekers do not accept reports about *any* Divine codes at face value. They do not ignore objective evidence that a so-called Divine code is false. A Divine code is meant to strengthen the faith of *any* believer. Information that a code is false should not weaken one's faith in God. Such information *confirms* that God is in total control. Almighty God protects sincere seekers from Satan's ploy to deceive them by concocting bogus codes and miracles. The proven Miraculous Code in the Quran is for *all* people, regardless of individuals' religions.

The Divine scriptures revealed to Jews, Christians, and Muslims were written in Hebrew, Arabic, and possibly Aramaic. The letters of the Hebrew and Arabic alphabets have letter-specific distinct mathematical values. The extensive distortion of the text of the Bible rules out any possibility that the Bible contains a miraculous code or miraculous letter-sequence system. Nevertheless, by God's leave, the Bible does contain many elements of Divine guidance found in authentic scriptures. Objective Christian and non-Christian scholars acknowledge that the Bible is not an intact Divinely revealed scripture. Scholars agree that the Bible is not the authentic Gospels revealed to Prophet Jesus nor does it contain authentic text of the Torah or Statute Book revealed to

Moses. The Bible was written by multiple authors. As previously stated, a revealed scripture is not composed of different versions supposedly written by different authors. When the text of a Divine scripture is altered by addition or omission of any original text, the mathematical-letter code embedded in the scripture is compromised. In such cases, a glitch in an authentic miraculous code proves that the text of a Divine scripture has been distorted.

There are two kinds of biblical distortions: explicit distortions which are directly related to clear changes in the text, which arise through alteration, omission or addition to the original text; and implicit distortions which are brought about by deliberate misinterpretation without any actual textual change. **There is no dispute over the existence of such distortions in the Bible since all Christians, both Protestants and Catholics, admit their existence.** [Bold text added]

> According to them the verses of the Old Testament containing references to Christ and the injunctions which were, to the Jews, of perpetual value were distorted by the Jews through misinterpretation. Protestant theologians claim that the Catholics have distorted many texts of both the Old and the New Testament. The Catholics similarly accuse the Protestants of having distorted the text of the Bible. We therefore do not need to include demonstrations of implicit distortions as they have already been provided by the Christians themselves.
>
> As far as textual distortion is concerned, this kind of distortion is denied by the Protestants and they offer false arguments and misguiding statements in their writings in order to create doubts among the Muslims. It is therefore necessary to demonstrate that all the three kinds of textual distortion, that is, alterations in the text: the deletion of phrases and verses from the text; and later additions to the original texts are abundantly present in both the Old and the New Testaments.[15]

Michael Drosnin[16] is a well-known author of two best selling books wherein he purports to have discovered a Bible code. His discovery has now paled in obscurity due to its highly flawed nature. Discounting the fact that there are major omissions and distortions in the Hebrew text,

Distortions of Christianity

he used a widely-used method in Bible code research called Equidistant Letter Sequence (ELS). The flaws uncovered in attempts to find Bible codes are enumerated below.

The Bible code by Michael Drosnin, however, has gained widespread popularity first, until many scientists and researchers produced similar codes in any regular book using the system that Michael Drosnin used. Since the code claimed in the Bible or similar books were discovered using the same system, they all shared in the same flaws that we will discuss next. The purpose behind the Bible code was to find secret or hidden messages or codes in the Bible and use these messages to try to prove that the Bible has to be the word of God. Here are the flaws in the system used to develop the Bible code and other codes and their hidden messages that use the same pattern.

1. The Code employed: The Bible code as used by Drosnin is based on what is now known as (ELS), short for Equidistant Letter Sequence. It works by eliminating spaces between words. It is a man made idea put into use, but has no mention or support in the Bible itself. Using this technique the researcher can produce what he is looking for, specially now with the help of the computer and the free hand in using any (ELS). The researcher has only to keep trying different ELS values until he/she gets what he/she wants.

2. The Writing of the Scripture : Hebrew, the original language of the Bible, is written from right to left. However, Drosnin and most of those who claimed the presence of the biblical code worked out the code analysis left to right opposite to the writing of the Hebrew scripture or at least the Divine intention of writing it.

3. Original Text: The Hebrew Bible has been written and re-written many times and has additions, corrections or commentaries added by pious Rabbis over the years. This means that the claim of Drosnin and others to use a "universally accepted original Hebrew text" as the basis for their studies has no basis. There does not exist an original Hebrew Bible. In other words, Drosnin and others were searching a totally man altered book and not an original scripture of Divine nature.

4. Added words: The student of the Bible will find out that there are numerous biblical manuscripts where the order of words

is not the same in all documents. In some others an explanation, correction or addition was added by a scribe writing at a later date. It is not unusual to see the remark "was not in the earliest manuscript." written in many Bibles.

5. Deliberate alterations of translations: A very important note by Ronald Hendel, about the manipulation used in getting some results in the Bible code shed some light for us. He wrote in *Bible Review*, August, 1997, that deliberate mistranslations had been used to get desired results. One example Hendel gave was Genesis 25:11 where your Bible will say "After Abraham's death" Drosnin used "After the death of the Prime Minister." The Hebrew Abraham was divided to Ab and raham making two words, and the ELS connection was Rabin! [17]

In his *Scientific American* journal article, Michael Sheimer[18] gave an appraisal of the purported Bible Codes. He wrote:

> According to proponents of the Bible Code--itself a subset of the genre of biblical numerology and Kabbalistic mysticism popular since the Middle Ages--the Hebrew Pentateuch can be decoded through an equidistant-letter-sequencing software program. The idea is to take every nth letter, where n equals whatever number you wish: 7, 19, 3,027. Print out that string of letters in a block of type, then search left to right, right to left, top to bottom, bottom to top, and diagonally in any direction for any interesting patterns. Seek and ye shall find.

Sheimer noted that science is a sure means to decipher any genuine physical pattern or code:

> Given our propensity to look for patterns in a superfluity of data, is it any wonder that so many are taken in by such codified claptrap? The problem is pervasive and a permanent part of our cognitive machinery. The solution is science, our preeminent pattern-discriminating method and our best hope for detecting a genuine signal within the noise of nature's cacophony.[19]

In his on-line review of Drosnin's Bible Code, the physicist Dr. Randall Ingermanson[20] echoed conclusions drawn by many open-minded scientists:

> In fact, the overwhelming majority of scientists and Biblical scholars reject the Bible code. Barry Simon's web site contains the names

of more than 50 mathematicians who have personally investigated the Bible code and found it not credible. Drosnin is completely wrong. He implies also that most nonscientists accept the codes. Again, he is flat-out wrong...

But what is even worse is that Drosnin is lumping together his own fantasy-based attempts with the work of Eliyahu Rips, Doron Witztum, and Yoav Rosenberg. Rips, Witztum, and Rosenberg published a much-debated scientific paper in 1994. Though it has failed to gain scientific acceptance, it was at least presented as a true scientific experiment. Drosnin's work is not. His "codes" are not science. They are not codes. They are so bogus it hurts.[21]

The unmasking of any fraudulent scriptural code serves all sincere seekers. Fraudulent codes are used as means to further deceive people about true worship, God's signs to humanity, and reconfigure human events as to serve one's prejudices, predictions, and false beliefs. The mathematical Code in the Quran meets all the scientific tests of a *valid* mathematical system embedded in the text of scripture. The mathematical Code is a *miraculous* example of the "genuine signal" that Michael Scheimer hopes to detect or examine.

Christmas and Easter: Pagan Holidays

Christmas has nothing to do with the worship of God or the Prophet Jesus. It is a pagan celebration thousands of years old that was modified to blend in with distorted teachings of Christianity. Jesus was not born in December, there were no wise men who saw a star and traveled to a manger, Jesus did not have a father (Mary was a virgin when he was born!), and he was not the "son of God." Jesus was born sometime between late September and early October. The Quran points out that, after giving birth to Jesus, Mary shook some date palm branches and dates fell to the ground. Dates only ripen enough to fall to the ground during a short period between late September and early October.

From the Quran:

When she bore him, she isolated herself to a faraway place. The birth process came to her by the trunk of a palm tree. She said, "(I am so ashamed;) I wish I were dead before this happened, and completely forgotten." (The infant) called her from beneath her, saying, "Do not grieve. Your Lord has provided you with a stream. "If you shake the trunk of this palm tree, it will drop ripe dates for you. (5:72)[22]

Pagan Romans worshiped the sun. December 21 is the date of the winter equinox or solstice when the sun crosses the equator, and spring is only three months away. Pagans called the winter solstice "the birth of the *sun* of God," not s-o-n of God. In celebrating the winter solstice, pagans would cut off branches from evergreen trees as symbols of everlasting life and put the tree branches in their homes. During his lifetime, Jesus warned his followers not to be like pagans who cut down tree branches and put them in their homes. The pagans also put eggs throughout their homes as symbols of fertility and life. The inventors of the tales and myths surrounding the Trinity doctrine wanted pagans to embrace the Roman Church. The mythmakers incorporated the idea of sun worship into church doctrine by claiming that Jesus was the "son of God." The word "Christmas" means "mass of Christ." The Church held mass on December 25, a few days after the winter solstice, in order to attract the pagan sun worshipers to the Church.

In their article *Why Christmas Is So Important to God*, the authors Carl Hilliker and Mark Jenkins [23] stated:

> The *Encyclopedia Britannica* states, "The reason why Christmas came to be celebrated on December 25 remains uncertain, but most probably the reason is that the early Christians wished the date to coincide with the pagan Roman festival marking the 'birthday of the unconquered sun.'...." "Christmas was not instituted by Jesus Christ, nor was it observed by any of the apostles personally instructed by Christ...." The truth is early Christians did not observe birthdays—not even Christ's birth.... The *Catholic Encyclopedia* also states, "Pagan

Distortions of Christianity

customs [not Christian customs] centering around the January calender gravitated to Christmas." [24]

Regarding the Christmas tree, Hilliker and Jenkins wrote:

> Semiramis [author of a "mystery" religion that was to become widespread] also claimed that a full-grown evergreen tree sprang up over night from a dead stump symbolizing the new life of Nimrod. She claimed that Nimrod would visit and leave gifts on each anniversary of his birth, which happens to be on December 25. This is the true origin of the Christmas tree, and the pagan history behind the gifts people place there to this day! This is why the Prophet Jeremiah knew of the "Christmas tree" so long before Jesus Christ was ever born. [25]

The Christmas tree has become central to the celebration of Christmas. At first glance, it seems to pose no harm by using it to symbolize what is characterized as "a season of giving and sharing with others." Like many symbols of corrupt religion, it appears to be an innocent custom. Innocent it is not. In their on-line article, *The Plain Truth About Christmas*, the Cornerstone Evangelical Association[26] points out that the Bible contains a clear prohibition against fashioning Christmas trees.

> ...it [Bible] does have something to say about the Christmas tree! This will come as a real surprise to many. But here it is: Jeremiah 10:2-6: "Thus saith the Lord, Learn not the way of the heathen . . . for the customs of the people are vain: for one cutteth a tree out of the forest, the work of the hands of the workman, with the axe. They deck it with silver and with gold; they fasten it with nails and hammers that it not move." There is a perfect description of the Christmas tree, termed by the Eternal as "the way of the heathen . . . the customs of the people." We are commanded not to learn that way or follow it. It is also viewed in this passage as idolatry. The fifth verse shows that these trees cannot speak-cannot walk-must be carried." Be not afraid of them; for they [the trees] cannot do evil, neither also is it in them to do good." They are not gods to be feared. Some people misread this to make it to say that there is no harm in having a Christmas tree, but that is not what it says.[27]

The Cornerstone Evangelical Association quotes another author as saying:

> Even the lighting of fires and candles as a Christmas ceremony is merely a continuation of the pagan custom, encouraging the waning sun-god as he reached the lowest place in the southern skies!...The use of Christmas wreaths is believed by authorities to be traceable to the pagan customs of decorating buildings and places of worship at the feast which took place at the same time as Christmas.[28]

What about "Santa Clause" or "Saint Nicholas?" Hilliker and Jenkins wrote:

> Nicolas is derived from the Greek words *nikos* and *laos,* which together mean conqueror or destroyer of people. The original conqueror or destroyer of people was Nimrod. Yet another of Nimrod's names was *Sanctus* or *Santa* which means saint.... The facts show that Nimrod is the true origin of the widely accepted "Saint Nicholas" or the " Santa Claus" that is so central to Christmas observances around the world. Any other explanations—and there are a number of them—are simply modern-day versions that conceal the truth behind these ancient "mysteries."...When Jesus Christ said that the "doctrine of the Nicolaitans" was a "thing I hate" (Rev. 2:15), He was condemning the same Nimrod-inspired Babylonian mysteries that had become a counterfeit "Christianity" for thousands of years.... Today, those same doctrines are still deceiving people who think their Christmas customs are pleasing to God.[29]

On Christmas and the "myth of the three wise men," the authors wrote:

> When Jesus Christ was born, there were in the same country shepherds abiding in the field, keeping watch over their flock by night (Luke 2:8). December is in the midst of a cold, rainy season in Judea. The shepherds always brought their flock in from the fields and mountains to be corralled by mid-October at the latest, for their protection... shepherds would not have been in open fields on December 25.[30]

In fact, we are told that "The word for Christmas in late old English is *Cristes Maesse*, the mass of Christ, *first found in 1038*." That is 1,000 years *after* the death of Christ.

> Christmas is a pagan festival. That is absolute fact. Research any Christmas custom and you quickly discover the pagan origin. Some people, unfortunately, take offense when these things are pointed out, but God commands His faithful Church to proclaim such things. (Isa. 58:1) [31]

In the final analysis, the Christmas-Santa Claus myth with all of its embellishments exacts a blow on many children's sense that the world can be trusted (it had that effect on me). A child may not immediately exhibit the impact of discovering that a belief purported to be so dear to so many, including one's parents, is a lie! A child may later ask, "Why did my parents tell me this lie?" Youngsters innocently embrace a contrived reality that they enjoy. Even after learning that the Christmas-Santa Claus myth is a lie, many of them later pass it on to their children. The inter-generational transmission of the myth reflects a personal resignation to a religious falsehood, and an unwillingness to depart from majority behavior. The Cornerstone Association notes that:

> Through the year, parents punish their children for telling falsehoods. Then, at Christmas time, they themselves tell their little children this Santa Claus lie! Is it any wonder that many of them, when they grow up and learn the truth, begin to believe God is a myth too... Is it Christian to teach children myths and falsehoods? God says, "Thou shall not bear false witness!" It may seem right, and be justified by human reason, but God says, "There is a way that seemeth right to a man, but the ends thereof are the ways of death!" [32]

Let alone celebrate the alleged birthday of Jesus, an *exaggerated* celebration of birthdays runs counter to the worship of God alone. Birthday celebrations are woven into the very fabric of life in many societies. Most people who have been raised in America and other western societies have not known a time in their lives when birthday celebrations were questioned or frowned upon. Nevertheless, one must be cautious. There are persons who prohibit what God has made lawful and encourage what God has made unlawful. It is important that such occasions not be transformed into idolatrous adoration of creatures (e.g., our selves, children, relatives, friends, celebrities, historical figures, etc.). The remembrance of a person's birthday should also be cause to praise and glorify God, The Creator and Giver of all life. The Cornerstone Association points out that:

> The apostles and early Church never celebrated Christ's birthday at any time. There is no command or instruction to celebrate it in the Bible. Rather the celebration of birthdays is a pagan, not a Christian custom, believe it or not.[33]

From the Quran:

He created you from one person (Adam). Subsequently, He gives every man a mate to find tranquility with her. She then carries a light load that she can hardly notice. As the load gets heavier, they implore God their Lord: "If You give us a good baby, we will be appreciative." But when He gives them a good baby, they turn His gift into an idol that rivals Him. God be exalted, far above any partnership. (7:189-190)[34]

Easter

Church doctrine supports the innovation that Easter is associated with the death and resurrection of Jesus. Easter is a pagan festival. The spring equinox occurs on March 21, three months after the winter equinox. During the spring equinox, pagans would collect eggs, rabbits, and don new clothes as a symbol of the earth flowering again during the onset of spring. Since rabbits cannot lay eggs, why did pagans associate them together? *Rabbits and eggs are pagan symbols of life and fertility.*[35] The ancient Persian-Zoroastrian practice of collecting and coloring eggs dates back hundreds of years before the birth of Jesus. The Christian celebration of Easter in the Roman Church takes place in April instead of March in order to distance the Christian Easter from its pagan origins. This artificial separation of the Christian Easter from its pagan roots does not diminish the pagan character of Easter. It remains a blasphemy and a form of idolatry. In her article, *The Pagan Origins of Easter*, Royce Carlson [36] wrote,

> Easter celebrations were held hundreds of years before Christ was born as festivals of spring honoring Eostre, the great mother goddess of the Saxons.... In the Mediterranean region, there was a pre-Christian spring celebration centered around the vernal equinox (March 20 or 21) that honored Cybele, the Phrygian goddess of fertility. Cybele's consort, Attis, was considered born of a virgin and was believed to have died and been resurrected three days later. Attis derived his mythology from even earlier gods... who also were supposed to have been born of a virgin and suffered death and resurrection as long as 500 years before Christ was born.[37]

Carlson also pointed out that:

> There are other Easter traditions that are pagan in origin. The Easter sunrise service is derived from the ancient pagan practice of welcoming the sun on the morning of the spring equinox, marking the beginning of spring. What we now call Easter lilies were revered by the ancients as symbols of fertility and representative of the male genitalia. The ancient Babylonian religions had rituals involving dying eggs as did the ancient Egyptians.[38]

Supporting their disclosures with Biblical verses against practicing Easter, Timothy A. and Kimberly B. Southall[39] explain why the Easter celebration is pagan. Here are some of their examples (underlining in original quotes):

> <u>Origin of Hares</u>. (Bunnies) and Eggs. According to Teutonic myth, the hare was once a bird whom Eostre changed into a four-footed creature. Thus it can also lay eggs....

> <u>Origins of Lent</u>. The word "lent" is of Anglo-Saxon origin meaning "spring." Lent developed from the pagan celebration of weeping, fasting, and mourning for 40 days over the death of Tammuz (one day for each year of his life). Tammuz (the son/husband of the Babylonian idol Ishtar)....

Origins of Hot Cross Buns and Fires. Cakes bearing a cross-like symbol representing the pair of cow-horns on the moon goddess, Isis, were offered by ancient Egyptians. The cakes which Greeks offered to Astarte and other divinities were called bous or boun, from which the word "bun" is derived. The Babylonians/Chaldeans offered similar cakes to the "Queen of Heaven." Fires were lit atop mountains and had to be kindled from new fire, drawn from wood by friction. The fire was then used to bake cakes in sacrifice to Semiramis, the "Queen of Heaven."...

Who celebrates Easter? Witches, who base their celebrations (including Halloween) on the phases of the moon, celebrate Easter. Christians, however, are clearly forbidden from observing this pagan celebration (Deuteronomy 12:30-31; Luke 4:8; I Corinthians 10:20-22; Ephesians 5:11). There is a good reason why the early church never spoke of Easter and why there is absolutely no indication of the observance of the Easter festival in the New Testament. (The only exception is a mistranslation of the King James version of Acts 12:4, where it gives the word "Easter" instead of the correct translation "Passover.") It was not an oversight on God's part; Christians are simply not to celebrate Easter, a pagan festival.[40]

Consistent with the universal message of all revealed scriptures, the Southalls cite a Biblical verse enjoining Christians to worship God alone:

Decision to make. You now have a decision to make concerning Easter. In the oft-quoted words of Joshua: "Now fear the Lord and serve Him with all faithfulness. Throw away the gods your forefathers worshiped beyond the River and Egypt, and serve the Lord. But if serving the Lord seems undesirable to you, then choose for yourselves this day whom you will serve, whether the gods your forefathers served beyond the River, or the gods of the Amorites, in whose land you are living. But as for me and my household, we will serve the Lord."(Joshua 24:14-15 NIV) [41]

Recall that the word "Lord" (with a capital R in the word "Rabb") in an original scriptural text can only mean the one God, not Lord as in "father of Jesus."

The commemoration of spring and the change of the seasons are signs of God and His promise to revive the dead on the Day of Resurrection. With spring comes the blossoming of flowers, the greening of barren wintered lands and trees, and the invigoration of millions of creatures in the animal kingdom. Humans are filled with joy and a sense of renewal. These phenomena remind Submitters to worship God alone.

From the Quran:

He is the One who sends the winds with good omens of His mercy, and we send down from the sky pure water. With it, we revive dead lands and provide drink for our creations—multitudes of animals and humans. (25:48-49)

God is the One who sends the winds to stir up clouds, then we drive them towards barren lands, and revive such lands after they were dead. Thus is the resurrection. (35:9)[42]

Jesus: Misquoted and Misrepresented

Vicarious atonement is the notion that Jesus died for the sins of humanity. Vicarious atonement mirrors the pagan practice of making blood sacrifices and offerings in order to cleanse oneself of sin and appease the gods. For example, among pagan peoples, an individual might sacrifice his or her own child or someone else as expiation for transgressions or to insure the pleasure of the gods. *The notion that God "sacrificed his son so that humanity could be saved" is in line with pagan beliefs about the purpose of blood sacrifice.* In the Roman Catholic Church, the "blood of Christ" is represented in the consumption of wine and the "body of Christ" is represented in the consumption of wafers. This ritual mirrors the pagan belief and practice that through the consumption of the blood and flesh of a sacrificed innocent or "holy" person, those who complete the ritual become part of the "pure" one who was sacrificed.

The belief that Jesus died in order that humans could attain spiritual salvation is firmly entrenched in the minds of most Christians. Pointing out that the idea that "Jesus died for the sins of humanity" is false usually engenders intense hostile responses. First, it is received as a gross blasphemy and demonic. The truths that vicarious atonement is false and the fact that Jesus is not Divine are perceived as attempts to wholly invalidate the Christian faith. Individuals who communicate the truth about Jesus are labeled as part of an "anti-Christ," agents of the Devil, or evil individuals attempting to rupture each Christian's faith in God. Due to the fear of displeasing the true God (in their heart of hearts) and priming by some misguided religious leaders, some Christians shy away from anyone who communicates the truth about the "Jesus-as-Savior" doctrine. Such behavior is understandable. A sincere person does not just abandoned cherished beliefs on a whim. To speak the *truth* about Jesus' mission is to honor him as having been one of God's prophets and messengers. The truth about Jesus' identity and his mission cannot and does not undermine the innermost belief of any Christian or anyone who sincerely seeks to worship the one and only God and Lord of creation.

From the Quran:

They worship beside God idols that possess no power to harm them or benefit them, and they say, "These are our intercessors at God!" Say, "Are you informing God of something He does not know in the heavens or the earth?" Be He glorified. He is the Most High; far above needing partners. (10:18)

When they are told, "Follow these revelations of God," they say, "No, we follow only what we found our parents doing." What if the devil is leading them to the agony of Hell? (31:21)

God is the One who created the heavens and the earth, and everything between them in six days, then assumed all authority. You have none beside Him as Lord, nor do you have an intercessor. Would you not take heed? (32:4)

They are like the devil: he says to the human being, "Disbelieve," then as soon as he disbelieves, he says, "I disown you. I fear God, Lord of the universe." (59:16)[43]

Second, such startling information is alarmingly uncomfortable for anyone who has invested his or her spiritual salvation in the belief that Jesus died for human sin. Fear is a great mover and the Devil knows it. Enveloped by fear and anger, many Christians refuse to research the facts about vicarious atonement. Like victims of distorted Judaism and Islam, misguided Christians close their hearts and minds when challenged with a truth about the worship of God that exposes false practices. They seek refuge in misguided clergy and their fellows. *This distortion of Jesus' identity and his role is very serious.* At no time did Jesus ever utter that he was God, the "son of God," or that he came to die for human sins. A closer reading of the Bible and of authentic scripture makes this quite clear to anyone who genuinely seeks to worship God in the correct manner. The Gospel of Barnabas, a non-canonical gospel rejected by early Church counsels, presents an enlightening contrast to the notion that Jesus died for human sin.

From the Bible:

Yahshua [Jesus] said to her, "Do not cling to Me, for I have not yet ascended to My Father; but go to My brethren and say to them, 'I am ascending to My Father and your Father, and to My God and your God.' "(John: 20:17)[44]

From the Gospel of Barnabas:

Then God, seeing the danger of his servant, commanded Gabriel, Michael, Rafael, and Uriel, his ministers, to take Jesus out of the world. The holy angels came and took Jesus out by the window that looks toward the South;. They bare him and placed him in the third heaven in the company of angels blessing God for evermore. (Excerpt, Number 215)

Jesus replied, embracing his mother: 'Believe me, mother, for truly I say to you that I have not been dead at all; for God has reserved me till near the end of the world.' And having said this he prayed the four angels that they would manifest themselves, and give testimony how the matter had passed...

Thereupon the angels manifested themselves like four shining suns, insomuch that through fear every one again fell down as dead. Then Jesus gave four linen cloths to the angels that they might cover themselves, in order that they might be seen and heard to speak by his mother and her companions. And having lifted up each one, he comforted them, saying: 'These are the ministers of God: Gabriel, who announces God's secrets; Michael, who fights against God's enemies; Rafael, who receives the souls of them that die; and Uriel, who will call every one to the judgment of God at the last day. Then the four angels narrated to the Virgin how God had sent for Jesus, and had transformed Judas, that he might suffer the punishment to which he had sold another...

And though I have been innocent in the world, since men have called me "God," and "Son of God," God, in order that I be not mocked of the demons on the day of judgment, has willed that I be mocked of men in this world by the death of Judas, making all men to believe that I died upon the cross. (Excerpts, Number 220)

And he reproved many who believed that he had died and risen again, saying: "Do you hold me and God for liars? I said to you that God has granted to me to live almost to the end of the world. Truly I say to you, I did not die; it was Judas the traitor. Beware, for Satan will make every effort to deceive you. Be my witnesses in Israel, and throughout the world, of all things that you have heard and seen."

And having said this, he prayed God for the salvation of the faithful, and the conversion of sinners and [then], his prayer ended, he embraced his mother, saying: "Peace be to you, my mother. Rest in God who created you and me." And having said this, he turned to his disciples, saying: "May God's grace and mercy be with you." Then before their eyes the four angels carried him up into heaven. (Number 221)

After Jesus had departed, the disciples scattered through the different parts of Israel and of the world, and the truth, hated of Satan, was persecuted, as it always is, by falsehood. For certain evil men, pretending to be disciples, preached that Jesus died and rose not again. Others preached that he really died, but rose again. Others preached, and yet preach, that Jesus is the Son of God, among whom is Paul deceived. But we - as much as I have written - we preach to those that fear God, that they may be saved in the last day of God's Judgment. Amen. (Number 222) [45]

From the Quran:

Thus, God said, "O Jesus, I am terminating your life, raising you to Me, and ridding you of the disbelievers. I will exalt those who follow you above those who disbelieve, till the Day of Resurrection. Then to Me is the ultimate destiny of all of you, then I will judge among you regarding your disputes. (3:55)

And for claiming that they killed the Messiah, Jesus, son of Mary, the messenger of GOD. In fact, they never killed him, they never crucified him - they were made to think that they did. All factions who are disputing in this matter are full of doubt concerning this issue. They possess no knowledge; they only conjecture. For certain, they never killed him (4:157) [46]

A Minister Admits to Misleading Others

When I was a college professor, I invited a minister to visit me in my office during open house activities for visiting parents. At the time, the minister was the father of one of my students. I unabashedly asked him, "Since you know that the Trinity is false and Jesus was not the son of God, why do you continue to preach these lies to your congregation?"

I did not know what he believed or said to his congregation. I took a chance. I thought that he might conclude that I investigated the history of the Trinity doctrine. His response to my question startled me. I did not exhibit any outer signs of surprise. The minister said,

> I tell them that because that is all plain folk can understand. They need something they can see and relate to [referring to images of Jesus]. They need to believe that they can get to someone closer. In their minds, God is just too far away. You have to tell them that Jesus died for their sins or else they will feel too overburdened with guilt. The idea of the oneness of God is too heavy for them.

The minister was an educated family man who lived in a middleclass community where he was respected and admired. He seemed to be completely at home with personally acknowledging the one indivisible God but telling others to believe in the Trinity. He did not exhibit any guilt or second thoughts about lying to his congregation. I felt that he was instructed to "keep it simple" for the uninitiated and the spiritually unlettered. In those few moments with the minister in my office, all that I had read and known about the Trinity as a false doctrine suddenly became a reality presented in vivo by someone who is supposed to represent spiritual truth. In a way of speaking, I was hearing it from the "horse's mouth." As I sat listening, I thought about how grave and satanic it is for clerics of any religion to knowingly mislead millions of people about the worship of God. Submitters to God alone do not knowingly allow anyone to tamper with their spiritual well-being. They do not intentionally lie to others about the worship of God.

From the Quran:

Among them are those who twist their tongues to imitate the scripture that you may think it is from the scripture, when it is not from the scripture, and they claim that it is from God, when it is not from God. Thus, they utter lies and attribute them to God, knowingly. (3:78)

Pagans indeed are those who say that God is a third of a TRINITY. There is no god except the one god. Unless they refrain from saying this, those who disbelieve among them will incur a painful retribution. (5:73)

Who is more evil than one who lies about God, or rejects His revelations? The transgressors never succeed. (6:21)

We have permitted the enemies of every prophet- human and jinn devils- to inspire in each other fancy words, in order to deceive. Had your Lord willed, they would not have done it. You shall disregard them and their fabrications. (6:112)[47]

The Revealed Sabbath is Saturday

The word "Sabbath" means "seven." The seventh day of the week is Saturday,[48] not Sunday. In the Greco-Roman tradition, Saturday is named after the seventh planet Saturn (Saturn-day). However, in authentic Judaism, its number identifies the seventh day (and other days of the week). There is no basis in the scriptures for "naming" the days of the week after anyone or anything. Sunday is actually the first day of the week. The Roman Emperor Constantine altered the calendar and designated Sunday or the "sun day" as the seventh day of the week. Monday or the "moon day" became the second day of the week. Evidently, Emperor Constantine was attempting to blend aspects of Judaism and pagan Roman practices. In almost all accounts, the early Roman church was a consolidation of polytheistic beliefs and distorted Judaism tailored for pagan converts. In many non-Western cultures, a new day traditionally begins on the sunset of the proceeding day. For example, Saturday or the Sabbath day begins at sunset on the proceeding Friday. Early followers of Jesus continued to observe Saturday as the seventh day of the week. They sought refuge from Constantine in his campaign to kill anyone, especially true followers of Jesus' teachings, who did not heed the dictates of the official Church of the Roman Empire. Today, many Jewish individuals, Eastern Orthodox Christians, and some denominations in the West correctly observe the Sabbath on Saturdays. In an online excerpt from the book *God's Law &*

The Ten Commandments, the Dasyd Ministry [49] points out that the idea that Sunday is the Sabbath is an innovation by the early Roman church.

> The word **"Sunday"** does not appear anywhere in the Bible simply because this day was named after the Greek **"Sun god."** The phrase "first day of the week" is used in the Bible eight times in the New Testament only. They are as follows: Matt. 28:1, Mark 16:1-2, 24:1, Luke 24:1, John 20:1, and 19, Acts 20:7-8, and 1 Cor 16:1-3. If our day of worship was to be changed from Saturday Sabbath to SUNDAY (first day of the week) then this change would have to obviously appear in one of the eight passages ….
>
> Another reason why our Sabbath day was changed was because the early Christian missionaries faced an uphill battle with the pagan beliefs everywhere. The pagans were reluctant to give up their false gods and ancient practices. So, the missionaries, unable to convert them easily to an entirely new code of worship, did what they thought was the next best thing. They took the pagan holy days and festivals as they were, and gradually grafted the observances of the new faith onto those festivals with the rites and customs surrounding them. They assumed that years later, as the pagans worshiped the new Christian God, they would dissolve the pagan holy days and festivals and get back to true Biblical traditions; but this never happened, in fact, the opposite occurred!…
>
> The Catholic Church, for over one thousand years, by virtue of her Divine mission, changed the Sabbath day to SUNDAY. The Protestant world, at its birth, found the Catholic Pagan Sabbath too strongly entrenched to run counter to its existence. The Catholic Sabbath kept by most churches today, is in fact the acknowledged offspring of the Catholic church. Therefore, for centuries, most deceived Believers have kept the pagan SUNDAY as a "Biblical" Sabbath. It is however clearly neither Biblical nor Sabbath." [50]

A partner to the distortion of the Jewish Sabbath is the notion that God needs rest or "rested" after creating the universes. The idea that the Supreme Being needs anything, let alone rest, is nonsense. The Quran clarifies that an ancient Jewish community was commanded by God to desist from fishing (i.e., working) on the Sabbath. That specific community failed the test but Submitter Jews have always adhered to the Divine command to observe their Sabbath.

From the Quran:

And we raised Mount Sinai above them, as we took their covenant. And we said to them, "Enter the gate humbly." And we said to them, "Do not desecrate the Sabbath." Indeed, we took from them a solemn covenant. (4:154)

Remind them of the community by the sea, who desecrated the Sabbath. When they observed the Sabbath, the fish came to them abundantly. And when they violated the Sabbath, the fish did not come. We thus afflicted them, as a consequence of their transgression. (7:163)[51]

The Christian Cross

The centerpiece and symbol of Christianity, the Christian cross symbolizes the major doctrines of the religion. The cross was adopted by the Roman church after Jesus' alleged crucifixion. Authors of the on-line article, *The Sign of The Cross*[52] point out that:

> In the Papal system, as it is well known, the sign of the cross and the image of the cross are all in all. No prayer can be said, no worship engaged in, no step can be taken, without frequent use of the sign of the cross. [53]

Contrary to what many may believe, the religious feelings about the Christian cross did not originate from any sayings of the Apostle Paul. As a religious symbol, the cross predates the monotheistic religions.

> There is hardly a Pagan tribe where the cross has not been found. The cross was worshiped by the Pagan Celts long before the incarnation and death of Christ.... It [cross] was worshiped in Mexico for ages before the Roman Catholic missionaries set foot there, large stone crosses being erected, probably to the "god of rain." The cross thus widely worshiped, or regarded as a sacred emblem, was the unequivocal

symbol of Bacchus, the Babylonian Messiah, for he was represented with a headband covered with crosses.... When, therefore, multitudes of the Pagans, on the conversion of Constantine, flocked into the Church, like the semi-Pagans of Egypt, they brought along with them their predilection for the old symbol . . . Thus, by the "sign of the cross," Christ has been crucified anew by those who profess to be His disciples. [54]

Any credible account of the emergence of the cross in Christianity, including the story of Emperor Constantine's alleged vision of a cross, supports the fact that the cross is an ancient symbol representing the sun and life.

> The same sign of the cross that Rome now worships was used in the Babylonian Mysteries, was applied by Paganism to the same magic purposes, was honored with the same honors. That which is now called the Christian cross was originally no Christian emblem at all, but was the mystic Tau of the Chaldeans and Egyptians—the true original form of the letter T—the initial of the name Tammuz.... Whether the Maltese cross, which the Romish bishops append to their names as a symbol of their episcopal dignity, is the letter T, may be doubtful; but there seems no reason to doubt that the Maltese cross is an expression of the sun. The mystic Tau, as a symbol of the great divinity, was called "the sign of life." ...borne by Osiris and all the Egyptian gods; and the ansa or "handle" was afterwards dispensed with, and it became the simple Tau, or ordinary cross, as it appears today, and that the design of its first employment on the sepulchers, therefore, could have no reference to the crucifixion of the Nazarene [Jesus], but was simply the result of the attachment to old and long-cherished Pagan symbols, which is always strong in those who, with the adoption of the Christian name and profession, are still, to a large extent, Pagan in heart and feeling. This, and this only, is the origin of the worship of the *"cross."*... This, no doubt, will appear very strange and very incredible to those who have read Christian history, as most have done to a large extent, even among Protestants, through Romish spectacles.... [55]

Claude, a bishop of Turin, Italy in the eight-century said:

> If we are to worship a cross because Jesus died on one, we should worship a manger because he lay in one or a donkey because he rode on one.[56]

Clarifying that the cross is a religious symbol that predated Christianity, Alexander Hislop said:

> It is a fact, …not less remarkable and well-attested, that the Druids in their groves were accustomed to select the most stately and beautiful tree as an emblem of the Deity they adored, and having cut the side branches, they affixed two of the largest of them to the highest part of the trunk, in such a manner that those branches extended on each side like the arms of a man, and, together with the body, presented the appearance of a HUGE CROSS…It was worshipped in Mexico ages before the Roman Catholic missionaries set foot there, large stone crosses probably being erected, probably to the "god of rain." …This symbol of the Babylonian god is reverenced at this day in all wide wastes of Tartary, where Buddhism prevails, and the way in which it is represented among them forms a striking commentary on the language applied by Rome to the Cross.[57]

The Christian crucifix is a cross with the figure of the body of Jesus on it.[58] It is one of the most important sacraments of the Roman Church and is required over the altar in Catholic churches. There is hardly a Christian church where a picture of Jesus on a cross (crucifix), or a metal or wooden cross is not the centerpiece of the altar or on the main wall. Ancient altars were simply flat rocks or table-like surfaces for making blood sacrifices to gods or to a deity. The ancient sacrificial altar has been replaced by table-like horizontal surfaces of various sizes in many Christian churches. Human blood has been substituted with red wine or grape juice. The altars, doctrines, and symbolic rituals associated with the beliefs that Jesus is "the son of God" and Jesus died for human sin are blasphemous. The symbols and rituals reflect the preservation of pagan practices in the Christian church.

Upon reflecting on these distortions of Christianity, many Christians may ask, "What is left of our religion?" What remains is the right path—God's authentic guidance and the true teachings of Prophet Jesus—the authentic Gospels revealed to him. Sincere Christians do not attempt to convince themselves that distortions are acceptable as long as one "believes in one's heart." Nor do they avoid the responsibility that comes along with awareness of false doctrines by claiming that disclosure of false teachings "will destroy our way of life."

Known by millions in America, Canada, and Europe, the late Canadian evangelist Charles Templeton eventually acknowledged the corruption of the Bible, denounced the Trinity doctrine, and abandoned the pulpit. In his last book, *Farewell to God*, Templeton [59] said:

> I oppose the Christian Church because, for all the good it sometimes does, it presumes to speak in the name of God and to propound and advocate beliefs that are outdated, demonstrably untrue, and often, in their various manifestations, deleterious to individuals and to the society. [60]

Templeton advocated examining scientific truths that contradicted Biblical stories instead of outright rejection of scientific facts. Templeton also encouraged people to inquire about possible parallels between the Bible's account of creation and what is proven scientific fact. The results of his own inquiries led Templeton to ask himself and others this question:

> Should one continue to base one's life system of belief... that for all its occasional wisdom and frequent beauty... is demonstrably untrue? [61]

At different times during the remainder of his life, Templeton is reported to have described himself as an atheist, an agnostic, and a humanist. To neutralize the impact of Templeton's disconnect from distorted Christianity, some influential Christian religious leaders trumpeted the notion that Templeton compromised his faith in God's Word by accepting man-made theories. *Just the opposite is true!* Corrupt religious leaders have elevated innovations, sanctified man-made religious doctrines, and claim that it all is the word of God!

From the Quran:

Among them are those who twist their tongues to imitate the scripture that you may think it is from the scripture, when it is not from the scripture, and they claim that it is from God, when it is not from God. Thus, they utter lies and attribute them to God, knowingly. (3:78)

Who is more evil than one who lies about God, or rejects His revelations? The transgressors never succeed. (6:21)[62]

Submitter Christians

Since the time of Jesus, Submitter Christians have sought out and held fast to the true worship of God and the *authentic* message revealed to Jesus. In the early years of the Roman Church, thousands of Christian Submitters were killed because they held fast to the truth, including the worship of God alone. Submitter Christians, who are not a few, understand this and journey beyond the distortions of Christianity. They realize that each soul's true happiness lies in the worship of God alone. Like their counterparts in any religion, Submitter Christians do not preserve false doctrines and institutions. They realize that no spiritual good can accrue to a soul that knowingly chooses a way of life apart from the right spiritual path. They understand that there is no real gain treading down a vast spiritual obstacle course. Genuine submitters understand that God's favor is worth far more than any position, long-held tradition, acceptance by and association with a misguided congregation, privilege, popularity, or prestige in this life.

From the Quran:

Surely, those who believe, those who are Jewish, the Christians, and the converts; **anyone who (1) believes in God, and (2) believes in the Last Day, and (3) leads a righteous life,** *will receive their recompense from their Lord. They have nothing to fear, nor will they grieve. (2:62)*

*When Jesus sensed their disbelief, he said, "Who are my supporters towards God?" The disciples said, "We are God's supporters; we believe in God, and bear witness that **we are submitters."** (3:52)*

They are not all the same; among the followers of the scripture [Jews and Christians], *there are those who are righteous. They recite God's revelations through the night, and they fall prostrate. They believe in God and the Last Day, they advocate righteousness and forbid evil, and they hasten to do righteous works. These are the righteous. Any good they do will not go unrewarded. God is fully aware of the righteous. (3:113-115)* [63]

...And you will find that the closest people in friendship to the believers are those who say, "We are Christian." This is because they have priests and monks among them, and they are not arrogant. (5:82, partial) [64]

Notes

[1] C.L. Barnhart and J. Stein, *The American College Dictionary*. (New York: Random House, 1964).

[2] Ibid, 191.

[3] Ibid, 856.

[4] Mordeci Alfandari, *Light of Israel: the great lie rejected*, <http://www.karaite-korner.org.light-of-Israel/great_lie_rejected.shhtml.> (2 June 2003).

[5] In the dictionary, the "Antichrist" is defined as the "archenemy of Christ." The real archenemies of Prophet Jesus are Satan, those who deny that Jesus was a Prophet of God, and those who knowingly perpetuate the myth that Jesus is God or the "son of God."

[6] Khalifa, *Quran*, 4:171, 5:73, and 9:30.

[7] *A Reader's Guide to the Holy Bible*. (New York: Thomas Nelson, Inc.1972).

[8] Khalifa, *Quran*, 19: 23-24 and 29-37.

[9] In the *Oxford American Desk Dictionary*, the term, "christ," is defined as "a title, also now treated as a name given to Jesus of Nazareth."

[10] Khalifa, *Quran*, 3:45.

[11] Stoop and Arterburn, *Recovery Bible*, 1120.

[12] John Hicks, *Myth of God Incarnate*, (Louisville: Westminister John Knox Press, 1977).

[13] Stoop and Arterburn, *Recovery Bible*, 1354.

[14] Khalifa, *Quran*, 5:17-19.

[15] *Human Distortion of the Bible*, <http://www.islam4all.com/human_distortion_of_the_bible.htm> 30 January 2003.

[16] Michael Drosnin authored two books, *The Bible Code and The Bible Code II*.

[17] Ahmed Okla, "Bible Code versus Quran Code," In *Submitter Perspective* (on-line). <http://www.submission.org/miracle/bible_code.html> (30 January 2003).

[18] Michael Scheimer, "Codified Claptrap," In *Scientific American* (May 12, 2003) <http://www.sciam.com/print_version.cfm?articleID=0005467F-2891-1EB7-BDC0809EC588EEDF> (5 July 2004).

[19] Ibid, 1.

[20] Randall Ingermanson, *A Review of: The Bible Code II by Michael Drosnin* <http://www.rsingermanson.com/html/drosnin2.html> (July 5, 2004). In 1999, Dr.

Ingermanson wrote a book entitled *Who Wrote the Bible Code*, wherein he elaborated on the myth of the Bible Code.

[21] Ibid, 1.

[22] Khalifa, *Quran*, 5:72.

[23] C. Hilliker and M. Jenkins, "Why Christmas Is So Important To God," *The Philadelphia Trumpet*, 13 (10), 2002.

[24] Ibid, 23.

[25] Ibid, 24.

[26] Cornerstone Evangelical Association, *The Plain Truth About Christmas*, <http://www.cornerstone1.org/b-Christmas.htm> (23 December 1999).

[27] Cornerstone Evangelical Association, *Truth About Christmas*, 5.

[28] Ibid.

[29] Hilliker and Jenkins, *Why Christmas*, 25.

[30] Ibid, 23.

[31] Ibid, 23 and 25.

[32] Cornerstone Evangelical Association, *Truth About Christmas*, 5.

[33] Ibid, 4.

[34] Khalifa, *Quran*, 7:189-190.

[35] In pagan mythology, the sun rises in spring from the death of winter to give life to the fertile earth once again.

[36] Royce Carlson, *The Pagan Origins of Easter, Zenzibar Alternative Culture*, 8 April 2001, <http://www.zenzibar.com/articles/Easter.asp> (18 December 2002).

[37] Ibid, 1.

[38] Ibid, 1.

[39] Timothy and Kimberly Southhall, *"The Truth About Easter,"* 9 January 2001, <http://www.bright.net/~1wayonly/easter.html> (18 December 2002).

[40] Ibid, 2-3. The exchange of the word "Easter" for "Passover" in this verse is a repeated mistranslation of the Bible. Such a mistranslation is consistent with a broad effort by distorted Christianity to convey the falsehood that Jesus' life (including his death) represents God's mercy upon humanity by "sending His son to die for human sin."

[41] Ibid, 2-3.

42 Khalifa, *Quran*, 25:48-49 and 35:9.

43 Ibid, 10:18, 31:21, 32:4, and 59:16.

44 *A Reader's Guide to the Holy Bible.* (New York: Thomas Nelson, Inc.1972).

45 Gospel of Barnabas <http://www.barnabas.net/barnabasP220.html> and <http://www.barnabas.net/barnabasP215.html> (6 July 2004).

46 Khalifa, *Quran*, 3:55.

47 Ibid, 3:78, 5:73, 6:21, and 6:112.

48 This is a scientific astronomical fact only disputed by uninformed individuals. Informed individuals are aware that the Christian Sabbath is a man-made doctrine.

49 Dasyd Ministry, *Sunday—first day of the week*, July 2002, <http://www.geocities.com/dasyd ministries/sunday.html> (18 December 2002).

50 Ibid, 1 and 3.

51 Khalifa, *Quran*, 4:154 and 7:163.

52 William Branham, *"The Sign of The Cross,"* <http://biblebelievers.org.au/2bab028.htm> (18 December 2002).

53 Ibid, 1.

54 Ibid, 1, 2, and 4.

55 Ibid, 2.

56 Ibid, 2.

57 Hislop, *Babylons*, 199.

58 Unlike a cross, a crucifix is a cross used to crucify or execute someone.

59 Charles Templeton, *Farewell to God: My Reasons for Rejecting the Christian Faith.* (Toronto: McClelland and Stewart, 1999)

60 Ibid, 7.

61 Ibid, 218.

62 Khalifa, *Quran*, 3:78 and 6:21.

63 Ibid, 3:52; 3:113-115.

64 Ibid, 5:82 (partial).

Four

Distortions of Islam

Traveling a spiritual path now more laden with doctrinal weeds and thorns, we reach a point associated with the advent of a prophet who came after Jesus. Jesus foretold of a prophet who would come after him. Scholars differ as to whether the translated Greek name of the prophet after Jesus is "Periklutos" (i.e., "highly praised one"), or "Parakletos" (i.e., "counselor," "comforter,"or "advocate").[1] Many Christian scholars seem to have misinterpreted the meaning of the name due partially to a change in vowel sounds from "u" in Periklutos to "e" in Periklutos.

From the Bible:

"But when the Counselor [parakletos] comes, whom I shall send to you from the Father, even the Spirit of Truth, who proceeds from the Father, he will bear witness to me; and you also are witnesses" (John 15:26-27 RSV)

"Nevertheless I tell you the truth: it is to your advantage that I go away, for if I do not go away, the Counselor [parakletos] will not come to you; but if I go, I will send him to you. And when he comes, he will convince the world concerning sin and righteousness and judgment" (John 16:7-8 RSV)[2]

Jesus clearly spoke about *someone human other than himself* who would be a prophet. Despite this fact, many Christian scholars of religion have falsely attributed the name "Paraclete" to God, to the Holy Spirit, and even to Jesus. The definitions of "Paraclete" vary from one source to another source. One distorted definition of "Paraclete" in a reader's guide[3] to a translation of the Bible states:

> Paraclete (para-clete) A Greek word, applied to Jesus Christ to indicate His function in making intercession for the people with

God the Father. It implies one who pleads for, counsels, strengthens, comforts.[4]

This definition contradicts proven truth that Jesus was not an intercessor between God and mankind. In addition, Jesus is not going to return to earth before the Day of Judgment to "plead, counsel, strengthen, and comfort" human beings. The Holy Spirit is the Angel Gabriel who comes into this world to deliver revelation to prophets, not to "convince the world concerning sin, righteousness, and judgment." Jesus could not "send God" anywhere. Certainly, the verses John 16:7-8 could not mean that Jesus would send himself back to earth. That would be like you saying to someone, "I am sending myself back to the store." On all accounts, even the inaccurate definition of Paraclete does not refer to Jesus, the Holy Spirit, or God. Nevertheless, the debate and polemics continue.

A simple correction of vowels in the Greek name makes a *crucial significant* difference in its meaning and connotation. *Unlike the name "Parakletos," the correct Greek name "Pariklutos" is identical to the Arabic name, "Ahmad" or" Praised."* Over the course of twenty-three years, the Prophet Muhammad received the verses that constitute the Quran. In his last years of earthly life, per Gabriel's instructions, Muhammad wrote the verses down in the arrangement and order that we have today. The authenticity and preservation of the Quran is confirmed by the miraculous mathematical Code embedded in its text. Prior to the revelation of the Quran, Muhammad practiced the religion of his Bedouin community - a *distorted* version of the religion practiced by the Prophet Abraham. The religion of Abraham is true Islam. The universal message of the Quran is identical to the Divine command revealed to all Prophets of God – *there is no god but the One God*. Submission to God alone *is* the religion of creation. However, weapons of mass distortion and deceit are also deployed against those who say that Islam is their religion and the Quran is their scripture.

The word Islam, or its equivalent in any language, does not refer to a religion separate from other divinely revealed religions. Islam encompasses all ways of life rooted in the worship of God alone. It does not matter whether you call it Islam, peace, or submission. It does not matter what language you speak. It is the same truth. The Arabic word "muslim" literally means *"submitter"* or *one who submits to God.* An individual can be a Buddhist Muslim, a Hindu Muslim, a Christian Muslim, a Jewish Muslim, a Muslim Muslim, or any other kind of Muslim if the person submits to God alone, obeys His commandments as revealed in authentic scriptures, believes in the Hereafter, and leads a righteous life. At different periods in the history of mankind, God revealed divine scriptures to prophets. In turn, the prophets taught the scriptures to their followers.

From the Quran:

The only religion approved by God is "Submission." Ironically, those who have received the scripture are the ones who dispute this fact, despite the knowledge they have received, due to jealousy. For such rejectors of God's revelations, God is most strict in reckoning. (3:19)

Surely, those who believe, those who are Jewish, the converts, and the Christians; any of them who (1) believe in God and (2) believe in the Last Day, and (3) lead a righteous life, have nothing to fear, nor will they grieve. (5:69)

He decreed for you the same religion decreed for Noah, and what we inspired to you, and what we decreed for Abraham, Moses, and Jesus: "You shall uphold this one religion, and do not divide it." The idol worshipers will greatly resent what you invite them to do. God redeems to Himself whomever He wills; He guides to Himself only those who totally submit. (42:13)

Muslims throughout the world view the scripture of Islam as the least corrupt scripture of the three monotheist religions. Objectively speaking, the tenets of Islam *in the Quran* are wholly intact and the authentic guidance and commands revealed to mankind in the Quran have not been lost. *The Quran was revealed for all people.*

From the Quran:

In their history, there is a lesson for those who possess intelligence. This is not fabricated Hadith; this (Quran) confirms all previous scriptures, provides the details of everything, and is a beacon and mercy for those who believe. (12:111)

A.L.R. These (letters) are proofs of this scripture; a profound Quran. (15:1)

Absolutely, we have revealed the reminder, and, absolutely, we will preserve it. (15:9)[5]

Islam after Hislam

When it comes to the creation of laws and practices never revealed or authorized by God, Islam is no less distorted than the other two monotheistic religions. Distorted Islam is filled with its share of "weeds and thorns." Contemporary Islam is replete with rituals, beliefs, and practices never ordained by God. The innovations of distorted religions are too numerous to detail in this book. Distorted Islam is divided into hundreds of sub-sects under the contrived main branches of Shiite and Sunni Islam. There are some groups located outside of traditional Muslim countries whose members are *not* traditionally enjoined to read and study the Quran, and *not* taught the obligatory duties of Islam (e.g., salat prayers, Zakat, etc.). In the groups, members are expected to strictly follow their leaders' beliefs and directives, at the expense of not understanding the tenants of Islam. The groups adopt the names, "Muslim" and "Islam," their members adopt Arabic names, and a few outward practices to conjure up a semblance of an Islamic group. Actually, the groups are branches of Hislam. Members of such groups are instructed to shy away from individuals and information that challenge their counterfeit claims of practicing and representing Islam.

In the West, too few Muslim leaders have taken any broad initiatives to educate the public about the true teachings of Islam. As a result, when many people think of Islam, their *local* references may be misinformed groups that claim to represent Islam. God guides sincere leaders and members of such groups to a clearer understanding of true Islam. A world-known example of such a conversion was Malcolm X.[6] After making the Pilgrimage to Mecca, Malcolm X (Malik Shabazz) realized that he had been deceived about the teachings of Islam. In contrast to what he had been taught, he was especially moved by the sense of one humanity– no racism and other artificial distinctions between people. He was also moved when he learned that there is but *one God for all humanity*. In the remainder of his life, he continued to advocate for African American rights and began to speak in support of the dignity of *all* people. Like misguided Jews and Christians, misguided Muslims are hoodwinked into embracing distortions about Islam and the teachings of the Quran. The distortions are as varied as the distorters want the distortions to be.

From the Quran:

Those who divide themselves into sects do not belong with you. Their judgment rests with God, then He will inform them of everything they had done. (6:159)

(Do not fall in idol worship,) like those who divide their religion into sects; each party rejoicing with what they have. (30:32)

Ironically, they broke up into sects only after the knowledge had come to them, due to jealousy and resentment among themselves. If it were not for a predetermined decision from your Lord to respite them for a definite interim, they would have been judged immediately. Indeed, the later generations who inherited the scripture are full of doubts. (42:14)[7]

Islam gave birth to the greatest period of learning, intellectual inquiry, inter-cultural harmony, and pursuit of truth in human history. This four-hundred year period ended due to the corruption of the *teachings and practice* of Islam alongside the emergence of an authoritarian clerical aristocracy. Music, the arts, and any activity deemed by the clergy as "distracting one from thinking about God" were prohibited. This is one reason why when you visit a museum or read a book that displays arts and crafts from different civilizations and cultures, Islamic art is traditionally confined to elaborate beautiful calligraphy, prayer rugs, and vessels for drinking tea. Photographs and pictures of humans were not allowed. The 'music' of Islam is traditionally confined to the recitation of the Quran.[8] These prohibitions have nothing to do with true Islam.

From the Quran:

Say, "Who prohibited the nice things God has created for His creatures, and the good provisions?" Say, "Such provisions are to be enjoyed in this life by those who believe. Moreover, the good provisions will be exclusively theirs on the Day of Resurrection." We thus explain the revelations for people who know. (7:32)

They made for him anything he wanted—niches, statues, deep pools, and heavy cooking pots. O family of David, work (righteousness) to show your appreciation. Only a few of My servants are appreciative. (34:13)

They follow idols who decree for them religious laws never authorized by God. If it were not for the predetermined decision, they would have been judged immediately. Indeed, the transgressors have incurred a painful retribution. (42:21)[9]

Islam does not separate spiritual consciousness from political and national life. Nor does Islam sanction the establishment of a government comprised of an ecclesiastical order of clergy. Nevertheless, such governmental clerical systems have arisen in corrupt Islam. The influence of the *ulama* or religious clergy in distorted Islam is akin to the past pervasive dictatorial arm of the historical Church of Rome and historical Church of England in the West. One of the most widely read scholars of Near Eastern Studies, Dr. Bernard Lewis,[10] roughly but accurately characterized the emergence of a clerical order in Islam as Islam's "infallible popes and college of cardinals." I would extend that to include legions of bishops (sheiks) and with their own catechism.

Islam's catechism consists of rulings (fat'was), and writings of its clergy over centuries and the sanctification of Hadith and Sunna as sources of religious guidance. In his on-line paper entitled *Rise and fall: Islamic apathy vs. 400 years of forgotten renaissance*, Iqbal Latif [11] comments on the current picture of Islam seen by millions in the world. He said:

> Is Islam about public flogging, hand chopping, denial of basic human rights to women and all human beings, and above all, denial of inquiry into human thought processes? Certainly not. The extremist fringe has mutilated the true picture of Islam and its historical benevolence and patronage of culture and science. The Islamic revolutions, with Shiacentric and Sunnicentric governments in Tehran and Kaul, are at each other's throats accusing each other of revisionism with both proclaiming to be the standard-bearers of Islam. [12]

Regarding the corrupt attitude towards learning and inquiry, Iqbal Latif said:

> Today's intolerance is based on heresy, fanatical Puritanism, and bigotry where modern knowledge is scorned like, take for example, the Internet banned by the Taliban as a serious encroachment on Islamic thought, though sharing of knowledge through the Internet can only be a threat to a totalitarian system like the one supported by the fundamentalists who represent the present day graduates of "Darul Ulooms" [houses of wisdom or alleged Islamic knowledge] mushrooming all over the Islamic world and engulfing moderate reason-based Islamic thinkers. These Darul Ulooms claim to represent true Islamic thought and movement. Such claims in light of historical facts are devoid of truth. History does not support their argument.[13]

From the Quran:

God brought you out of your mothers' bellies knowing nothing, and He gave you the hearing, the eyesight, and the brains, that you may be appreciative. (16:78)

> *You shall not accept any information, unless you verify it for yourself. I have given you the hearing, the eyesight, and the brain, and you are responsible for using them. (17:36)*
>
> *He is the One who granted you the hearing, the eyesight, and the brains. Rarely are you appreciative. (23:78)*[14]

Many people in Muslim societies refer to themselves as "born Muslims." Given the fact that the entire creation is Muslim, people born in non-Muslim societies are obviously "born Muslims" too. No human being is born into any religion, other than the religion of creation. From the religion of creation, each person embarks on a course to re-affirm their submission to God or tread down another course. Some Muslims believe that their ethnic identity and language define them as Muslims. A few even go so far as considering themselves to be the only true Muslims. Some Muslims from Arabic-speaking countries or who have learned Arabic believe that you cannot understand Islam and the Quran unless you can speak the Arabic language. They revere the Arabic language. Arabic, the language of the Quran, has been promoted by some Muslims as the language of Islam. *Islam has no official language.*

From the Quran:

> *We did not send any messenger except (to preach) in the tongue of his people, in order to clarify things for them. God then sends astray whomever He wills, and guides whomever He wills. He is the Almighty, the Most Wise. (14:4)*
>
> *If we made it a non-Arabic Quran they would have said, "Why did it come down in that language?" Whether it is Arabic or non-Arabic, say, "For those who believe, it is a guide and healing. As for those who disbelieve, they will be deaf and blind to it, as if they are being addressed from faraway." (41:44)*[15]

Similar to the distortion of Judaism into an ethno-cultural designation, Islam has been falsely presented in some quarters as primarily an Arab or Middle Eastern religion. When many Westerners think of Islam, they think of terrorists with a blind ambition to impose their view of religion and Islam on the "infidels," picture veiled women, camels, prayer rugs, a man chanting from a high tower, and people prostrating in prayer. In recent times, some elements in the Western media have promoted a distorted picture of Islam. The picture has included news clips of head-wrapped bearded clerics denouncing the West as "the great Satan," women being admonished or beaten in the street for allowing their hair to be seen beneath a head cover or scarf, and hordes of individuals parading in streets and engaging in self-injury, praying to dead saints, and exalting their religious leaders.

Contemporary, distorted Islam is besieged by small cadres of fanatical terrorists who, under the banner of representing Islam, engage in violence, subterfuge, intimidation, and murder to advance what they believe is their God-given mission to rid the world of infidels (i.e., anyone who does not "accept Islam" as they define it). In many places worldwide, the very word "Islam" has come to represent fear instead of calm, violence instead of virtue, religious racism instead of inclusiveness, the worship of Arabism instead of an appreciation and respect for all cultures and languages, the denial of women's God-given rights instead of equal spiritual partnership as companions with different qualities in this life, and theocratic tyranny instead of Quran-based systems of democratic representative Providence-guided governments. Yet, make no mistake about it. As is the case in deluded fanatical Judaism and Christianity, terrorist elements in Muslim communities do not mirror true Islam or Submission. Paranoid at the slightest thought that they may be misguided, such persons of any faith suppress any feelings that invite them to re-examine their beliefs and actions. They plunge deeper into an abyss of aberrant self-righteous behavior. Satan loves the extreme, the bizarre, and the outrageous, especially when it is mistaken for religious sincerity and zeal. Deluded into believing that they are the only true Muslims and cut off from the light of the Quran, such persons like to play "watchdog" over other Muslims' religious practices and censure anyone who violates Islamic law (i.e., Shari'ah) as they define it.

Distortions of Islam

1. Confession of Faith

Each one of the five basic obligatory duties of Muslims has been distorted. First, the confession or statement of faith, known as the *Shahada*, has been changed. The word shahada simply means a testimonial, confession, or oath. The confession is: *"I bear witness that there is no god but the One God."* According to the Quran, the angels and all creatures with knowledge bear witness that there is One God. This sacred testimony has been corrupted by the addition of the phrase, *"and Muhammad is the Prophet of God."*

From the Quran:

*God bears witness **that there is no god except He**, and so do the angels and those who possess knowledge. Truthfully and equitably, He is the absolute god; there is no god but He, the Almighty, Most Wise. (3:18)*

When God alone is mentioned, the hearts of those who do not believe in the Hereafter shrink with aversion. But when others are mentioned beside Him, they become satisfied. (39:45)

The places of worship belong to God; do not call on anyone else beside God. (72:18)[16]

2. Five Daily Prayers

Muslims in corrupt Islam no longer simply repeat the specific words that God ordained to be repeated in the daily obligatory prayers. During prayers, many prayer leaders recite additional verses and chapters of the Quran, rather than hold fast to the seven verses that constitute the first chapter of the Quran, *Al-Fatihah: The Key or The Opener.*

From the Quran:

In the name of God, Most Gracious, Most Merciful.
Praise be to God, Lord of the universe.

Most Gracious, Most Merciful.
Master of the Day of Judgment.
You alone we worship; You alone we ask for help.
Guide us in the right path;
the path of those whom You blessed; not of those who have deserved wrath, nor of the strayers.

When a prayer leader completes his recitation, many Muslims repeat the phrase, "Amen"—a Greek phrase repeated in Christian prayers and liturgies. The phrase is not part of *Al-Fatihah* or the salat prayers. Many Muslims are taught that they can make up obligatory prayers that they missed during specified time periods. Not true. Instead of only making the required number of rotations and prostrations, Muslims in corrupt Islam are taught that it is acceptable and even laudable in some instances to make extra rotations and prostrations after completing a required prayer. Instead of only uttering the ordained words for prayer, many prayer leaders spend exorbitant amounts of time during prayer reciting additional Quran verses. As a result, they make what God has made easy into something difficult.

From the Quran:

We never burden any soul beyond its means, and we keep a record that utters the truth. No one will suffer injustice. (23:62)

Some individuals compete with each other and want to impress others with their recitation of the Quran during prayer. As a result, their prayers are nullified. Some people argue that a supplicant's ability to be patient while a long chapter of the Quran is being recited reflects the supplicant's piety. Not true. Prayers are not tests of worshipers' physical endurance. *The purpose of prayer is to glorify God and make contact (i.e., salat) with God, not to show off behind a facade of humility or knowledge of the Quran.* Some Muslims make additional supplications during a required prayer, ignorant of the fact that they should not subtract or add anything to a required prayer. This situation reminds me of the time when Rabbi Judah expressed concern about some Jews in France during the twelfth century

Distortions of Islam

who altered their morning prayers. Prophet Jesus cautioned his followers not to alter their prayers or seek recognition from others for performing their prayers.

From the Quran:

The hypocrites think that they are deceiving God, but He is the One who leads them on. When they get up for the Contact Prayer (Salat), they get up lazily. That is because they only show off in front of the people, and rarely do they think of God. (4:142)

And woe to those who observe the contact prayers (Salat)—who are totally heedless of their prayers. They only show off. (107:4-6)[17]

From the Bible:

And now about prayer. When you pray, do not be like the hypocrites who love to pray publicly on street corners and in the synagogues where everyone can see them. I assure you, that is all the reward they will ever get...When you pray do not babble on and on as people in other religions [non-Jewish pagan religions] do. They think their prayers are answered only by repeating their words again and again. Do not be like them because your Father (Lord) knows exactly what you need even before you ask Him. (Matthew, 6:5, 7)[18]

3. Fasting

In distorted Islam, one must physically see or receive a report from someone who has physically seen the crescent moon of the ninth lunar month before starting the Ramadan fast. This man-made rule is treated as a divine command. As is the case with other Islamic practices, many misguided Muslims rely on Hadith detailing how one should verify the presence of the new moon. In an age when the start date of any new month is readily available on the Internet, in newspapers, in libraries, and in precise astronomical tables even available in hand-held computers, some Muslims still insist on sighting the ninth crescent moon. Before the development of these technologies, it made complete sense to look for the crescent moon as an indicator of a new lunar month. But, the widely-upheld "fat'wa" that the visual sighting of the crescent moon is mandatory before starting the Ramadan fast is a fabrication. It contradicts God's command in the Quran to learn how to calculate the passage of time.[19]

From the Quran:

The count of months, as far as God is concerned, is twelve. This has been God's law, since the day He created the heavens and the earth. Four of them are sacred. This is the perfect religion; you shall not wrong your souls (by fighting) during the Sacred Months. However, you may declare all-out war against the idol worshipers (even during the Sacred Months), when they declare all-out war against you, and know that God is on the side of the righteous. (9:36)

He is the One who rendered the sun radiant, and the moon a light, and He designed its phases that you may learn to count the years and to calculate. God did not create all this, except for a specific purpose. He explains the revelations for people who know. (10:5)[20]

4. Obligatory Charity

Many Muslims pay the obligatory charity or Zakat from their savings only once a year, at the end of the month of Ramadan. In the Quran, God commands each Muslim to pay the obligatory charity of 2.5% each time he or she receives "harvest." In modern times, harvest is the same as income. A Muslim should pay Zakat whenever he or she receives any income. Zakat is to be paid from earnings, not savings. In January 2003, I met a sincere Muslim man from a Middle East country who insisted that the Zakat is 5% of one's income. In response to my question about the source of such a ruling, he told me that the religious scholars encourage giving 5% of one's income in Zakat. He added that the Zakat is paid to the imams and religious scholars to be distributed in the community. I asked him on what basis did the religious scholars justify giving Zakat to them, since no such command is in the Quran. I reminded him that it is each Muslim's individual duty to give Zakat to the persons specifically identified in the Quran. Zakat is distinct from *Sadaqa* or voluntary charity. Sadaqa can be given at any time, there is no specific percent or amount that must be given, and the recipients of Sadaqa are not specifically identified.

From the Quran:

They ask you about giving: say, "The charity you give shall go to the parents, the relatives, the orphans, the poor, and the traveling alien." Any good you do, God is fully aware thereof.(2:215)

He is the One who established gardens, trellised and untrellised, and palm trees, and crops with different tastes, and olives, and pomegranates—fruits that are similar, yet dissimilar. Eat from their fruits, and <u>give the due alms on the day of harvest</u>, and do not waste anything. He does not love the wasters. (6:141)

And they give their obligatory charity (Zakat). (23:4)

Therefore, you shall give the relatives their rightful share (of charity), as well as the poor, and the traveling alien. This is better for those who sincerely seek God's pleasure; they are the winners. (30:38)[21]

5. Hajj or Pilgrimage to Mecca

If possible, a Muslim should make the pilgrimage to the Kabaah in Mecca, Saudia Arabia during his or her lifetime. God prescribed the specific months to make the Hajj. The twelfth lunar month of the Islamic calender is called Zul-Hijja. The Hajj period begins at the beginning of Zul-Hijja and extends through the third lunar month. This specific time period for Hajj has been altered and compressed by Muslim clerics from four months into the first ten days of the twelfth lunar month. The Muslim clerics justified their distortion of the Hajj period by twisting the meaning of the phrase *"They shall commemorate God's name during the specified number of days."* The Hajj can be completed by a pilgrim in five days. Note that in the following verse, the word *"months"* (*ash'hur"*) is in the text, not the words "month"(*shahr*) or "day"(*ya'um*). So, how could one claim that the Hajj period is confined to less than a month?

From the Quran:

Hajj shall be observed in the specified months [ash'hur"]. Whoever sets out to observe Hajj shall refrain from sexual intercourse, misconduct, and arguments throughout Hajj. Whatever good you do, God is fully aware thereof. As you prepare your provisions for the journey, the best provision is righteousness. You shall observe Me, O you who possess intelligence. (2:197) [22]

Women's Dress

In many traditional Muslim communities, women are compelled to wear head and facial covers. Despite centuries-old claims that this restriction in women's dress is found in the Quran, *it is not in the Quran*. In the Quran, mention is made of a wife of the prophet Muhammad speaking to others "from behind a barrier" (Khalifa translation). The word *hijab* means a barrier, partition, cover or curtain. The word *khimar* means cover as in a headcover or scarf. According to the Quran, one should not enter the home or private quarters of another adult person without permission. This is especially true with respect to not violating the privacy of members of the opposite sex.

From the Quran:

O you who believe, do not enter the prophet's homes unless you are given permission to eat, nor shall you force such an invitation in any manner. If you are invited, you may enter. When you finish eating, you shall leave; do not engage him in lengthy conversations. This used to hurt the prophet, and he was too shy to tell you. But God does not shy away from the truth. If you have to ask his wives for something, ask them from behind a barrier (hijab). This is purer for your hearts and their hearts. You are not to hurt the messenger of God. You shall

> not marry his wives after him, for this would be a gross offense in the sight of God. (33:53) [23]

Instead of correctly explaining the meaning as a curtain or cover separating the private quarters from the outside, innovators described this verse as a divine command that women must cover their faces and heads and remain secluded from public areas. For centuries, this distortion has been presented by misguided Muslim clergy to Muslim masses as an immutable divine command.

Head and facial covers are considered part of the cultural dress for Muslim women. An entire industry of manufacturing so-called religious headscarves and facial covers exists due to this fabricated doctrine. In some Muslim societies, the removal of the headscarf in public is considered a crime and a sign that a woman is "unrighteous." The absence of a head cover on older Muslim girls and women is traditionally associated with a lack of morality, being unchaste, and objection to Islamic law. In distorted Islam, the head cover is a symbol of a woman's role and status. It reflects a pervasive distortion of Quranic guidelines on dress code. Twenty years ago, Andrea Rugh,[24] an author and researcher on the Egyptian family, cited an article in the *Egyptian Gazette* acknowledging that the idea that Muslim women must wear head covers is an innovation. The article indicated that:

> As it turns out, the ugly costume they have come up with has nothing to do with Islam in any case; it is a relic of pre-Islamic ignorance…Apart from being utterly silly in its own right…it gives rise to equally silly and needless controversy at home and invites ridicule from thoughtless writers around the world.[25]

In America and other western countries, some Muslim women are having problems acquiring drivers' licenses and identification cards because the women refuse to remove headscarves and facial covers in order to take license photographs. In every case, the women argue, "This is my religion." In one sense, they are correct. This practice they cling to is part of *their perception of Islam.* Their passionate objections to requests to remove their head covers reflect the fact that they have been convinced since childhood that "fake flowers are real roses". An obligation to wear head covers is not a part of true Islam. Many states in the U.S. are *no longer* modifying their drivers' license guidelines in order to accommodate a religious innovation. For thousands of years before the revelation of the Quran, indigenous peoples, men and women, living in arid desert regions have worn head and facial covers to protect themselves from the sun's heat, hot air, and blowing sands. In disfigured Islam (i.e., a form of Hislam), the wearing of head covers suddenly became a "divine obligation" on women.

Men's Dress

Prior to becoming a Muslim Submitter, I would frequently don a long one-piece pajama-like garment called a *jalabi'a*. The jalabi'a is a form of dress worn by male inhabits of Saudi Arabia, the Middle East, and other desert areas for thousands of years. However, upon embracing traditional Islam, many males from non-Muslim cultures are led to believe that the jalabi'a is an Islamic dress for men.

From the Quran:

Tell the believing men that they shall subdue their eyes (and not stare at the women), and to maintain their chastity. This is purer for them. God is fully Cognizant of everything they do. And tell the believing women to subdue their eyes and maintain their chastity. They shall not reveal any parts of their bodies, except that which is necessary. They shall cover their chests and shall not relax this code in the presence of other than their husbands, their fathers, the fathers of their husbands, their sons, the sons of their husbands, their brothers, the sons of their brothers, the sons of their sisters, other women, the male servants or employees whose sexual drive has been nullified, or the children who have not reached puberty. They shall not strike their feet when they walk in order to shake and reveal certain details of their bodies. All of you shall repent to God, O you believers, that you may succeed. (24:30-31) [26]

Distortions of Islam

Hadith and Sunna: Man-Made Sources of Religious Law

Having abandoned the Quran alone as the sole source of Islamic law, corrupt Islam created its own body of laws and sources of religious guidance called the *shari'ah*. Two major elements of the shari'ah are the *Hadith* and *Sunna*. Hadith and Sunna are presented as elements of divine guidance. The *Hadith* are thousands of purported sayings of the prophet Muhammad about virtually every aspect of life. Many Muslim religious leaders acknowledge that most Hadith are spurious. Hadith that have been deemed "authentic" ("saheeh" in Arabic) are codified into Islamic law. Many Hadith are simply historical accounts of past events. Hadith contradict each other, some contradict common sense and scientific facts, and some reflect superstitions. The Quran does not need to be supplemented by any book or writings by religious scholars about how to understand the Quran. In His infinite knowledge, God knew that followers of corrupt Islam would invent *Hadith* instead of relying solely on the Quran as their source of religious guidance. The word *Hadith* is specifically used in Quranic verses that foretell and expose this practice. God reveals that He is the Teacher of the Quran.

From the Quran:

This Quran could not possibly be authored by other than God. It confirms all previous messages and provides a fully detailed scripture. It is infallible, for it comes from the Lord of the universe. (10:37)

In their history, there is a lesson for those who possess intelligence. This is not <u>fabricated Hadith</u>; this (Quran) confirms all previous scriptures, provides the details of everything, and is a beacon and mercy for those who believe. (12:111)

Among the people, there are those who uphold <u>baseless Hadith</u>, and thus divert others from the path of God without knowledge and take it in vain. These have incurred a shameful retribution. (31:6)

<u>God has revealed herein the best Hadith</u>; a book that is consistent and points out both ways (to Heaven and Hell). The skins of those

who reverence their Lord cringe therefrom, then their skins and their hearts soften up for God's message. Such is God's guidance; He bestows it upon whoever wills (to be guided). As for those sent astray by God, nothing can guide them. (39:23)

These are God's revelations that we recite to you truthfully. In which <u>Hadith</u> other than God and His revelations do they believe?(45:6)

[God] Teacher of the Quran. (55:2)

What <u>Hadith</u> other than this [Quran], do they uphold? (77:50)

On the Day of Judgement, the Prophet Muhammad will utter the following words:

From the Quran:

The messenger said, "My Lord, my people have deserted this Quran." (25:30) [27]

Followers of distorted Islam have abandoned the Quran for Hadith, Sunna, and the edicts of their clergy. At the time Prophet Muhammad departed from this world, his followers were holding fast to the Quran and did not add anything to it. But, things soon changed. Factions and false leaders emerged claiming that they were the rightful heirs to true Islam. Like all departed souls, Muhammad has no awareness of what has transpired in this world since his departure. He will be surprised to find out that people substituted the Quran with other writings known as "Hadith," a body of narrations never authorized by God.[28]

For example, one Hadith, reported to have met a stringent test of acceptance, alleges that the prophet Muhammad said that "the earth is supported on the back of a whale." No prophet or messenger of God would utter such nonsense. Another Hadith cautions that dogs are forbidden, possess evil spirits, and are unclean. Yet, there is a historical account in the Quran of the seven Christian sleepers of Ephesus and their dog who

Distortions of Islam

sought refuge in a cave from Roman idolaters. In another verse, God confirms that dogs can be trained and used in hunting animals for food.

From the Quran:

They consult you concerning what is lawful for them; say, "Lawful for you are all good things, including what trained dogs and falcons catch for you." You train them according to God's teachings. You may eat what they catch for you, and mention God's name thereupon. You shall observe God. God is most efficient in reckoning. (5:4)

You would think that they were awake, when they were in fact asleep. We turned them to the right side and the left side, while their dog stretched his arms in their midst. Had you looked at them, you would have fled from them, stricken with terror. (18:18)

We caused them to be discovered, to let everyone know that God's promise is true, and to remove all doubt concerning the end of the world. The people then disputed among themselves regarding them. Some said, "Let us build a building around them." Their Lord is the best knower about them. Those who prevailed said, "We will build a place of worship around them."...Some would say, "They were three; their dog being the fourth," while others would say, "Five; the sixth being their dog," as they guessed. Others said, "Seven," and the eighth was their dog. Say, "My Lord is the best knower of their number." Only a few knew the correct number. Therefore, do not argue with them; just go along with them. You need not consult anyone about this. (18:21-22) [29]

Scientists have now confirmed that dogs can smell the presence of cancerous abnormal proteins in human urine and in skin moles.[30] The canine sense of smell is as much as one hundred thousand times greater than the human olfactory sense. In numerous instances, dogs owners who did not know that they had skin cancer reported that their canine friends would incessantly sniff cancerous skin moles and ignore other moles on their owners' bodies. When the cancerous moles were removed, the dogs would stop sniffing or attempting to bite the areas. With accuracy greater than chance, dogs can distinguish between specimens of human urine that contain cancerous proteins and human urine specimens that do not. For some of the dog owners cited in the studies, their dogs' strange behavior led to early medical interventions to treat serious cancers. The fact that the dogs seem to care about removing unfamiliar substances from the bodies of their owners wholly contradicts the notion that canines are full of evil spirits. These scientific findings along with the Quran verses 18:18 and 18: 21-22 clearly reveal that the supposedly pure reliable Hadith that describe dogs as forbidden and harbors of evil spirits, are fabrications.

Men may lie but God does not. Facts in the Quran and scientific investigations of the soundness of many "sahih Hadith" confirm that Hadith are not a source of religious law or guidance. One cannot simply extract Hadith that seem logical and reasonable and classify them as "pure or unsullied," with the intent of defining them as sacred directives. Unfortunately, following tradition rather than God's commands, many people in Muslim societies and communities continue to regard Hadith as a source of sacred guidance. Yet, there are many Muslims who question and no longer regard Hadith as sacred. Many of these Muslims choose not to voice their opinion openly, due to intensely negative reactions from misguided Muslims.

Miraculous Code Exposes Tampering with the Quran

Two false verses were added to the end of the ninth chapter of the Quran. It is the only chapter (114 chapters) that does not begin with the *Basmalah*, the 19-Arabic lettered phrase *"In the name of God, Most Gracious, Most Merciful."* The *Basmalah* is the foundation of the Miraculous Code. God knew that hypocritical Muslims would tamper with the Quran. God placed the missing *Basmalah* that is absent from chapter nine in the text of chapter 27 (27:30). Chapter 27 also begins with the *Basmalah*. Thus, the total count of the *Basmalah* in the Quran is intact – 114 (19 x 6). When the false verses are included in the Code counts, the Code is "compromised." This inconsistency in the 19-based Code is meant to prove once and for all that verses 128-129 of chapter nine are innovations.

The Miraculous Mathematical Code provides Muslim scholars with an opportunity to close centuries of debate and orchestrated conjecture about the validity of the two bogus verses. Informed Muslim religious scholars have always held the two verses suspect. The scholars have yet to take advantage of this opportunity. Most of them choose not to acknowledge the Mathematical Code as an indisputable fact. If the religious leaders accept the Code, they fear loss of power and loss of control over the uninformed Muslim masses. Some leaders delude themselves into believing that they are preserving the Quran. God alone preserves the Quran and the miraculous mathematical Code.

From the Quran:

Absolutely, we have revealed the reminder, and, absolutely, we will preserve it [Quran]. (15:9)

Indeed, it is a glorious Quran. In a preserved master tablet. (85:21-22) [31]

Even though, for centuries, thousands of Muslims have attempted to decipher the meaning of the Code letter combinations, Muslim religious leaders now suddenly warn that any attempts or claims to have unraveled the meaning of the letter combinations are counterfeit and a sin. For example, a 1997 English translation of the Quran prepared by Saheeh International and published by the Abul-Qasim Publishing House in Riyadh, Saudia Arabia, contains the following footnote in reference to the first set of initials (A.L.M. - Alif, Lam, Meem):

These are among the fourteen opening letters which occur in various combinations at the beginning of twenty-nine surahs of the Quran. Although there has been much speculation as to their meaning, it was not in fact revealed by Allah to anyone and is known only to Him.

The wording, "it was not in fact revealed by Allah (the word, "Allah," means the one and only God) to anyone," clearly shows that this misleading warning is a response to the discovery of the Miraculous Code. The warning is written and endorsed by individuals who may possibly belong to the *same* Muslim religious institutions that initially acknowledged the veracity of the Code. One purpose of the Code is to expose those who would deny it and discourage others from examining it. Note the following portion of verse 30 of chapter 74, where the number 19 is mentioned.

From the Quran:

... (5) *to expose those who harbor doubt in their hearts, and the disbelievers; they will say, "What did God mean by this allegory?" God thus sends astray whomever He wills, and guides whomever He wills*... *(74:30, partial)*

Is it possible that some individuals seek to discourage others from investigating the Miraculous Code in the Quran? Yes. Any camouflaged characterization of the miraculous Code as "speculation"[32] is a distortion and denial of one of God's greatest miracles to mankind. The Arabic word "Saheeh" means "authentic or pure." A name like Saheeh International, is possibly meant to relieve readers of any doubt about the quality and integrity of the publications, including the publication of an English translation of the Quran. Hundreds of years ago, some Muslim scholars designated spurious irrational "Hadith" or alleged sayings of Prophet Muhammad as "Saheeh."

Many Muslim men attempt to mimic the reported dress, appearance, and behavior of Prophet Muhammad because they are taught that it is the "sunna of the Prophet." For example, some individuals attempt to eat in a manner that mimics what they believe to be the way that Prophet Muhammad ate his food. They wear full beards, sleep on their right sides, individuals enter a restroom with their left foot and exit with their right foot, do not wear silk, do not wear watches or rings made of gold, and wear shirts without neckties. These stereotyped behaviors are associated with the "sunna of the Prophet." At one time, I engaged in this behavior. Some Muslims incorrectly deem the Prophet Muhammad as "the perfect man." There is not nor was there ever a "perfect man." Even Jesus was not perfect. If we were perfect humans, we would not be living in this dimension.[33] A righteous man of high moral character with strengths and weaknesses, Prophet Muhammad made mistakes during his lifetime. Here are some examples *from the Quran.*

From the Quran:

They almost diverted you from the revelations we have given you. They wanted you to fabricate something else, in order to consider you a friend. If it were not that we strengthened you, you almost leaned towards them just a little bit. Had you done that, we would have doubled the retribution for you in this life, and after death, and you would have found no one to help you against us. (17:73-75)

Say, "I have been <u>enjoined from</u> worshiping the idols you worship beside God, when the clear revelations came to me from my Lord. I was commanded to submit to the Lord of the universe." (40:66)

He (Muhammad) frowned and turned away. When the blind man came to him. How do you know? He may purify himself. Or he may take heed, and benefit from the message. As for the rich man. You gave him your attention. Even though you could not guarantee his salvation. The one who came to you eagerly. And is really reverent. You ignored him. (80:1-10)[34]

"Norm Troopers" Enforce Innovations

I recall conversations with a Muslim man who had been pressured by some members of his community that it is unlawful (i.e., *haram* in Arabic) for him to wear a necktie. We had many in-depth discussions about distortions of Islam, spiritual development, and the Miraculous Code. I gave him a copy of the Quran translated by Dr. Khalifa, and materials about the Code and how Islam has been distorted. Several weeks later, he returned the Quran and the materials to me. He told me that he was threatened by some individuals in his religious community that if he continued reading the materials or if he adopted any of the corrections noted in the materials, he would be designated an apostate from Islam and possibly be separated from his family. I was upset that the kind intelligent brother had been threatened because he was merely examining the evidence and information. I told him that he was not in a country where authoritarian clergy dictate religious practice and self-appointed "norm troopers" enforce clerical innovations. In this case, the norm troopers' threats and behavior are not only criminal, but their behavior is also based on a *distortion* of a Quran verse (2:221) that prohibits marriage between disbelievers (i.e., atheists, idolaters) and believers (i.e., people who worship the One God). In America, regardless of some individuals' negative conduct, people have freedom of religion and the right to express their spiritual views without harassment. Informed religious and non-religious Americans who understand the American Constitution and their rights do not tolerate the importation of such nonsense. This nation came into being in a struggle against such tyranny. God willing, this society will not tolerate the importation of strong-arm Hislamic practices disguised as Islam.[35] Like submitters of other faiths in America, American Muslims are in a unique position to promote the true worship of God alone should they choose to abandon centuries-old distortions.

Primitive Justice System

In some communities within corrupt Islam, the thief's hand is cut off, the adulterer and adulteress are stoned to death, anyone considered an apostate is executed, persons who do not pray are imprisoned or executed, a man who believes that his wife is not obedient to him or fails to follow his directives may subject her to his physical beatings, and a woman who reveals her hair in public is subject to imprisonment and whipping. When questioned by non-Muslims about such archaic measures, many Muslims nurtured in distorted Islam respond,

> I know it looks strange to you but this is what we have to do. We follow Allah's (God's) revealed commands regarding punishment. We

cannot question God's commands. You do not understand our system of law. Because we follow God's laws, our societies are free of many of the crimes you have in western societies.

Not one of the consequences mentioned above is in the Quran. The punishments were invented by individuals who distorted verses in the Quran and followed centuries of man-made traditions, some practices predating the revelation of the Quran. Yet, the punishments are incorrectly deemed as part of Islamic law. The Quran and nothing but the Quran is the religious law in authentic Islam.

In the Quran, the hand of a thief who repeatedly steals without justification is permanently marked—not cut off. This is supported by the fact that the *same* word for cutting or marking (*qata'a*) is also used in a verse (12:31) that describes a group of women who were so startled by the handsomeness of Joseph that the women cut themselves, resulting in self-inflicted hand wounds. In his translation of the Quran, Dr. Khalifa explained how the Miraculous Code exposes the innovation of cutting off the hand of a thief.

> The practice of cutting off the thief's hand, as decreed by the false Muslims, is a satanic practice without Quranic basis. Due to the special importance of this example, God has provided mathematical proof in support of marking the hand of the thief, rather than severing it. Verse 12:31 refers to the women who so admired Joseph that they "cut" their hands. Obviously, they did not "cut off" their hands; nobody can. The sum of sura and verse numbers are the same for 5:38 and 12:31, i.e., 43. It is also the will and mercy of God that this mathematical relationship conforms with the Quran's 19-based code. Nineteen verses after 12:31, we see the same word in 12:50.[36]

From the Quran:

The thief, male or female, you shall mark their hands as a punishment for their crime, and to serve as an example from God. God is Almighty, Most Wise. If one repents after committing this crime, and reforms, God redeems him. God is Forgiver, Most Merciful. (5:38)

When she heard of their gossip, she invited them, prepared for them a comfortable place, and gave each of them a knife. She then said to him, "Enter their room." When they saw him, they so admired him, that they cut their hands. They said, "Glory be to God, this is not a human being; this is an honorable angel." (12:31)

The king said, "Bring him to me." When the messenger came to him, he said, "Go back to your lord and ask him to investigate the women who cut their hands. My Lord is fully aware of their schemes." (12:50)[37]

In a society that follows God's system of assistance to the poor, individuals are not compelled to steal necessities of life like food and money from others. Individuals who can be clearly identified without any doubt as engaging in extra-marital and premarital sex are flogged before an audience and separated from the society as a health measure. The flogging should be painful but not debilitating. Public humiliation and isolation serve as greater punishments. The humiliation and isolation presuppose that one is living in a society where chastity is considered an important moral virtue, not a stigma. Persons are quarantined because they may be carriers of sexually transmitted diseases (STDs). The HIV-AIDs epidemic should serve as ample notice that such behavior has severe consequences. Men do not have the right to beat their wives. A woman or man should not be punished for not following a man-made prohibition against a behavior never discouraged or prohibited by God.

From the Quran:

There shall be no compulsion in religion: the right way is now distinct from the wrong way. Anyone who denounces the devil and believes in God has grasped the strongest bond; one that never breaks. is Hearer, Omniscient. (2:256)

O you who believe, it is not lawful for you to inherit what the women leave behind, against their will. You shall not force them to give up anything you had given them, unless they commit a proven adultery.

You shall treat them nicely. If you dislike them, you may dislike something wherein God has placed a lot of good. (4:19)

The adulteress and the adulterer you shall whip each of them a hundred lashes. Do not be swayed by pity from carrying out God's law, if you truly believe in God and the Last Day. And let a group of believers witness their penalty. The adulterer will end up marrying an adulteress or an idol worshiper, and the adulteress will end up marrying an adulterer or an idol worshiper. This is prohibited for the believers. Those who accuse married women of adultery, then fail to produce four witnesses, you shall whip them eighty lashes, and do not accept any testimony from them; they are wicked. If they repent afterwards and reform, then God is Forgiver, Merciful. (24:2-5)

As for those who accuse their own spouses, without any other witnesses, then the testimony may be accepted if he swears by God four times that he is telling the truth. The fifth oath shall be to incur God's condemnation upon him, if he was lying. She shall be considered innocent if she swears by God four times that he is a liar. The fifth oath shall incur God's wrath upon her if he was telling the truth. This is God's grace and mercy towards you. God is Redeemer, Most Wise. (24:6-10) [38]

The Star and Crescent

A single star alongside a crescent moon has become a universal symbol of Islam throughout the world. Like the star of David in Judaism and the Cross in Christianity, the star and crescent is found on flags, jewelry, cards, clothing, buildings, on towers atop mosques, schools, and on government buildings and vehicles in many Muslim countries. However, the Quran is replete with verses that warn against composing religious idols, symbols, and images. The religion of Islam did not have any physical symbols or icons. Most Muslims are unaware that the crescent and star are ancient symbols adopted by peoples of Central Asia and Siberia in their worship of the sun, moon, and sky gods. In 330 A.D., Emperor Constantine rededicated the city of Istanbul, Turkey to the virgin Mary (i.e., Mary-mother of Jesus) whose "star symbol" was added to the crescent moon symbol. The "star symbol" refers to the myth about shepherds seeing a lone bright star in the night sky when Jesus was born. The crescent moon is an ancient symbol of the Byzantium goddess, Diana, goddess of the hunt. The ancient name of Istanbul was Byzantium, a metropolis in the Eastern Roman Empire. After defeating Emperor Constantine, Mahomett II and the Ottoman Empire first hoisted a *flag* of the crescent and star as a symbol of Islam. The use of the crescent and star as a symbol of religious and cultural beliefs was carried over from the ancient Roman and Byzantine Empires. The crescent and star have served as a logo of Islam for more than a thousand years. Prior to Mahomett II's defeat of the Roman Emperor Constantine, Muslim armies and caravans only used solid-colored pennants and flags with no markings or symbols to identify themselves.

In explaining the context in which this "logo" or "emblem" of Islam emerged, the authors of one web site said:

> Legend holds it that the founder of the Ottoman Empire, Osman, had a dream in which the crescent moon stretched from one end of the earth to the other. Taking this to be a good omen, he chose to keep the crescent and make it a symbol of his dynasty. There is speculation that the five points on the star represent the five pillars of Islam, but this is pure speculation.... Based on this history, many Muslims reject the crescent moon as a symbol of Islam.[39]

Several words the authors used in this description bear noting—legend, dream, omen, and speculation. Any so-called Islamic practice based on the above experiences is suspect to begin with. Legends and even Hadith about the crescent moon and its emergence as a symbol of Islam have apparently become enmeshed in the minds of many Muslim clergy and their followers.

Muslim Submitters

Submitter Muslims share the same traits as Submitters of other faiths. In religious matters, they only follow what God has ordained in His scriptures and worship Him alone. They make no distinction among God's messengers and prophets. Muslim Submitters do not identify with a very small minority in the traditional Muslim community who claim to follow the Quran but attempt to force their religious beliefs on others, commit unjustified violence against innocents, subjugate women, engage in terror, maintain and promote bogus so-called Islamic laws and traditions, attempt to sabotage every initiative to establish Scripture-based and representative governments in their societies, and promote idolatries in the form of the worship of saints and the worship of Prophet Muhammad. Expressions of Hislam in Islam are obviously not unique to Islam. Muslim Submitters heed God's system in life in their affairs without infringing on the rights of others. They also identify with Submitters of other prophetic traditions and realize that each religious community will be judged based upon the authentic revelation and knowledge revealed to the communities.

From the Quran:

Surely, those who believe, those who are Jewish, the Christians, and the converts; anyone who (1) believes in God, and (2) believes in the Last Day, and (3) leads a righteous life, will receive their recompense from their Lord. They have nothing to fear, nor will they grieve. (2:62)

Say, "We believe in God, and in what was sent down to us, and in what was sent down to Abraham, Ismail, Isaac, Jacob, and the Patriarchs; and in what was given to Moses and Jesus, and all the prophets from their Lord. We make no distinction among any of them. To Him alone we are submitters." (2:136) [40]

Notes

1. John Renard, *Responses to 101 Questions on Islam*, (Mahwah, N.J.: Paulist Press, 1998).
2. *A Reader's Guide to the Holy Bible*, (New York: Thomas Nelson Publishers, 1972).
3. Ibid, 102 (New Testament section).
4. Ibid, Dictionary-Concordance, 43.
5. Khalifa, *Quran*, 3:19, 5:69, 42:13, 12:111, and 15:9.
6. Alex Haley, The *Autobiography of Malcolm X* (New York: Ballantine Books, Inc., 1992 – Commemorative Edition).
7. Khalifa, Quran, 6:159, 30:32, and 42:147.
8. During the rule of the Taliban in Afghanistan, the citizenry was not allowed to listen to birds sing. A person who violated this prohibition was subject to arrest.
9. Khalifa, Quran, 7:32, 34:13, and 42:21.
10. Dr. Bernard Lewis is Cleveland E. Dodge Professor of Near Eastern Studies Emeritus at Princeton University.
11. Iqbal Latif, Rise and fall: Islamic apathy vs. 400 years of forgotten renaissance. *The Iranian*, <http://www.iranian.com/opinion/2001/August/Islam/> (28 December 2002).
12. Ibid, 1.
13. Ibid, 2.
14. Khalifa, *Quran*, 6:78, 17:36, and 23:78.
15. Ibid, 14:4 and 41:44.
16. Ibid, 3:18, 39:45, and 72:18.
17. Ibid, 23:62, 4:142, and 107: 4-6.
18. Stoop and Arterburn, *Recovery Bible*, 1122.
19. The Arabic word for month occurs in the Quran twelve times and the Arabic word for day occurs 365 times.
20. Khalifa, *Quran*, 9:36 and 10:5.
21. Ibid, 2:215, 6:141, 23:4, and 30:38.
22. Ibid, 2:197.
23. Ibid, 33:53.
24. Andrea Rugh, *Family in contemporary Egypt*. (Cairo: The American University

Press, 1985).

[25] Ibid, 233.

[26] Khalifa, *Quran*, 24:30-31.

[27] Ibid, 10:37, 12:111, 31:6, 39:23, 45:6, 55:2, 77:50, and 25:30.

[28] In God's presence, there is no time and space. All events in this dimension, including the future and the Day of Judgement have already happened. This is why verse 25:30 is written in the past tense.

[29] Khalifa, *Quran*, 5:4, 18:18, and 21-22.

[30] *"Study shows dogs able to smell cancer,"* In USA Today (on-line edition), <www.usatoday.com> September 24, 2004.

[31] Khalifa, *Quran*, 5:9 and 85: 21-22.

[32] The disguised specific characterization of the miraculous Code as "speculation" is parallel to the phrase, "What did God mean by this allegory [referring to the Code]?" in verse 74:31 of the Quran.

[33] This life is an opportunity for us to merit God's Mercy by worshiping Him alone. Each human has to decide to admit his or her crime of doubting God's Omnipotence and submit to God alone or continue rebelling against God's system and His commands.

[34] Khalifa, *Quran*, 17:73-75, 40:66, and 80: 1-10.

[35] Informed Muslims (Submitters) in America should not align themselves with centuries-old traditions and practices that violate God's commands in the Quran. Some Muslims in America are attempting to establish a clerical ruling class in the States. Leaders of corrupt Islam feel that Muslims in America need a group of religious scholars and imams endorsed by "official sources" to teach and interpret their version of Islamic law and life in America. Most traditional Muslims rely on misguided clergy and so-called "schools of thought" instead of God's guidance in the Quran.

[36] Khalifa, *Quran*, Footnote to verse 5:38.

[37] Ibid, 5:38 and 12:31, 50.

[38] Ibid, 2:256, 4:19, and 24:2-5, 6-10.

[39] Tracy Pearson, *Crescent Moon: Symbol of Islam?* <http://islam.about.com/library/weekly/aa060401a.htm> (28 December 2002)

[40] Khalifa, *Quran*, 2:136.

Five

Distortions in Other Religions

It is estimated that there are at least 4,222 religions, including different denominations, sects, and local belief systems in the world.[1] The spiritual path that we all started out on has branched off into hundreds of trails. Most travelers on each trail believe that they are practicing the truth. In many respects, the *original* teachings of other religious systems also contain aspects of the Abrahamic tradition.[2] Some of these systems contain similar teachings to those found in the authentic scriptures revealed to prophets in Islam, Judaism, and Christianity. Almighty God *sends messengers to every community on earth.* Messengers deliver the truth in the languages and cultures of their communities.

From the Quran:

We do not send the messengers except as deliverers of good news, as well as warners. Those who believe and reform have nothing to fear, nor will they grieve. (6:48)

O children of Adam, when messengers come to you from among you, and recite My revelations to you, those who take heed and lead a righteous life, will have nothing to fear, nor will they grieve. (7:35)

To each community, a messenger. After their messenger comes, they are judged equitably, without the least injustice. (10:47)

We did not send any messenger except (to preach) in the tongue of his people, in order to clarify things for them. God then sends astray whomever He wills, and guides whomever He wills. He is the Almighty, the Most Wise. (14:4)

Distortions in Other Religions

> *We have sent a messenger to every community, saying, "You shall worship God, and avoid idolatry." Subsequently, some were guided by God, while others were committed to straying. Roam the earth and note the consequences for the rejectors. (16:36)*[3]

In the case of every prophet or messenger, Satan, or the Devil, has disfigured and corrupted the pure message to worship God alone. Nevertheless, at no time did God *not* have control. In this life, each person has a representative of Satan as well as a warner from God. Life is a series of tests along the path (and trails) to grant us opportunities to exercise our free will and to learn from mistakes. Each person must choose to embrace the truth and proven evidence from God presented to him or her or embrace distortions and lies. God does not interfere with an individual's decision either to worship Him or practice idolatry in its many forms. Otherwise, if God interfered, we would not have free will. There are millions of humans born in different cultures with different languages and religious systems but we all are on the same path called life in this world.

> *We did not send before you any messenger, nor a prophet, without having the devil interfere in his wishes. God then nullifies what the devil has done. God perfects His revelations. God is Omniscient, Most Wise. (22:52)* [4]

The larger of Eastern religious systems not typically associated with the Abrahamic tradition today include Hinduism, Buddhism, Shinto, Taoism, Sikhism, and Baha'i. Sikhism and Baha'i are clearly derived from Islam. Religious systems that reflect divine guidance contain moral principles and guidelines, standards for appropriate behavior, and enjoin righteousness. An individual can evaluate the authenticity of *all* religions based on the same criteria: the worship of God alone, belief in the Day of Judgment, belief in the Hereafter, belief in prophets and messengers of God, living a righteous life, and enjoining righteousness. To the extent that these cardinal tenets are not central in the teachings of a religion, the religion is distorted, disfigured, or altogether counterfeit. There possibly have been divine scriptures revealed to some of the earliest human generations preceding Judaism, Christianity, and Islam. As stated in chapter 3, divine scriptures are not written down for the first time *after* the departure of a messenger or prophet of God. Revealed scriptures are complete, do not require supplemental texts, nor do they require refinement or revision. Revealed scriptures *never* include beliefs and practices that run counter to God's commands and guidance. Legitimate religious communities never condone any beliefs and practices that contradict God's commands.[5] The One Supreme Being is beseeched in different names by different people but all refer to the One God.

From the Quran:

God has chosen Adam, Noah, the family of Abraham, and the family of Amram (as messengers) to the people. (3:33)

Messengers to deliver good news, as well as warnings. Thus, the people will have no excuse when they face GOD, after all these messengers have come to them. GOD is Almighty, Most Wise. (4:165)

O children of Adam, when messengers come to you from among you, and recite My revelations to you, those who take heed and lead a righteous life, will have nothing to fear, nor will they grieve. (7:35)

We have sent (messengers) before you to the communities in the past. (15:10)

To God belongs the most beautiful names; call upon Him therewith, and disregard those who distort His names. They will be requited for their sin. (7:180)

Say, "Call Him God, or call Him the Most Gracious; whichever name you use, to Him belongs the best names." You shall not utter your Contact Prayers (Salat) too loudly, nor secretly; use a moderate tone. (17:110)[6]

The presence of spiritual beliefs among *all* people confirms that humans are endowed with an innate propensity to contact and connect to something or someone greater than themselves. The authentic straight path of submission to God alone was later riddled with mysteries, sorcery, magic, spiritualism, superstition, occult practices, and a fear of unseen forces. *The facts run counter to the claim that the spiritual practices of primitive communities reflect the earliest expression of religion among mankind.* The claim that the religions of primitive peoples have evolved into the modern religions is based on the false notion that early man did not have the knowledge, intelligence, or ability to worship the Creator. How could such be the case, when Adam and Eve were taught by God how to worship Him? (see verses 2:37 and 7:172) For sure, Adam and Eve were cautioned *not* to practice idolatry (e.g., harbor superstitions, depend on forces and powers other than God, not to pay homage to nature spirits, or not to make or worship images). Contemporary religions are no more aligned on the straight path than the religions of earlier communities. The Quran indicates that there are more people among the earliest followers of each messenger or prophet of God who practice authentic religion than the number of followers who later join the ranks.

From the Quran:

Then, Adam received from his Lord words, whereby He redeemed him. He is the Redeemer, Most Merciful. (2:37)

Recall that your Lord summoned all the descendants of Adam, and had them bear witness for themselves: "Am I not your Lord?" They all said, "Yes. We bear witness." Thus, you cannot say on the Day of Resurrection, "We were not aware of this." (7:172)

We passed the scripture from generation to generation, and we allowed whomever we chose from among our servants to receive it. Subsequently, some of them wronged their souls, others upheld it only part of the time, while others were eager to work righteousness in accordance with God's will; this is the greatest triumph. (35:32)

Ironically, they broke up into sects only after the knowledge had come to them, due to jealousy and resentment among themselves. If it were not for a predetermined decision from your Lord to respite them for a definite interim, they would have been judged immediately. Indeed, the later generations who inherited the scripture are full of doubts. (42:14)

Such are the ones stamped as disbelievers among <u>every</u> generation of jinns and humans; they are losers. (46:18)

Many from the first generations. Few from the later generations. (56:13-14)[7]

Like distorted Judaism, Christianity, and Islam, tenets of Hinduism, Buddhism, Shinto, Taoism, Sikhism, and Baha'i contain truth mixed with falsehood. Such a mixture proves to be more effective and appealing than rank falsehood. It seems that humans can more easily recognize out-and-out spiritual falsehoods. Satan assumes that the human ability to recognize spiritual falsehood is degraded as more elements of a truth are added to a lie. For example, most people say they believe in God or The Supreme Being. In Hislam, people are taught to worship others alongside The Supreme Being. The others are deities of their own making – the self, unseen forces, products of their own imagination and thoughts, other humans, animals, heavenly bodies, objects, symbols, prophets and messengers, etc. In order to clearly decipher spiritual truth from falsehood, a person has to heed God's guidance

From the Quran:

Do not confound the truth with falsehood, nor shall you conceal the truth, knowingly. (2:42)

Instead, it is our plan to support the truth against falsehood, in order to defeat it. Woe to you for the utterances you utter. (21:18)

This is because those who disbelieve are following falsehood, while those who believe are following the truth from their Lord. God thus cites for the people their examples. (47:3) [8]

Distortions in Other Religions

Hinduism (4000 BC to Present)

The origins of Hinduism can be traced to the Indus Valley civilization sometime between 4000 and 2500 BCE. Though believed by many to be a polytheistic religion, the basis of Hinduism is the belief in the unity of everything. This totality is called Brahman. The purpose of life is to realize that we are part of God and by doing so we can leave this plane of existence and rejoin with God. This enlightenment can only be achieved by going through cycles of birth, life and death known as samsara. One's progress towards enlightenment is measured by his karma. This is the accumulation of all one's good and bad deeds and this determines the person's next reincarnation. Selfless acts and thoughts as well as devotion to God help one to be reborn at a higher level. Bad acts and thoughts will cause one to be born at a lower level, as a person or even an animal. Hindus follow a strict caste system which determines the standing of each person. The caste one is born into is the result of the karma from their previous life. Only members of the highest caste, the brahmins, may perform the Hindu religious rituals and hold positions of authority within the temples.[9]

Possibly due to later flawed doctrine, Hinduism's description of the Supreme Being as a nebulous totality and unity of all things, its doctrine of reincarnation, the presence of a caste system, and the notion that only members of the highest caste qualify as religious leaders all reflect the fact that contemporary Hinduism is vastly distant from its authentic teachings (e.g., see the Yajur and the Rig Vedas).

Buddhism (560 to Present)

According to the BBC World Service publication, *Your Guide to the Religions of the World*,

Buddhism developed out of the teachings of Siddhartha Gautama who, in 535 BCE, reached enlightenment and assumed the title Buddha. He promoted 'The Middle Way' as the path to enlightenment rather than the extremes of mortification of the flesh or hedonism. Long after his death, the Buddha's teachings were written down. This collection is called the Tripitaka. Buddhists believe in reincarnation and that one must go through cycles of birth, life, and death. After many such cycles, if a person releases their attachment to desire and the self, they can attain Nirvana. In general, Buddhists do not believe in any type of God, the need for a savior, prayer, or eternal life after death. However, since the time of the Buddha, Buddhism has integrated many regional religious rituals, beliefs and customs into it as it has spread throughout Asia, so that this generalization is no longer true for all Buddhists. This has occurred with little conflict due to the philosophical nature of Buddhism.[10]

Original Buddhism may have been the brainchild of a prophet or messenger of God. If such was the case, the original teachings of Buddhism seem to have been laid waste in a vast ocean of thousands of Buddhas in all shapes, colors, and sizes. Images and drawings of Buddha abound wherever a supplicant seeks prosperity, good fortune, and good health. The belief in reincarnation and literal cycles of life, disbelief in God, the early denial of a need for prayer, and disbelief in the Hereafter clearly indicate that Buddhism has been grossly distorted from its possible form as a God-inspired system of guidance. The fact that some of its adherents have 'borrowed' concepts from the monotheistic religions to give it a more religious character further points out that Buddhism may have originated as a disciplined philosophy of life containing some righteous teachings.

Shinto (500+ B.C. to Present)

According to the BBC World Service publication, *Your Guide to the Religions of the World*,

> Shinto is an ancient Japanese religion, closely tied to nature, which recognizes the existance of various "Kami", nature dieties. The first two deities, Izanagi and Izanami, gave birth to the Japanese islands and their children became the deities of the various Japanese clans. One of their daughters, Amaterasu (Sun Goddess), is the ancestress of the Imperial Family and is regarded as the chief deity. All the Kami are benign and serve only to sustain and protect. They are not seen as separate from humanity due to sin because humanity is "Kami's

Child." Followers of Shinto desire peace and believe all human life is sacred. They revere "musuhi", the Kami's creative and harmonizing powers, and aspire to have "makoto", sincerity or true heart. Morality is based upon that which is of benefit to the group. There are "Four Affirmations" in Shinto:

1. Tradition and family: the family is the main mechanism by which traditions are preserved.
2. Love of nature: nature is sacred and natural objects are to be worshiped as sacred spirits.
3. Physical cleanliness: they must take baths, wash their hands, and rinse their mouth often.
4. "Matsuri": festival which honors the spirits.[11]

Traditional Shinto is an "ethnic or cultural religious system" inasmuch as it seems exclusive to a specific group of people who embraced the idea that they and their ancestors are the 'offspring of deities.' In contrast to the worship of one God, the adherents of traditional Shinto believe in sacred spirits and worship nature. They revere family, cultural tradition, and their ancestors. It is not surprising that morality is primarily based upon what benefits the group. In such societies, the welfare of the group has traditionally taken precedence over the well-being and aspirations of an individual. Consistent with their traditional Shinto beliefs, individuals who wholly embrace traditional Shinto teachings are ethnocentric in the sense that they view themselves as superior to others, and frown on inter-ethnic unions.

According to the BBC World Service publication, *Your Guide to the Religions of the World*,

Taoism (440 CE to Present)

Taoism was founded by Lao_Tse, a contemporary of Confucius in China. Taoism began as a combination of psychology and philosophy which Lao_Tse hoped would help end the constant feudal warfare and other conflicts of his time. His writings, the Tao_te_Ching, describe the nature of life, the way to peace and how a ruler should lead his life. Taoism became a religion in 440 CE when it was adopted as a state religion.

Tao, roughly translated as path, is a force which flows through all life and is the first cause of everything. The goal of everyone is to become one with the Tao. Tai Chi, a technique of exercise using slow deliberate movements, is used to balance the flow of energy or "chi" within the body. People should develop virtue and seek compassion, moderation and humility. One should plan any action in advance and achieve it through minimal action. Yin (dark side) and Yang (light side) symbolize pairs of opposites which are seen through the universe, such as good and evil, light and dark, male and female. The impact of human civilization upsets the balance of Yin and Yang. Taoists believe that people are by nature, good, and that one should be kind to others simply because such treatment will probably be reciprocated.[12]

Many principles of Taoism are very similar to the teachings of the monotheistic religions. Tao is deemed the "first cause of everything." Obviously, God is the First Cause. Over time, people began to worship Lao-Tse, instead of the Tao or Supreme Being. Taoists also began to worship forces of nature. Taoists believe that good actions enable the soul to have a better life, and they encourage righteous deeds and self-control. Tai Chi is a highly effective technique of exercise, moderation, meditation, and promotion of a virtuous path. Taoism is essentially a philosophy of living later adopted as a state religion. Taoism does not include belief in a Day of Judgment, or belief in the Hereafter.

Sikhism (1500 CE to Present)

In 1500 CE The Sikh faith was founded by Shri Guru Nanak Dev Ji in the Punjab area, now Pakistan. He began preaching the way to enlightenment and God after receiving a vision. After his death a series of nine Gurus (regarded as reincarnations of Guru Nanak) led the movement until 1708. At this time these functions passed to the Panth and the holy text. This text, the Shri Guru Granth Sahib, was compiled by the tenth Guru, Gobind Singh. It consists of hymns and writings of the first 10 Gurus, along with texts from different Muslim and Hindu saints. The holy text is considered the 11th and final Guru.

Sikhs believe in a single formless God with many names, who can be known through meditation. Sikhs pray many times each day and are prohibited from worshipping idols or icons. They believe in samsara, karma, and reincarnation as Hindus do but reject the caste system. They believe that everyone has equal status in the eyes of God. During the 18th century, there were a number of attempts to prepare an accurate portrayal of Sikh customs. Sikh scholars and theologians started in 1931 to prepare the Reht Maryada— the Sikh code of conduct and conventions. This has successfully achieved a high level of uniformity in the religious and social practices of Sikhism throughout the world. It contains 27 articles. Article 1 defines who is a Sikh:

"Any human being who faithfully believes in:
* One Immortal Being,
* Ten Gurus, from Guru Nanak Dev to Guru Gobind Singh,
* The Guru Granth Sahib,
* The utterances and teachings of the ten Gurus and
* the baptism bequeathed by the tenth Guru, and who does not owe allegiance to any other religion, is a Sikh.[13]

An amalgamation of two religious cultures in India, Sikhism contains elements and teachings of Islam and Hinduism. Sikhism teaches belief in one God, the prohibition against idolatry, the prohibition of discrimination and racism (e.g., caste system), and daily prayer. Sikhism parts from the teachings of the revealed scriptures by presenting the idea that one of its Gurus completed a holy text (there is no revealed scripture or holy text after the Quran), its belief in reincarnation including claims that some of its leaders were literal "reincarnations" of its founder, and the construction of a religious hierarchy that composed a set of social customs, conduct, and conventions. It appears that Sikhism has its own man-made religious laws. It would also appear that the founder of Sikhism possibly realized that both Hinduism and Islam in their current forms had been distorted, but he or some of his followers perpetuated or introduced innovations in Sikhism.

Bahá'í (1863 CE to Present)

In the 1800s, the Bahá'í Faith arose from Islam. It is now a distinct worldwide faith. The faith's followers believe that God has sent nine great prophets to mankind through whom the Holy Spirit has revealed the "Word of God." This has given rise to the major world religions. Although these religions arose from the teachings of the prophets of one God, Bahá'í's do not believe they are all the same. The differences in the teachings of each prophet are due to the needs of the society they came to help and what mankind was ready to have revealed to it. Bahá'í beliefs promote gender and race equality, freedom of expression and assembly, world peace and world government. They believe that a single world government led by Bahá'ís will be established at some point in the future. The faith does not attempt to preserve the past but does embrace the findings of science. Bahá'ís believe that every person has an immortal soul which cannot die but is freed to travel through the spirit world after death.[14]

Many of the general tenets of the Bahá'í religion are consistent with the teachings of the revealed scriptures. The major tenet of Bahá'í is the oneness of humanity. Now five million in number throughout the world, Bahá'ís have established their own physical organizational structure, shrines, and guidelines for branches throughout the world. Bahá'í scared writings consist mainly of the words of its founder, Baha'ullah, who Bahá'ís believe was a messenger of God.[15] An abandonment of the Quran for the writings (e.g., hadith) of its founder, the dismissal of religious obligatory duties, and the establishment of an organizational structure not unlike those in distorted religious systems are all counter to authentic revealed scripture. Baha'is may have possibly "embraced" the findings of science as an alternative to corrupt practices, beliefs, and teachings in distorted Islam and Hinduism. Bahá'ís believe that religion and science are complimentary. In the process of abandoning some corrupt teachings in distorted Islam and Hinduism, Bahá'ís seem to have "thrown the baby out with the bathwater," in the sense that they have discarded divinely-ordained obligations of worship revealed in the authentic scriptures.

Upon surveying religious systems in the world, an objective inquirer realizes that most people in all times have been satisfied with their opinions, traditions, conjecture, and guessing. Most people take comfort in the widely-upheld false religious views in their groups and cultures.

From the Quran:

Surely, those who believe, those who are Jewish, the Christians, and the converts; anyone who (1) believes in God, and (2) believes in the Last Day, and (3) leads a righteous life, will receive their recompense from their Lord. They have nothing to fear, nor will they grieve. (2:62)

The idols you invoke besides God are creatures like you. Go ahead and call upon them; let them respond to you, if you are right. (7:194)

They disbelieved, followed their opinions, and adhered to their old traditions. (54:3)

If you obey the majority of people on earth, they will divert you from the path of God. They follow only conjecture; they only guess. (6:116)[16]

Notes

1. Authors of the website (Adherents.com) describe the website as "an Internet initiative and is not affiliated with any religious, political, educational, or commercial organization." See <http://www.adherents.com> (16 September 2003).

2. The tradition of Abraham is to only worship the one God. All the duties of worship were revealed to Abraham, and the duties were later distorted or lost. The knowledge of the one God is innate (Quran, 7:172). Humans have the freedom of will to cultivate this knowledge or ignore and distort it.

3. Khalifa, *Quran*, 7:35, 10:47, 14:4, and 16:36.

4. Ibid, 22:52.

5. No matter how wise sounding its espoused principles, how large in numbers, or how lofty it may appear to be, any religious community that condones discrimination, disrespects others' rights, advocates irrational dogmas, views itself as select, and denounces others as inferiors could not possibly be a God-inspired community. It is a community that embraces false doctrines (i.e., "fake flowers") masked as appealing truths (i.e., "roses").

6. Khalifa, *Quran*, 3:33, 4:165, 7:35, 15:10, 7:180, and 17:110.

7. Ibid, 2:37, 7:172, 35:32, 42:14, 46:18, and 56: 13-14.

8. Ibid, 2:42, 21:18, and 47:3.

9. BBC World Service, *"Your Guide to the Religions of the World."* <http://www.bbc.co.uk/worldservice/people/features/world_religions> (3 June 2003). The summaries of any one religion in this section of the book are derived from material drawn from several internet websites.

10. Ibid, 1

11. International Shinto Foundation, *"What is Shinto in Brief."* <http://www.shinto.org/brief-e.html> (16 September 2003).

12. The Patience T'ai Chi Association, *"Taoism and Tai Chi Chuan."* <http://www.patiencetaichi.com/taoism.html> (16 September 2003).

13. BBC World Service, *Religions of the World.*

14. The Bahá'í World: Official Site of Bahá'í Faith, <http://www.bahai.org/article-1-2-0-1.html>, (16 September 2003)

15. Recall that God revealed that messengers of God shall be sent to every community, even after the departure of Muhammad, the final prophet to humanity. True messengers of God meet specific criteria outlined in the Quran.

16. Khalifa, *Quran*, 7:194, 54:3, and 6:116.

Six

Professional Clerics: A Bogus Institution

Since our sojourn as a species began in this world, individuals have always studied the revealed scriptures and sought spiritual guidance. All righteous people study the authentic scriptures. God has ordained that such should always be the case. There must be individuals who are aware of the scriptures and can share the content of the scriptures with others. This was especially important in societies based on an oral transmission of information, and when few people knew how to write.

From the Quran:

When the believers mobilize, not all of them shall do so. A few from each group shall mobilize by devoting their time to studying the religion. Thus, they can pass the knowledge on to their people when they return, that they may remain religiously informed.[1]

True Religious Leaders Never Ask for Wages

The establishment of a professional clergy that welcomes and receives income or wages from its congregations is a violation of divine law. Anyone who sincerely seeks spiritual truth has access to divine guidance. There is no need to turn to professional clergy to explain or teach what God has revealed to humanity. Man concocts ideas that a person must take special courses, read special texts, receive a certificate or degree of divinity, be ordained, or become an ascetic in order to explain the contents of revealed scriptures. When God revealed the scriptures to humanity, He did not say, "In order to understand My guidance, you have to depend on someone who has received special training, and been taught how to explain My guidance to you. You should pay the person wages and a livelihood because the person has forsaken the wages of this world to administer to you." A former Christian minister for twenty years, a fellow Submitter who is well versed in the Bible told me that many misguided Christian clergy justify receiving wages or income based on Biblical verses 17-18 of 1 Timothy, Chapter 5.

From the Bible:

Elders who do their work well should be paid well (actual Greek reads "should be worthy of double honor"), especially those who work hard at preaching and teaching...(I Timothy, Chapter 5: 17-18)... And in another place, "those who work deserve their pay![2]

A hired man, who is not a teacher and whose students are not his own, sees a wolf coming and leaves the students and runs away, and the wolf catches and scatters them. This is because he works for pay and has no concern for the students. (Chapter 45, p 152)

As translated and interpreted, these Biblical verses are inconsistent with the rule in authentic scriptures, including the Quran, against clergy accepting wages.

From the Quran:

O you who believe, many religious leaders and preachers take the people's money illicitly, and repel from the path of God. Those who hoard the gold and silver, and do not spend them in the cause of God, promise them a painful retribution. (9:34)

O my people, I do not ask you for any wage. My wage comes only from the One who initiated me. Do you not understand? (11:51)

"I do not ask you for any wage. My wage comes from the Lord of the universe. (26:109)

"Follow those who do not ask you for any wage, and are guided. (36:21)

This is the good news from God to His servants who believe and lead a righteous life. Say, "I do not ask you for any wage. I do ask each of you to take care of your own relatives." Anyone who does a righteous work, we multiply his reward for it. God is Forgiver, Appreciative. (42:23)[3]

A person should never ask or create a scheme to get remuneration, gifts, or wages for sharing divine truth and guidance with others. The clergy of corrupt religions solicit funds from their followers on a routine basis. In some of the small community churches in my childhood neighborhood, ministers subtly threatened their followers with retribution from God, some induced guilt in their congregations, and some insisted that they only wanted paper money to be placed in offering plates. Some congregations are coerced into remaining at worship services until they give a certain amount for the offering. Clergy retire from active ministries and receive retirement benefits. I recall a couple of childhood friends who, in order to make a livelihood, became professional ministers and established their own churches. They did not declare that their actual intent was to earn a living by becoming ministers. Some congregations compete with each other in lavishing their ministers with expensive cars, homes, and clothing. In fairness, a significant number of clergy do not use their religious roles as a means of income.

On a larger scale, huge sums of money are given to institutional religions and their enterprises, charities, and projects. In God's system, money and aid are given directly to individuals who need it, not to clergy, the church, or "building funds." Solicitation of funds in religion also takes the form of buying penance and forgiveness, and purchasing religious rulings (e.g., called *fat'was* in corrupt Islam).

A prophet of God receives a divine revelation from God. The revelation is in the form of a scripture or book of guidance. The prophets spent a significant portion of their remaining lives spreading the message revealed to them. Some of the prophets include Abraham, Jesus, Moses, David and Muhammad. In each case, God blessed a prophet with a skill, craft, or trade as a means of making a living. In some cases, a prophet could no longer continue his craft or trade because of the growing responsibilities related to delivering a revelation to his community. Nevertheless, all provisions come from God. Despite the prohibition against a salaried professional clergy, some corrupt elements of Judaism, Christianity, and Islam have established broad networks of professional clerics. No doubt, there are persons among the clergy who are sincere and genuine in their worship of God alone. The current clerical institution they embrace has veered far from its role as defined in the authentic scriptures.

From the Quran:

We have sent down the Torah, containing guidance and light. Ruling in accordance with it were the Jewish prophets, as well as the rabbis and the priests, as dictated to them in God's scripture, and as witnessed by them. Therefore, do not reverence human beings; you shall reverence Me instead. And do not trade away My revelations for a cheap price. Those who do not rule in accordance with God's revelations are the disbelievers. (5:44)

If only the rabbis and the priests enjoin them from their sinful utterances and illicit earnings! Miserable indeed is what they commit. (5:63)

They have set up their religious leaders and scholars as lords, instead of God. Others deified the Messiah, son of Mary. They were all commanded to worship only one god. There is no god except He. Be He glorified, high above having any partners. (9:31)[4]

Although there are exceptions, many clerics feel compelled to uphold false doctrines. Clergy, evangelists, and religious leaders are victims of the false doctrines they perpetuate. They are acutely fearful and timid when it comes to openly acknowledging that they and their followers believe and preach man-made doctrines. To admit such would result in scorn and rejection, a dread of having previously committed themselves to false doctrines, and a fear of God's punishment. When offered opportunities to correct their behavior and beliefs, many clerics feel that the truth would undermine their very existence. Some clergy assume an attitude of futility. It is just too late to disconnect. They resign themselves to the belief that a religion's superstructure is too powerful, vast, and interwoven into a society. For example, when invited to embrace the truth about the miraculous Code in the Quran, the truth about Jesus' identity, and to worship God alone, a nationally known cleric in America said, "This will destroy our way of life!" Pharaoh uttered a similar response when he witnessed the nine miraculous signs that accompanied Moses.

From the Quran:

Pharaoh said, "Let me kill Moses, and let him implore his Lord. I worry lest he corrupts your religion, or spreads evil throughout the land." (40:26)[5]

Similar responses were uttered by contemporary Muslim clerics when they were informed about the miraculous Code in the Quran, invited to worship God alone, and invited to discard man-made sources of Islamic law (e.g., Hadith, Sunna).

Some clergy belong to guilds and societies[6] composed of their peers, high-ranking clergy, and influential lay persons. The guilds typically mirror the rank and classes of clergy in their clerical orders. Thus, there are core networks less visible than the surface church or religious structures known by lay persons. When inducted into certain closed groups, new members are told that the Trinity doctrine is false and they have been accepted as a member of an elite select group of persons who are capable of grasping the truth. To ease their shock upon hearing this information, novices are told that their presence in the group is God's will and it is their responsibility to make sure that lay people or commoners hear God's word, even if it means continuing to openly endorse the Trinity. In short, it is *not* the internalization of true spiritual teachings that really counts in such groups. Many individuals seek favor and advancement from group members who reward them for promoting formal doctrine. In some guilds and groups, a cleric's sermons and lessons are monitored by elders to make sure that official accepted beliefs are presented properly.

There are groups that mainly consist of lay persons who also know that any departure from total belief in the One God is false and a blasphemy. Members of the closed lay groups vocalize belief in spurious religious doctrines when amidst non-group members in outer social circles but reaffirm their belief in the one God in closed meetings. Similar to secret clerical guilds, initiates in closed lay groups are also told that they are capable of grasping the truth. Unfortunately, most members of elite clerical and lay groups are unaware of the fact that they actually promote Hislam. A closed lay group may be comprised of members from religions that do not even remotely share the same beliefs.

From the Quran:

Do they not realize that God knows their secrets, and their conspiracies, and that God is the Knower of all secrets? (9:78)

The only ones who fabricate false doctrines are those who do not believe in God's revelations; they are the real liars. (16:105)

O you who believe, if you have to confer secretly, you shall not confer to commit sin, transgression, and to disobey the messenger. You shall confer to work righteousness and piety. You shall reverence God, before whom you will be summoned. Secret conspiracy is the devil's idea, through which he seeks to hurt those who believed. However, he cannot hurt them against God's will. In God the believers shall trust. (58:9-10) [7]

No Divine Commandment to Practice Celibacy

Individuals who choose to become priests and monks should not exclude themselves from interactions with their societies. The popular notion of a priest or monk being indefinitely isolated from normal life is inconsistent with the active, involved roles that Prophets and messengers of God had in their communities. God never ordained humans to abstain from marriage and sex between marriage partners. Celibacy is not a litmus test for the worship of God. The practice of celibacy as a means of attaining spiritual enlightenment predates the monotheistic religions. It is an ancient practice associated with the false idea that denial of physical and sexual appetites leads to a higher state of spiritual consciousness or enlightenment. In some cultures, celibate priests, spiritual leaders, and healers are perceived as closer to the spiritual or karmic self whereas persons who accommodate their sexual urges are viewed as controlled by so-called baser bodily appetites. The Roman Church claimed that celibacy was supported and promoted by Jesus. Jesus never supported or promoted the celibate lifestyle as an index of spiritual commitment and growth.

From the Quran:

Subsequent to them, we sent our messengers. We sent Jesus the son of Mary, and we gave him the Injeel (Gospel), and we placed in the hearts of his followers kindness and mercy. But they invented hermitism which we never decreed for them. All we asked them to do was to uphold the commandments approved by God. But they did not uphold the message as they should have. Consequently, we gave those who believed among them their recompense, while many of them were wicked. (57:27) [8]

Contrary to a popular belief that celibacy in the Roman Church was primarily instituted for reasons of spiritual advancement of its clergy, Raymond A. Grosswirth,[9] once an aspirant to the priesthood, identifies a very secular reason for the man-made doctrine of celibacy in the Church.

> When one looks at the history of celibacy in the Catholic Church, it soon becomes apparent that this state of life became mandatory due to financial considerations, not because priests were supposed to emulate Christ by remaining single.... A controversy arose when married priests in turn left this [church property] to their heirs. To make a long story short, celibacy soon followed as a requirement of

ordination, so as to prevent such property exchanges between heirs. (There was nothing theological in the celibacy directive.) [10]

This canon of celibacy was instituted in 1139. Gosswirth points out that the Inquisition coupled with the ruling of the Council of Trent sought out priests who married in secret. The Nicene councils echoed the edict that married men were no longer allowed to become priests. In his on-line article entitled *Clerical Celibacy,* Dr. Ian Paisley[11] notes that:

> Not only is there no Scripture which admits of being so perverted on its behalf, but there is explicit and emphatic Scripture against it [celibacy]. It is expressly foretold, that among the evil deeds of the Man of Sin, would be the prohibition against marriage.... The Council of Trent, in its twenty-fourth session, 1563, dealt largely with the question of marriage.... Such, from that hour, has been the law of the Romish Church respecting the marriage of the clergy. All ecclesiastics, of whatever order or degree, are bound to celibacy, and the penalty of marriage is instant excommunication.[12]

Dr. Paisley further states that the prohibition of marriage involving priests and nuns...

> was one of the most immoral and pernicious institutions of the Popedom. It deserves remarks that the laity in general-strangely, and to their own grievous hurt- sided with the Vatican, and took part against the married priests, whom they persecuted in all possible ways, covering them with odium, and even reducing them to the sad alternative of starvation, or separation from their families...married ministers, in many places, were thus driven out, and no numbers came forth to take their places....[13]

Referring to celibate clergy, Dr. Paisley quoted William of Paris, a highly esteemed Monkish historian described as a "lover of truth and virtue."

> The clergy, according to him [Paris], "have neither piety or learning, but rather the foul vices of devils, and the most monstrous uncleanliness and crimes! Their sins are not mere sins, but rather the

prodigious and dreadful crimes! They are not the Church, but rather Babylon, Egypt, and Sodom" [14]

In April 2002, Grosswirth said:

> As I present this updated thesis on celibacy, we are in the midst of a pedophilia crisis in the Catholic church. For the record, I try to distance two issues. While I don't label celibacy as the cause of pedophilia, an all-male celibate clergy does provide an attractive secretive environment in which potential pedophiles can easily hide. [15]

The crisis that Grosswirth spoke of in 2002 has now been exposed to be a pervasive practice of many priests, cardinals, and bishops in thousands of parishes in the United States and other countries. Victims' rewards from litigations have placed a significant strain on the monetary resources of the Vatican.

A lifetime member of the Canon Law Society of America and an emeritus professor of religion, Dr. James E. Biechler[16] pointed out that:

> Celibacy is not the cause of pedophilia. But celibacy as idealized, institutionalized and mandated by the church provides an ideal environment for those men whose sexuality (and personality) development has been arrested at an immature level leading to their inability to establish intimate relations with another adult. Surely we should ask whether the seminary system, especially the minor seminary, may not be a factor inhibiting the development of mature heterosexual personality. At a crucial stage of personal development the young seminarian is formed in a culture of denial. He must deny his natural feelings, he must downgrade the natural order which includes those feelings, he must deny the importance of his natural family, he must relegate marriage and the procreation of children to an inferior level of life, and so he must even see children in a diminished light. When the worth of children is diminished and sexuality is immature, the distance to pedophilia is short.[17]

Dr. Biechler's observation echoes the position of many theologians, mental health professionals, formerly celibate clergy, and lay persons who recognize the relationship between celibacy and some individuals' propensity towards pedophilia. Stated bluntly, sexual urges and tensions are satisfied by some so-called celibate individuals via their molestation of minors. Sexual abstinence is no guarantee that a person develops a greater awareness of appropriate sexual conduct and knowledge of wholesome non-sexual adult-child relations. For more than a few individuals, sexual abstinence heralds in the opposite of wholesome adult-adult and adult-child relationships.

Not all nations and provinces under the sway of the Roman Church and its hundreds of offshoots accepted celibacy as a requirement for ordination. In modern times, the prohibition against married clergy has been revised, modified, and even eliminated in some quarters. Yet, celibacy remains a prominent feature of the Catholic priesthood and some Christian and non-Christian denominations.

Throughout the ages, there have been and are hundreds of thousands of *sincere* individuals in all faiths who feel a special calling to be witnesses of spiritual truths and righteousness. But, they do not regard themselves as "clerics" in the Hislamic sense. As *Submitter* witnesses, they hold fast to their responsibilities as defined in authentic scriptures, seek spiritual guidance from God, never explicitly or indirectly solicit wages, payment, or any form of *personal* compensation for sharing revealed spiritual truth with others. They define their endeavors to advocate righteousness as simply born of a desire to please God, not as a profession or self-promotion. They bear witness to divine truth, do not promote false doctrines, and do not invent and support laws and rituals that God never ordained. They do not resign themselves to institutional religious practices that violate God's commands. They never knowingly distort or blatantly lie about the worship of the One God.

From the Quran:

You are not responsible for guiding anyone. God is the only one who guides whoever chooses (to be guided)... (2:272, partial)

Let there be a community of you who invite to what is good, advocate righteousness, and forbid evil. These are the winners. (3:104)[18]

Notes

1. Khalifa, *Quran*, 9:122.
2. Stoop and Arterburn, *Recovery Bible*, 1464.
3. Khalifa, *Quran*, 9:34, 11:51, 36:21, and 42:23.
4. Ibid, 5:44, 63; and 9:31.
5. Ibid, 40:26.
6. In the Christian church, clerics of any standing in their communities belong to groups wherein they are sworn to preach and promote specific interpretations and doctrines mutually agreed upon. For sure, this practice is not limited to Christianity.
7. Khalifa, *Quran*, 9:78, 16:105, and 58:9-10.
8. Ibid, 57:27.
9. R. A. Grosswirth, *Celibacy*. <http://www.angelfire.com> (28 January 2003).
10. Ibid, 1.
11. Ian R.K. Paisley, *A Clerical Celibacy.@* http://www.ianpaisley.org, 18 August 2000, (28 January 2003).
12. Ibid, 1.
13. Ibid, 2.
14. Ibid, 4.
15. Grosswirth, *Celibacy*, 1.
16. James E. Biechler, *"A Question of Rights: Celibacy and Pedophilia"* <http://astro.temple.edu/~arcc/rights7.htm> (10 November 2003)
17. Ibid, 2.
18. Khalifa, *Quran*, 2:272 and 3:104

Seven

Truth about Religion: A Matter of National Security

The truth about the worship of God is a matter of national security. A nation's internal spiritual security ultimately rests upon the spiritual knowledge and moral fiber of its people. A strong people do not shy away from spiritual truth and guidance. National security begins with the spiritual serenity and security of each individual. Everyone does not reach for or attain spiritual serenity and security. But, in truly secure societies, this goal is considered one of the most important pursuits in life. In the absence of sufficient numbers of people with divinely based moral values and spiritual security, collective perseverance in the face of internal and external threats is short-lived. Insecure people are unwilling to make the sacrifices and collective investment necessary in challenging times.

The gnawing absence of spiritual security is reflected in the increase in social problems, crime, family fragmentation, prevalence of addictions and emotional problems, rabid pursuit of material gain at the expense of wholesome self-development, the near worship of cult personalities in the media, and selfish disregard for others. In such an atmosphere, Hislam always attempts to take the high ground. Via Hislam, false doctrines are promoted with increased fervor. More people regard their break from religion and moral values as a "badge of honor." The church body looks more like a "cavalcade of stars" who appear on local and national entertainment shows. Mention of religion is taboo in the workplace and politically incorrect in government settings. Movies with distorted religious themes are quite profitable at the box office. Attendance at the box office to see such movies far exceeds attendance in places of worship. Amidst this spiritual morass, guardians of the spiritual status quo feel that the truth about the worship of God would put our nation in a tailspin.

Our nation is in a spiritual and social tail spin. God willing, many people will pull out of the tailspin by returning to *proven* Divine guidance. Deluded fanatical religious elements outside America's borders seek to import their corrupt visions of religion onto the American people and the rest of the world. Misguided professional religionists in the country want to maintain their hold on their faithful naïve flocks. *Such zealots, misguided professional religionists, and extremists are a serious threat to the security of a community or nation.* This condition is also present in other societies throughout the world. The adage, "You can't judge a book by looking at its cover," is apt in these cases.

In pointing out doctrinal distortions of religion along the path, my focus was on the "theology" of Hislam. *There is no "theology" on the right path that we started out on.* "Theology" complicates what God has made easy– the worship of God alone. Submitters and genuine seekers are *not* "theologians," in the traditional sense. In this chapter, attention is turned to the spiritually-destructive social debris (thorns and weeds) that are by-products of Hislam. Sincere seekers learn to recognize debris spread by persons and groups who coerce or convince the public to oppose God's guidance. The debris is presented in the form of lifestyles, philosophies, theories, ideas, and ways of thinking that supposedly advance social harmony and order.

Revealed moral codes are viewed as archaic, authoritarian, and obsolete. Proponents' of the debris are casts as dynamic creative intellectuals, social leaders, thinkers, and writers who are not afraid to challenge old rules. They are cast as social pioneers who breakdown barriers to human progress. A favorite tactic in presenting their reality view is to emphasize the "value of the self," and decry that people need to discover themselves and develop their full potential. Honest intellectuals, social leaders, writers, and thinkers utter similar words. Yet, the two groups are poles apart. It is important to remember that honest guided individuals who remove the debris are "roses." Individuals who deceive and mislead others are "fake flowers."

New Tyrants Replace Old Sovereigns

Historians and social philosophers have speculated that there are three elements of any society that an individual or group must highly influence in order to hold sway over a society. The elements are the means of economic exchange, religious belief and interpretation, and major communications media (i.e., information control). In times past, most communities in the world were controlled by individual leaders. People declared their total allegiance to monarchs, conquerors, and heirs to thrones. Allegiance to a leader meant allegiance to the leader's vision of reality, his or her dictates, religious beliefs, and schemes for economic prosperity. Most people marched lockstep behind their leaders along man-made spiritual paths inundated with 'weeds and thorns' (i.e., distortions and falsehood). Americans in particular and millions throughout the world seem to be more adept at recognizing *individuals* who attempt to suppress their freedoms.

In contemporary times, the new leader/usurpers of reason, morality, and freedom are not individuals. The new usurpers are politically correct views and beliefs that contradict God's laws. *The tyrants of our times are corrupt beliefs, the words used to communicate the beliefs, and the social and political pressures exerted to compel people to accept the beliefs.* "Norm troopers" in the guise of academic experts, media personalities, political figures, and opinion polls insure that such ideas are unwittingly or willfully embraced by the majority. Majorities are *not* always right. The majority *is* almost always misinformed, misguided, and manipulated. The majority routinely mistrusts and shuns those who reject cherished-but-false religious beliefs and practices. Despite being outnumbered, those who resist false majority views hold fast to their rightly-guided religious convictions.

From the Quran:

If you obey the majority of people on earth, they will divert you from the path of God. They follow only conjecture; they only guess. (6:116)

> *The majority of those who believe in God do not do so without committing idol worship.(12: 106)*
>
> *When our revelations are recited to them, clearly, those who disbelieve say to those who believe, "Which of us is more prosperous? Which of us is in the majority?" (19:73)*
>
> *By the afternoon. The human being is utterly lost. Except those who believe and lead a righteous life, and exhort one another to uphold the truth, and exhort one another to be steadfast.(103:1-3)* [1]

These verses inform us that, in any era at any place, most people are preoccupied with acquiring some form of recognition, influence, and prominence at the expense of spiritual development. Casting authentic worship aside, many people take the track to recognition, influence, and prominence more often than not. The decision entails aligning oneself with the prosperous and powerful in a community and engaging in conjecture about matters that are clearly spelled out in proven authentic scripture. Today, hardly any people who believe in God worship statues or pay homage to natural forces. Instead, many people tolerantly embrace and elevate popular opinions and practices (religious and non-religious) above God's commands. This is a form of idolatry.

Accumulated "social debris" and "fake flowers" contaminate youth. Youth are like fertile fields. Many youth are trusting and believe the words of misguided individuals who they admire. Youth seek noble causes and enterprises to invest their loyalty and change society for the better. But, many youth lack the maturity and perspective that comes with tested life experience. It is the responsibility of parents and elders to impart the importance of worshipping God alone to the young. Youth who heed God's guidance and the advice of submitter elders can more easily recognize Hislam disguised as overtures for social progress and creativity.

From the Quran:

Recall that Luqmān said to his son, as he enlightened him, "O my son, do not set up any idols beside God; idolatry is a gross injustice." (31:13)

"O my son, know that even something as tiny as a mustard seed, deep inside a rock, be it in the heavens or the earth, God will bring it. God is Sublime, Cognizant. "O my son, you shall observe the Contact Prayers (Salat). You shall advocate righteousness and forbid evil, and remain steadfast in the face of adversity. These are the most honorable traits. "You shall not treat the people with arrogance, nor shall you roam the earth proudly. God does not like the arrogant showoffs. "Walk humbly and lower your voice - the ugliest voice is the donkey's voice." (31:16-19)

Included in revealed scriptures, Luqman's advice to his son is the highest form of wisdom that elders can impart to the young. Luqman tells his son not to practice idolatry, nothing is hidden from God, all secrets and the truth will eventually be brought forward, to observe his prayers, advocate righteous and forbid evil, remain steadfast, do not think you are superior to others, do not be conceited, be humble, and speak in a moderate tone so as to control your temper and enable others to understand what you are saying, and do not act like a know-it-all who boasts and brags. As adults, youth who heed such guidance are the most emotionally and psychological stable members of society. They are not *overburdened* with personal and social issues that impede their own development and impede the development of others.

In settings where the debris of Hislam and the *absence* of wholesome spirituality prevail, a misguided parent's advice may sound very similar to the following remarks:

> *O my child, worship whatever you want to worship or do not worship at all…you can define religion as you please; if there is a god, understand that the god does not know or control everything; no one ever knows the whole truth about any matter; O my child, some people need religion but*

it is not necessary in order to have a successful life; do whatever you have to do to get what you deserve, do not cheat yourself out of any reward you think you should have; if you do not get it, someone else will; do not let others "scare" you with talk about morals, decide what is right and wrong for yourself; O my child, you are better than most people, be more self-confident, you do not have to apologize for that; speak loud enough to make people pay attention, you have important things to say, others should listen to you, do not be a wimp.

Does the misguided parent's advice sound more familiar than Luqman's advice? The misguided parent's advice is prevalent in societies that dismiss Divine guidance. The social and psychological consequences of inculcating such advice are widespread. Luqman's advice is deemed by misguided individuals as idealistic, immature, and naïve.

The Choice: Freedom or Free Doom

One purpose of government is to protect its citizens' right to worship or not worship as they please. The ultimate benefit of living in a free society is the opportunity to discover God's Truth unhampered by institutional maneuvers to remove God-consciousness from daily life. *People who embrace moral values understand the meaning of freedom.* People who dismiss moral values declare allegiance to the new tyrants. Free doom is not the result of a food or water shortage, the loss of civil liberties, widespread unemployment, or the emergence of an unpopular political party. *An ever-increasing rejection of God's laws and guidance leads to free doom. The use of spiritual weapons of mass distortion and deceit is also a time-tested means of bringing on destructive social conditions in a society.* Free doom is 'free' inasmuch as an individual is not forced to dismiss moral principles. It is *'doom'* inasmuch as the negative consequences of such behavior are clearly spelled out in *proven, confirmed* Divine scripture. People have distorted and ignored the consequences in order to avoid feeling anxious and fearful. Such persons want to feel at ease when they violate Divine commands.

Seemingly impressive speeches, arguments, articles, debates, and intellectualizing about so-called "outdated codes of morality" can never alter universal truth. Neither can large numbers of people who object to so-called "old fashion morals" change the Reality that encompasses them and their opinions.

From the Quran:

Many a community we have annihilated because of their wickedness. They ended up in ruins, stilled wells, and great empty mansions. (22:45)

Have they not roamed the earth and noted the consequences for those who preceded them? They used to be greater in number, greater in power, and possessed a greater legacy on earth. Yet, all their achievements did not help them in the least. When their messengers went to them with clear proofs, they rejoiced in the knowledge they had inherited, and the very things they ridiculed were the cause of their fall. (40:82-83)[2]

Tenets of free doom are presented to the public as realistic, suitable, and favored solutions for social problems and stagnation. Ironically, the rhetoric of free doom promises many rights, freedoms, and opportunities to anyone who rejects so-called antiquated prescriptions of moral behavior in the authentic scriptures. Many people accept the hype about so-called outdated moral laws and traditions because they want to be viewed as modern, open-minded, and informed. Wanting to be accepted and fit in, many people parrot *prevailing orthodoxy* about morality, religion, religious-minded people, and belief in God. In this case, prevailing orthodoxy refers to what is considered by perceived experts and persons with social influence and power to be correct and acceptable spiritual beliefs and behavior.

Theophobes Attempt to Create Godless Societies

Naïve misinformed members of society are subjected to collective attempts to suppress God-consciousness by individuals who I clinically describe as *Theophobes*.[3] The phrase *Theo* means God. A small *t* would be inappropriate here because the meaning of the term, Theophobe, is specifically related to the Supreme Being. In Greek, the word, *phobic*, means morbid fear or aversion. Psychological suppression involves *consciously* pushing back unacceptable thoughts, and striving to keep what is unacceptable out of one's mind or awareness. In cases of Theophobia, the unacceptable thoughts are comprised of moral principles and values, God-consciousness, and a sense of moral accountability. An atheist does not believe in a Supreme Being but most atheists do not engage in a crusade to eliminate all symbols of religion from the society. Theophobes make every effort to completely free themselves from thoughts about religion and God. Theophobes attempt to create a social reality that mirrors their godless mental state. When a Theophobe utters the politically-correct statement, "Religion is a private matter that must remain private," the Theophobe actually means,

> I do not want to have anything to do with notions of a Supreme Being or religion. I do not want any religious symbols or quotes from so-called revealed sacred texts placed in my view (or consciousness), especially when I enter any public arena. I have the right not to be reminded of what I wish to dismiss. It is the responsibility of government to insure that I am not imposed upon or harmed or offended by reminders of religion or notions of moral accountability. I believe that naïve unintelligent people need religion. I do not need religion. I accept the fact that many people are not as intelligent as I am. It is my responsibility to correct such situations. I must promote many unpopular ideas and practices even though others are not intelligent enough to recognize their benefits.

Modern psychiatry and psychology do not recognize or have a category for the symptoms and features of Theophobia. *Nevertheless, a chronic aversion towards God is a serious mental illness.* Many adherents of Freudian theory and ultra-secularists in the mental health field dispute the *fact* that Theophobia is a mental illness. Each individual has the right to become afflicted with Theophobia or tread a healthy path. Theophobia is not the same as a natural form of questioning the existence of God or scrutiny of religious themes. It certainly is not part of a genuine search for spiritual truth.

From the Quran:

As for those who disbelieve, it is the same for them; whether you warn them, or not warn them, they cannot believe.... God seals their minds and their hearing, and their eyes are veiled. They have incurred severe retribution. (2:6-7)

Some of them listen to you, but we place veils on their hearts to prevent them from understanding, and deafness in their ears. Thus, no matter what kind of proof they see, they cannot believe. Thus, when they come to argue with you, the disbelievers say, are tales from the past." (6:110)

When God alone is mentioned, the hearts of those who do not believe in the Hereafter shrink with aversion. But when others are mentioned beside Him, they become satisfied. (39:45)[4]

Theophobes are *not* bothered by artistic, visual, and written material about mythical gods, ghosts, wizards, witches, star worshippers, demonic cults, and idols. Found in every strata of society, Theophobes aspire towards opportunities that enable them to challenge or eradicate references to *revealed* religion. Died-in-the-wool Theophobes detest God-conscious people and attempt to portray them as immature, unintelligent, and narrow-minded.

From the Quran:

We have given you the truth, but most of you hate the truth. (43:78)

That is because they hated what God revealed and consequently, He nullifies their works... This is because they followed what angered God and hated the things that please Him. Consequently, He has nullified their works. (47:9, 28)

Why are they so averse to this reminder? Running like zebras. Who are fleeing from the lion! (74:49-51)

> *They hated them for no other reason than believing in God, the Almighty, the Praiseworthy. (85:8)*[5]

Hislamic beliefs and practices are used as a justification by Theophobes for dismissing authentic religion. Remember the person who rejected the entire food dish and refused to sample the good portions? Theophobes are *irreligious*. Irreligiosity can range from a lack of interest in spiritual matters to open hostility towards religion. The ultimate impact of irreligiosity on a community can be illustrated in a metaphorical *law of religiosity*. *The law of irreligiosity is* $w + f = e$. The w signifies weapons of mass religious distortion and deceit, f signifies free doom, and e signifies escape from God (i.e., aversion and suppression of God-consciousness). When w and f multiply and proliferate, the result is mass escape from God. Promoted by Theophobes of all stripes, mass escape from God conjures up confusion, injustice, and chaos on earth. Many people would argue that the decrease in moral conscientiousness in our educational, political, and economic systems, the creeping demise of the two-parent family, the increase in immoral themes in the media, and the loss of a sustained healthy sense of national purpose and unity are by-products of a *collective* escape from God-consciousness. The law of irreligiosity does not apply to persons and communities that heed God's guidance.

From the Quran:

> *Those who disbelieved are allies of one another. Unless you keep these commandments, there will be chaos on earth, and terrible corruption. (8:73)*

> *Indeed, if the truth conformed to their wishes, there would be chaos in the heavens and the earth; everything in them would be corrupted. We have given them their proof, but they are disregarding their proof. (23:71)*[6]

National leaders and public figures who submit to God alone do not promote Hislam and free doom. They do not succumb to new tyrants, and they do not fear Theophobes. They do not ferment animosities between people of different colors and creeds. They are not ashamed to openly profess their belief in God. They advocate righteousness, forbid evil, judge, and rule fairly, and set an example for their fellow citizens.

From the Quran:

The people of the Gospel shall rule in accordance with God's revelations therein. Those who do not rule in accordance with God's revelations are the wicked. Then we revealed to you this scripture [Quran], truthfully, confirming previous scriptures, and superseding them. You shall rule among them in accordance with God's revelations, and do not follow their wishes if they differ from the truth that came to you. For each of you, we have decreed laws and different rites. Had God willed, He could have made you one congregation. But He thus puts you to the test through the revelations He has given each of you. You shall compete in righteousness. To God is your final destiny—all of you—then He will inform you of everything you had disputed. (5:47-48)

They are those who, if we appointed them as rulers on earth, they would establish the Contact Prayers (Salat) and the obligatory charity (Zakat) and would advocate righteousness and forbid evil. God is the ultimate ruler. (22:41)

O David, we have made you a ruler on earth. Therefore, you shall judge among the people equitably, and do not follow your personal opinion, lest it diverts you from the way of God. Surely, those who stray off the way of God incur severe retribution for forgetting the Day of Reckoning. (38:26)[7]

History's most ruthless leaders (e.g., Pharaoh, Hitler) found support for their visions of an ideal society in the corrupt spiritual systems that they created, adopted, and subscribed to. Corrupt religious leaders and secularists reject authentic revealed scripture and bring disaster on themselves and their peoples. Hislam, deceit, and suppression of honest inquiry into spiritual truth go hand in hand. In some wayward societies, the triad of Hislam, deceit, and suppression of spiritual truth is more obvious than in other wayward societies. When you peel beneath outer layers of social culture, language, political life, and overt religiosity, the intrigues and schemes to shape the minds of the masses in matters of religion are quite apparent.

From the Quran:

If we are to annihilate any community, we let the leaders commit vast corruption therein. Once they deserve retribution, we annihilate it completely. (17:16)

The followers will say to their leaders, "It was you who schemed night and day, then commanded us to be unappreciative of God, and to set up idols to rank with Him." They will be ridden with remorse, when they see the retribution, for we will place shackles around the necks of those who disbelieved. Are they not justly requited for what they did? (34:33)

Invariably, when we sent a warner to any community, the leaders of that community would say, "We found our parents following certain practices, and we will continue in their footsteps." (43:23)[8]

Hislam Undercuts National Prosperity

A nation's *enduring* prosperity is directly related to the degree that its citizens follow God's laws. This truth is difficult for some people to grasp because they see that some nations and communities have exploited other communities. While inter-group exploitation does exist, beware of concluding that God approves of oppression and exploitation. In God's system, those who oppress others only signal their own destruction. In the Quran, God reveals that some unbelievers are decreed material wealth in this world but they have no share in the Hereafter. *Without a single exception, righteous God-fearing people have always been granted eventual victory over their enemies.* Some unrighteous nations and communities may have temporary wealth but, in the absence of submission to God, the downfall of such societies is inevitable. Historical examples include ancient Egypt and the Roman Empire. One case in point in the twentieth century is the rise and fall of Communism, an atheistic, political, and socialist ideology forced on nation-states in Europe and parts of Asia for fifty years. *Communist states have never known true prosperity for any significant period of time.*

From the Quran:

If it were not that all the people might become one (disbelieving) congregation, we would have granted everyone who disbelieves in the Most Gracious mansions with silver roofs, and stairs upon which they could climb. Their mansions would have impressive gates, and luxurious furnishings. Also many ornaments. All these are the temporary materials of this lowly life. The Hereafter—at your Lord—is far better for the righteous. (43:33-35)

There is no divine right or destiny to oppress others:
The leaders among Pharaoh's people said, "Will you allow Moses and his people to corrupt the earth, and forsake you and your gods?" He said, "We will kill their sons, and spare their daughters. We are much more powerful than they are." (7:127)

Such was the case with the people of Pharaoh and others before them. They first rejected the signs of their Lord. Consequently, we annihilated them for their sins. We drowned Pharaoh's people; the wicked were consistently punished. (8:54)

We willed to compensate those who were oppressed on earth, and to turn them into leaders, and make them the inheritors. (28:5)

Apathy about oppression is no excuse:
Those whose lives are terminated by the angels, while in a state of wronging their souls, the angels will ask them, "What was the matter with you?" They will say, "We were oppressed on earth." They will say, "Was God's earth not spacious enough for you to emigrate

therein?" For these, the final abode is Hell, and a miserable destiny. (4:97)

"Our Lord, let us not be oppressed by those who disbelieved, and forgive us. You are the Almighty, Most Wise." (60:5)[9]

Economic downturns do not occur by accident. As a community turns away from the worship of God alone, the community experiences greater degrees of hardship. Nationwide hardships are meant to remind people to return to God. God grants communities time to correct any departures from His guidance. In the absence of correction, the consequences that befall a community may include retribution in the form of a loss of security and peace, severe economic losses, droughts, floods, significant loss of life and destruction due to major natural disasters, widespread vice and crime, unforeseen incurable diseases, corruption of leaders, widespread family and social fragmentation, and intrusions from external enemies. Each wayward community assumes that it is an exception to the consequences of violating Divine guidance. *Such an assumption is a very serious threat to a nation's security.* A deceptive feeling of widespread non-accountability to God is reinforced by Theophobic forces intent upon negating the importance of the worship of our Creator.

From the Quran:

Many a community we annihilated; they incurred our retribution while they were asleep, or wide awake. (7:4)

Did the people of today's communities guarantee that our retribution will not come to them in the daytime while they play? (7:98)

When they disregarded what they were reminded of, we saved those who prohibited evil, and afflicted the wrongdoers with a terrible retribution for their wickedness. (7:165)

The disbelievers will continue to suffer disasters, as a consequence of their own works, or have disasters strike close to them, until

God's promise is fulfilled. God will never change the predetermined destiny. (13:31)

Did those who scheme evil schemes guarantee that God will not cause the earth to swallow them, or that the retribution will not come to them when they least expect it? (16:45)

God cites the example of a community that used to be secure and prosperous, with provisions coming to it from everywhere. But then, it turned unappreciative of God's blessings. Consequently, God caused them to taste the hardships of starvation and insecurity. Such is the requital for what they did. (16:112)

If we are to annihilate any community, we let the leaders commit vast corruption therein. Once they deserve retribution, we annihilate it completely. (17:16)

Many a community we have annihilated because of their wickedness. They ended up in ruins, stilled wells, and great empty mansions. (22:45)

Similarly, when the people of Noah disbelieved the messengers, we drowned them, and we set them up as a sign for the people. We have prepared for the transgressors a painful retribution. (25:37)

Many a community we annihilated for turning unappreciative of their lives. Consequently, here are their homes, nothing but uninhabited ruins after them, except a few. We were the inheritors. (28:58)

All those disbelievers were doomed as a consequence of their sins. Some of them we annihilated by violent winds, some were annihilated by the quake, some we caused the earth to swallow, and some we drowned. God is not the One who wronged them; it is they who wronged their own souls. (29:40)

We have annihilated many communities around you, after we had explained the proofs that they might repent. (46:27).[10]

The best stimulus package for a community experiencing sustained loss of provision would include a return to morals and ethical behavior in daily life. There is a significant number of people in our society who oppose any national rejuvenation plan associated with encouraging (but not forcing) people to heed God's authentic proven commands. Such persons are social toxins and constitute part of the human forces of Satan.

From the Quran:

"O my people, seek forgiveness from your Lord, then repent to Him. He will then shower you with provisions from the sky and augment your strength. Do not turn back into transgressors." (11:52)

Say, "My Lord is the One who controls all provisions; He grants the provisions to whomever He wills, or reduces them, but most people do not know." (34:36)

Who is there to provide for you, if He withholds His provisions? Indeed, they have plunged deep into transgression and aversion. (67:21)[11]

The longevity of a community or nation-state is ultimately an index of the people's recognition of and adherence to God's commands. All past great communities and civilizations have met their demise after failing to heed God's guidance. The path down the road to destruction includes adopting beliefs and behavior contrary to God's prescriptions for life. This pill may be hard to swallow for people who believe that their predecessors' hardships were *solely* brought on by environmental conditions, external invaders, or oppressors. Such communities fail to realize that these secondary causes of their predecessors' downfalls are natural consequences of abandoning God's guidance.

From the Quran:

Your Lord never annihilates any community unjustly, while its people are righteous. (11:117)

Shifts (of angels) take turns, staying with each one of you—they are in front of you and behind you. They stay with you, and guard you in accordance with God's commands. Thus, God does not change the condition of any people unless they themselves make the decision to change. If God wills any hardship for any people, no force can stop it. For they have none beside Him as Lord and Master. (13:11)

Many a community we annihilated because of their transgressions; we designated a specific time for their annihilation. (18:59)[12]

Satanic Hands

I use the phrase, *Satanic Hands*, to reflect individuals and groups who attempt to remove God-consciousness from daily national life.[13] One satanic hand belongs to fanatical, misguided religious groups. A second satanic hand belongs to rank atheists and God-haters. A third satanic hand reflects false religious doctrines. A fourth satanic hand reflects elements in the media, education institutions, and legal system that undermine and distort religion. All four hands have destroyed previous civilizations and have been attempting to choke the spiritual vitality out of this country. In the name of entertainment and first amendment rights, the mass media is used as a medium to promote lifestyles and behavior in opposition to the laws and guidance of God. Under the disguise of preparing informed, skilled, and open-minded citizens, hands in the education system promote philosophies, beliefs, and behaviors that debunk religious faith. Homosexuality and abortion are two examples of immoral behavior that are promoted as individual private rights that should be socially and legally sanctioned. Other popularized spiritually destructive practices include popularized infidelity among marriage partners, premarital sex, gambling, the consumption of alcoholic beverages, the belief that morality is relative, the belief that faith is inferior to reason and intellectual inquiry, and the notion that humans evolved from primate apes.

Under the guise of maintaining separation of church and state, satanic hands in the legal system attempt to remove all vestiges of moral law, authentic religion, and spirituality from schools, public institutions, and courts. A potential juror who openly verbalizes that he or she would refer to divine law in reaching a judgment about someone's guilt or innocence is subject to be excused from jury duty. Albeit their critical role in our legal system, the Supreme Court, and state and local court systems are viewed by some people as *substitutes for divine law*. The courts are used as an instrument to: 1) create and elevate a body of laws contrary to the laws of God, 2) eliminate any mention of God in political and public life, and 3) legalize behaviors (e.g., homosexuality, abortion) clearly against Divine law. The phrase "so help me God" has been removed from swearing-in procedures and legal proceedings in some court jurisdictions throughout the country. The phrase "under God" in the Pledge of Allegiance is being challenged as unconstitutional in the nation's courts. Legal challenges to the phrase "In God We Trust" on the nation's currency have been made.

Court judges and lawyers debate and conjecture about what constitutes right and wrong (in the absence of any reference to Divine guidance), guilt or innocence, and introduce all kinds of technicalities and hypothetical situations in a court case. One wonders whether some lawyers' attempts to refashion the court system have been to showcase their ability to write legal documents, argue, debate, and circumvent facts in court cases.

> Not only do they [lower court judges] *intentionally* pervert the course of justice but in so doing they create erroneous case law, which may be subsequently cited by other lower court judges. *This practice leads to a vicious cycle in which one erroneous ruling is piled on top of another, forming a judicial 'cancer'.* [14][italics added]

This situation is parallel to the conduct of corrupt religious leaders who pontificate and write their own body of laws and technicalities instead of making judgments that complement authentic Divine guidance.

Homosexuality: A Gross Sin

The people of the ancient communities of Sodom and Gomorrah were the first persons to ever practice homosexuality. The people openly displayed homosexual preferences and behavior, and attempted to convince others to, at minimum, tolerate homosexual behavior in their communities.

From the Quran:

Lot said to his people, "You commit such an abomination; no one in the world has done it before!" (7:80)[15]

According to Biblical accounts (e.g., Genesis, 19:23), the two communities were destroyed by fire from "out of the heaven." The Quran points out that Sodom and Gomorrah were destroyed by fire and rocks from heaven "designated by your Lord to strike the transgressors." In the same area where Sodom and Gomorrah were located, a team of archeologists, geologists, and climatologists discovered that the sediment rock contains compounds *found only in meteorites*![16] In 1997, The Jerusalem Report[17] published an article about the discovery, and points out that:

> Sodom and Gomorrah may have been destroyed by a meteorite—and not by an earthquake, as earlier suggested by some scholars according to new research to be presented at a conference on natural catastrophes at Cambridge University this summer.... One of the most compelling findings: samples of a calcite material unique to meteorites that were found in three Middle Eastern regions, including where the two cities would have stood, by French archeologist Marie Agnes Courty. That strengthens the theory that severe meteor showers bombarded parts of the earth in about 2000 BCE—the possible time of the cities' destruction, according to scholars who regard the Biblical account as having historical basis.... But, Prof. Arnon Dar of Haifa Technion's astrophysics department says, it's "absolutely reasonable that meteorites could have caused such destruction." He points to large meteorite-created craters, such as one in Arizona that is over a kilometer wide.[18]

Additional evidence of meteorite impact in that area has been gathered from information about the southern part of the Dead Sea:

There have been excavations on the Lisan peninsula, which nearly cuts the southern part of the Dead Sea off from the rest of it. It is also different from the main Dead Sea in that its mean depth is very different from the rest of the Dead Sea, only 10 m in average. It seems that there was a great catastrophe around 2200 BC that has destroyed Sodom and Gomorrah…If we take the story in Genesis for what it seems to indicate, the whole southern part of the Dead Sea may be an impact crater that was caused by a cosmic disaster, one piece in the 2200 BC disaster.[19]

The scientists' discoveries confirm scriptural accounts of the destruction of Sodom and Gomorrah. Due to their persistent abandonment of God's guidance and their transgressions, the people of Sodom and Gomorrah could no longer perceive the truth. They deluded themselves into believing that homosexuality is normal. In their self-imposed spiritual blindness, they beseeched and challenged God to rain down upon them "rocks from the sky" if God prohibited homosexuality (verse 8:32, "if this is really the truth from You…"). God answered their prayer! Their challenge to God to punish them is strikingly similar to the declarations of homosexuals and their supporters today who insist that homosexuality is not a sin, because God "created them (homosexuals) that way." *Note verses 8:32 and 11:82 cited below*[20]. The earth passes through orbits (dust and debris paths) of parent comets and meteorites. In addition to other areas impacted at that time, pieces of debris or meteorites headed directly towards Sodom and Gomorrah by God's command. God already knew the people's decision. God knows the past, present, and the future. There is no "time" as far as God is concerned. The ultimate proof about this retribution that befell the two cities is in the mathematically coded Quran:

From the Quran:

"You practice sex with the men, instead of the women. Indeed, you are a transgressing people." (7:81)

They also said, "Our god, if this is really the truth from You, then <u>shower us with rocks from the sky</u>, or pour upon us a painful punishment." (8:32)

His [Lot's] people came rushing; they had grown accustomed to their sinful acts. He said, "O my people, it would be purer for you, if you take my daughters instead. You shall reverence God; do not embarrass me with my guests. Have you not one reasonable man among you?" They said, "You know well that we have no need for your daughters; you know exactly what we want." (11:78-79)

When our judgment came, we turned it upside down, and we <u>showered it with hard, devastating rocks. Such rocks were designated by your Lord to strike the transgressors.</u> (11: 82-83)

He is the One who created the heavens and the earth in six days, then assumed all authority. He knows everything that enters into the earth, and everything that comes out of it, and everything that comes down from the sky, and everything that climbs into it. He is with you wherever you may be. God is Seer of everything you do. (57:4)[21]

Many professional associations (e.g., American Civil Liberties Union, American Psychiatric Association, American Psychological Association, National Association of Social Workers, Sexuality Information and Education Council of the United States) regard homosexuality as normal sexual behavior. By means of the media, the courts, professional associations, and the education system, individuals are encouraged to recognize homosexuality as an alternative lifestyle. An individual who does not accommodate or accept this so-called alternative lifestyle is labeled "homophobic." The word, "homophobia," is defined as an "unreasonable fear of homosexuals." When distorted by the 'wordsmiths' of the written and visual media as well as designated "politically correct" groups, the word "homophobic" suddenly implies *prejudice* against homosexuals. Persons who express an unrelenting rejection of homosexual behavior as a normal behavior are often given this label. The label is meant to suggest that there is something abnormal about having negative views about homosexuality. The altered popularized definition of "homophobic" tacitly labels persons who reject homosexuality as hating individuals who engage in the behavior. This strategy is meant to equate so-called "homophobes" as like persons who are racist and exhibit prejudice against ethnic minority groups. As a psychologist, I recognize how contempt for homosexuality is being associated with irrational fear and anger. If a person feels contempt for homosexuality, the individual should not be persuaded by the popularized social definition of homophobia into believing that he or she is biased and harbors an irrational attitude about this abominable behavior. The distortion of the terms homophobic and homophobia in the public arena is another example of how satanic hands attempt to shape public opinion in a direction of accepting behavior that violates Divine law.

Some health professions have started to offer treatment to help individuals overcome homophobia! According to a Fox News poll conducted in 2004, eighty-eight percent of national media professionals believe that society should accept homosexuality.[22] Some corrupt elements of Christianity and Judaism condone the behavior, even to the extent of accommodating homosexuals within their clergy. On February 4, 2004, the Massachusetts State Supreme Court ruled that government attorneys "failed to identify any constitutionally adequate reason" to deny them (lesbian and gay couples) the right (to marry)."[23] The Court's ruling is an example of how our courts are used as an instrument to create and elevate a body of laws contrary to the laws of God. Spurious case law and selective distortion of rights enumerated in the U.S. Constitution are made substitutes for Divine law. Many legal advocates of homosexuality and other violations of Divine law (e.g., abortion) exhibit features of Theophobia. On May 17, 2004, hundreds of homosexual couples in the state of Massachusetts were legally married by court officials.[24] This social climate is not far removed from the social climate that characterized Sodom and Gomorrah. Like the homosexuals and their sympathizers who lived in Sodom and Gomorrah, some of their modern-day counterparts are impervious to authentic Divine guidance and oblivious to advice to reexamine their immoral behavior. Some people make the absurd claim that discrimination against homosexuals is like discrimination against members of ethnic minority groups that are victims of racism and prejudice. Any objectively unjustifiable discrimination towards anyone is a sin. Promotion of the notion that homosexuality is an inborn trait like skin complexion, is an example of distortion of the truth to control and shape the opinions of naïve uninformed audiences. Homosexuality is an aberrant behavior of choice whereas a person's skin color, gender, and ethnicity are genetic characteristics. God created humans as males and females. There is no middle of the road in this matter.

From the Quran:

O people, we created you from the same male and female, and rendered you distinct peoples and tribes, that you may recognize one another. The best among you in the sight of God is the most righteous. God is Omniscient, Cognizant. (49:13)

We created a pair (male and female) of everything, that you may take heed.(51:49)

And Him who created the male and the female. (92:3)[25]

Despite the truth in the scriptures about this behavior, detractors attempt to argue that gender identity is not inherited and all gender-specific behavior is learned. Many homosexuals argue that they are born with innate homosexual preferences, and they are "just being themselves."

The push to scientifically validate the false notion that all sexual preferences are learned including homosexuality is very strong. In 1966, a physician-professor at the John Hopkins University attempted to change the anatomical and psychological gender identity of a twin baby boy, after the boy's penis was accidentally severed after birth.[26] The physician purposely mislead the infant's parents into believing that the infant would never be happy as a boy or man, and convinced the baby's parents to raise the baby boy as a girl. The naïve parents complied. They named their infant son "Brenda." Whenever the parents took the toddler to the physician's office, the physician coached the toddler and his twin brother to engage in sexual (homosexual?) play. For some time, counselors working with the treating physician simply mirrored the opinion of the physician, until the parents changed therapists. The attempt to alter the child's sexual identity included mental, social, and hormonal conditioning plus unsuccessful requests to get "Brenda" to agree to cosmetic surgery. The attempt continued until the child was fourteen years old. *The attempt failed.*

During the interim years, the physician ignored feedback from the child's parents that the experiment was not working – the boy was not acting like a girl. "Brenda" suffered from peer rejection, depression, and other emotional and psychological problems as a young child. His parents suffered from stress and severe mental problems due to their complicity, guilt feelings, and worry about "Brenda's" emotional problems. When the 14-year-old boy was finally told his correct gender identity, he said, "I'am not crazy…all along I knew I was not crazy." David had been led to believe that he should ignore and suppress any feelings or impulses he experienced towards masculine behavior. David immediately escalated his natural gender-consistent urges and relentlessly pursued all things manly and male. His parents changed his name from "Brenda" to David. David had surgery to restore his genitals and received long-term counseling.

David eventually married and raised three stepchildren. Later, David suffered from severe depression after the death of his twin brother and separation from his former wife. In May 2004, David committed suicide. He was 38 years old. The physician-professor who conducted the experiment has yet to admit that his efforts to change the gender of David failed. Instead, he blames David's parents for not fully cooperating with him. David's case is one among numerous attempts to groom and raise children to assume a gender identity opposite to their natural gender.

Some homosexuals feel that their behavior is such an abomination that it is futile to seek forgiveness and guidance from God. Others have either established their own places of worship or sought congregations that will accept them to fill a spiritual void in their lives. In so doing, some have inadvertently or willingly distorted religion and worship to accommodate their behavior. The distortions are "fake flowers" that look like roses. Some homosexuals secretly anguish over their condition and genuinely want release from such behavior. Satan and his compatriots encourage so-called closet homosexuals to step forward and, with confidence, openly declare their sexual preference. The individuals are counseled that they will feel better about themselves, no longer feel any anguish, and experience contentment. This is a trilogy of tragedies. The first tragedy is endorsing or practicing homosexuality. The second tragedy is an unwillingness to heed innate urges to stop the behavior. The third tragedy is being told by so-called experts that such behavior is normal and can contribute to better mental health. Such so-called expert advice reminds me of the Freudian notion that behavior prohibited in revealed scripture must be expressed to overcome neurotic guilt and anxiety.

Many people ask, "Is it possible for a person who practiced homosexuality to be forgiven by God?" Certainly. There is only one unforgivable sin if maintained until one's death – idolatry. A sincere person who seeks to correct his or her behavior must repent to God, desists from the sinful behavior, avoid situations and places where people gather for the purpose of having homosexual liaisons, avoid close relations with anyone who practices homosexual behavior, and lead a righteous life. This God-given formula holds true for all indiscretions a person commits in life. In journeying along this path, seekers engage in behaviors that they later regret, and they ask God to forgive them.

> *If they fall in sin or wrong their souls, they remember God and ask forgiveness for their sins - and who forgives the sins except God - and they do not persist in sins, knowingly. (3:135)*
>
> *God does not forgive idolatry, but He forgives lesser offenses for whomever He wills. Anyone who sets up idols beside God, has forged a horrendous offense. (4:48)*[27]

Divine Prohibition against Adultery and Premarital Sex

Rather than discouraging people from engaging in premarital and extramarital sex, health agencies promote "safe sex outside of marriage." Evidently, not a small number of people believe that what makes sex safe has nothing to do with moral values. In some quarters, adultery and fornication are presented as part of the drama of adult life. In schools and colleges, many students who choose to abstain from sex are ridiculed and stigmatized by their peers as "old-fashioned" and "behind the times."

The worldwide HIV-AIDS epidemic is both a consequence of widespread illicit sexual relations and a warning to desist from homosexuality and sex outside of lawful marriage. The fact that some individuals who do not engage in the aforementioned behaviors contract AIDS does not diminish the retributive nature of the epidemic. Thousands of people scoff at the truth that AIDS is a consequence and warning to mankind from our Creator. The impact of large numbers of people infected with the HIV virus is just beginning to take its devastating toll. The media presents the message, "Have sex, have protection." Some movies, TV programs, and commercials depict lovers overwhelmed with passion and preparing to engage in foreplay or sex. The public is bombarded with sex and sexually laden themes in the print, audio, and visual media. In the face of the promotion of illicit relationships, pornography, and homosexual unions, individuals are challenged to assume personal responsibility and exhibit the moral conviction and courage to resist the "sex-without-morals" movement in modern society.

From the Quran:

Today, all good food is made lawful for you. The food of the people of the scripture is lawful for you. Also, you may marry the chaste women among the believers, as well as the chaste women among the followers of previous scripture, provided you pay them their due dowries. You shall maintain chastity, not committing adultery, nor taking secret lovers. Anyone who rejects faith, all his work will be in vain, and in the Hereafter he will be with the losers. (5:5)

They never implore beside God any other god, nor do they kill anyone-for God has made life sacred—except in the course of justice. Nor do they commit adultery. Those who commit these offenses will have to pay. (25:68)[28]

Abortion is Murder

Advocates of abortion frame the taking of life in the womb as "a woman's right to choose," and argue that a woman "owns her body." Many people are hoodwinked into believing that they or "nature" created the life and can choose to eliminate it. Neither the woman nor the man whose sperm fertilized the egg can create anything. In couching this question strictly in legal terms and characterizing the situation as a personal and property rights issue, abortion advocates dismiss the divine prohibition against the murder of one's unborn children. In the landmark Supreme Court Case *Roe vs. Wade*, lawyers argued that Ms. McCorvey was raped and therefore had a "right" to an abortion. The truth is Ms. McCorvey was never even suspected of having been raped! *Ms. McCorvey never said that she was raped!* In her own words:

> "[The] experiment with legal abortion is an utter failure...It is my sincere prayer that there will be no 30th anniversary of Roe v. Wade."[29]

Ms. McCorvey is now a dedicated pro-life advocate and national spokesperson in the pro-life movement. Since learning that the pro-abortion lawyers knowingly lied about Ms. McCorvey, I wondered how this case even reached the Supreme Court. In a follow-up Supreme Court case *Doe vs. Bolton*, American Civil Liberties Union (ACLU) lawyers lied and said that that Ms. Sandra Cano (the "Doe" in the case) wanted to have an abortion and be sterilized. *Ms. Cano never said she wanted an abortion!* In her own words:

> "I'm just now learning a lot of the details, and I'm really shocked," Mrs. Cano, now 49, told WORLD. "Abortion is against every belief I have. I've never been for abortion. I never went for an abortion. I was not the person they say I was. This case was based on lies."[30]

The lawyers took this case to the Supreme Court based on lies.[31] When he testified at the Supreme Court in 1972, Dr. Bernard Nathanson, co-founder of the National Abortion Rights Action League, *intentionally* lied about the number of women who died from illegal abortions. He was attempting to buttress the case for legal abortion. When confronted later about this lie, Dr. Nathanson said,

> "We spoke of 5,000 – 10,000 deaths a year...I confess that I knew the figures were totally false...it was a useful figure, widely accepted, so why go out of our way to correct it with honest statistics?"[32]

Dr. Nathanson commented that his fabricated information "was a useful figure [and] widely accepted" reflects an abandonment of moral principle in the name of promoting a desired social agenda. Such behavior is increasingly commonplace in our nation's courts and society.

From the Quran:

Do not confound the truth with falsehood, nor shall you conceal the truth, knowingly. (2:42)

Are those enlightened by their Lord the same as those whose evil works are adorned in their eyes, and they follow their own opinions? (47:14)

In 2001, Congress passed the "Born Alive Infant Protection Act." The Act was passed to prevent induced labor abortions, a procedure that is nothing less than murder. A baby exits from the womb, feet, legs, and arms first. While the baby's head is in the birth canal, the baby's brain is bludgeoned with a sharp surgical instrument. The baby's brains are sucked out of its head.[33]

As of 2004, it is estimated that 43 million abortions have been performed in the United States. Medical science has proved that there is no point between conception and birth when there is not viable life in the womb. Abortion of the unborn and near-born has not gone on without abortion-related biological consequences befalling many of the women who have elected to eliminate the life in their wombs. A significant link has been established between abortion and breast cancer in women who have abortions. In her article, *Abortion-Breast Cancer Link Must Not be Ignored*, Elenor Schoen[34] convincingly stated that the truth has been hidden from the public about the link. She is not the only journalist, physician, or scholar who is aware of this cover-up. Here are some excerpts from her article:

> There seems to be a shocking reluctance in the media to investigate and report on the increasing evidence of a link between abortion and the incidence of breast cancer. The link was revealed as long ago as 1970 when the World Health Organization gathered data that "suggest increased risk associated with abortion."
>
> In 1981, a University of Southern California study found a 140 percent increased breast cancer risk among young women who had chosen to abort their first pregnancy. This was also reported in the British Journal of Cancer in the same year.
>
> Another study was conducted at the Fred Hutchinson Cancer Research Center in Seattle in 1994 by Dr. Janet Daling, a pro-abortion scientist. She found an overall 50 percent risk increase. Women who had an abortion before age 18 had a 250 percent risk increase. Women who had their first abortion after age 30 showed a 210 percent risk increase. In 1997, Daling stated: "I would have loved to have found no association between breast cancer and abortion, but our research is rock solid and our data is accurate. It's not a matter of believing it, it is a matter of what is."
>
> Dr. Angelo Lanfranchi, a breast surgeon from New Jersey, declared: "Over the past three or four years, I have spoken to many authorities and people in a position to be well-informed. They have stated they knew abortion was a risk factor but it was too political to speak about. They had found, as I did, that cases of breast cancer in young women are associated with an abortion history."
>
> Until June 2002, the National Cancer Institute Fact Sheet maintained that abortion is not a risk factor for breast cancer, but this fact sheet has now disappeared from the NCI Web site. Total funding for breast cancer research through the National Institutes of Health from fiscal years 1992 to 2001 equaled $4.2 billion.

Can an issue be so political, such a sacred cow that statistics and studies are hidden from the public and further investigation discouraged? Has the fact that abortion is a multimillion-dollar industry (numbered among the Fortune 500) have any connection with this cover-up? [35]

Members of the British Academy of Royal Medical Colleges noted that the condition known as the Abortion Breast Cancer syndrome (ABC) was not present among women in third world nations.[36] ABC is epidemic among women in the United States. To confirm their clue to the reason for this critical difference, controlled studies were conducted. In addition to publishing their findings about the abortion-cancer link, Elenor Schoen mentioned their findings in her article.

> The reasoned explanation for this link is that nature, through hormones, provides women in late stages of pregnancy with increased protection against tissue-susceptibility to cancer, carrying forward the recognized protective effects of early first childbirth. If pregnancy is suddenly ended through an induced abortion, the breast cells that make up the milk glands are unable to complete their maturation into cancer-resistant cells. During the remainder of a woman's reproductive life, the increased number of immature breast cancer cells will be exposed to high estrogen levels during each menstrual period. Estrogen, although normally found in the body, is carcinogenic in high doses because it stimulates cell division. While statistics about the carcinogenic effects of pollution, industrial waste, nuclear accidents, etc., are reported, the abortion-breast cancer link continues to be mostly ignored.[37]

In August, 2003, the Association of American Physicians and Surgeons highlighted research confirming ABC and echoing information about schemes to cover up the abortion-cancer link. In their article, *Politics Trumps Science in Abortion B Breast Cancer Link,* Association authors wrote:

> Scientists, women's groups, and the media have consistently suppressed or ignored research that establishes a direct link between abortion and breast cancer for their own political purposes. Further,

women considering abortion are not given true informed consent about the real risks of the procedure as a result of withholding this evidence.

[Karen] Malec shows how several studies conducted as early as 1957 showing the link were suppressed or ignored, as were later post-Roe studies that showed significantly higher rates of breast cancer in the "Roe Generation." For example, Brind et al estimated that in 1996 an excess of 5,000 cases of breast cancer were attributable to abortion, and that the annual excess would increase by 500 cases each year. They predicted 25,000 excess cases in the year 2036.

The scientific and medical community admits that the reasons for the suppression are political. The president of the American Society of Breast Surgeons said that she presented her concerns about getting information to the public about the abortion-breast cancer link, but the board felt it was "too political." The director of the Miami Breast Cancer Conference explained that there was no presentation on the program because it was "too political."

The author found that the web pages of the National Cancer Institute (NCI) and leading American and Canadian cancer organizations contain false statements, misrepresentation, and omissions in their discussions. Yet when pressured by scientists to post studies that show a 2.4 fold increase in breast cancer risk, pro-choice activists cried foul, accusing them of using "pro-life scare tactics." [38]

In the revealed religions, murder is a sin. Via scheming in the court system, and manipulation of public opinion, murder of this kind (abortion) is sanctioned and even encouraged by some groups. Women are not fully appraised about the lethal risks to themselves by having abortions. Satanic Hands scheme to hide the truth and promote social opposition to God's guidance and commands. Like their ancient counterparts, persons with Satanic Hands present themselves as knowledgeable and say they only seek the welfare of the people. They scheme to first divert people away from God's guidance and then convince people to adopt evil actions promoted as social and personal remedies. In many cases, the schemers seek recognition, political power, or profit from the evil actions.

From the Quran:

We allow the leading criminals of every community to plot and scheme. But they only plot and scheme against their own souls, without perceiving. (6:123)

When we bestow mercy upon the people, after adversity had afflicted them, they immediately scheme against our revelations! Say, "God's scheming is far more effective. For our messengers are recording everything you scheme." (10:21)

They resorted to arrogance on earth, and evil scheming, and the evil schemes only backfire on those who scheme them. Should they then expect anything but the fate of those who did the same things in the past? You will find that God's system is never changeable; you will find that God's system is immutable. (35:43)[39]

No unborn child should be harmed because: 1) a mother finds the pregnancy undesirable or inconvenient, 2) a mother does not want to bear the child of a divorced husband or estranged partner, or 3) the idea that the child would pose an economic hardship. Pregnancy is not caused by chance or the roll of dice. Despite the circumstances, no one is conceived by accident. God knows all things and creates all life. Misguided individuals and groups ignore these truths.

From the Quran:

The divorced women shall wait three menstruations (before marrying another man). **It is not lawful for them to conceal what God creates in their wombs if they believe in God and the Last Day.** *(In case of pregnancy,) the husband's wishes shall supersede the wife's wishes, if he wants to remarry her. The women have rights, as well as obligations, equitably. Thus, the man's wishes prevail (in case of pregnancy). God is Almighty, Most Wise. (2:228)*

God knows what every female bears, and what every womb releases, or gains. Everything He does is perfectly measured. (13:8)

You shall not kill your children due to fear of poverty. We provide for them, as well as for you. Killing them is a gross offense. (17:31)[40]

Divine Prohibition against Gambling and Consumption of Intoxicants

Even though intoxicants and gambling are forbidden in the revealed scriptures, both behaviors flourish in modern society. Alcoholism and drug abuse abound in developed nations and anywhere there is not a shared strong moral sanction against such behavior. Some states in the U.S. have adopted legalized gambling as a means of generating revenue. Again, courts are used as an instrument to create and elevate a body of laws contrary to the laws of God. In some municipalities, public work projects and social programs rest almost entirely on funds generated from state-sanctioned gambling enterprises. In some Hislamic religions, prophets of God and other pious people are portrayed in doctored scriptures as "becoming drunk and naked."

From the Quran:

They ask you about intoxicants and gambling: say, "In them there is a gross sin, and some benefits for the people. But their sinfulness far outweighs their benefit." They also ask you what to give to charity: say, "The excess." God thus clarifies the revelations for you, that you may reflect." (2:219)

O you who believe, do not observe the Contact Prayers (Salat) while intoxicated, so that you know what you are saying.... God is Pardoner, Forgiver. (4:43-partial)

O you who believe, intoxicants, and gambling, and the altars of idols, and the games of chance are abominations of the devil; you shall avoid them, that you may succeed. (5:90)[41]

Spiritual Truths Ignored in Academia

Many academics view religion as anti-intellectual and antithetical to scientific inquiry. I know this firsthand because I was an associate professor for ten years. Many teachers and students believe that religion is insignificant in the search for knowledge and personal fulfillment. Religion is seen as rooted in unproven premises about the purpose of life and origin of the universe. Misguided intellectuals cavalierly dismiss spiritual truths and dismiss the reality of a moral universe. Elevating a disjointed concept of science, such individuals focus only on phenomena that they can physically sense. If they cannot see it, smell it, taste it, dissect it, monitor it, count it, or measure it, it is nonexistent for them. Their science is disconnected from the Reality that created them, gave them senses, brains, minds, and the inspiration to conceive of science. Recognized by millions as one of the greatest scientist in the twentieth century, Albert Einstein unhesitatingly recognized the existence of God. Einstein said that neither perceived reality nor science can account for the whole of reality. Einstein referred to God as "the illimitable superior spirit."

> My religion consists of a humble admiration of the illimitable superior spirit who reveals himself in the slight details we are able to perceive with our frail and feeble mind… "Not everything that counts can be counted and not everything that can be counted counts." (Sign hanging in Einstein's office at Princeton University) [42]

A desire to separate scientific inquiry from Divine Truth stems from at least three factors: 1) the separation may be due to ignorance about the issues, 2) the separation may be born out of attempts by factions of Hislam to denounce scientific findings that contradict Hislamic teachings, and 3) the separation reflects the maintenance of a discourse that substitutes the reality of a *created purposeful* universe, with a discourse bereft of greater meaning and human connection to a higher intelligent Being.

From the Quran:

Among the people there is the one who argues about God without knowledge, and without guidance, and without an enlightening scripture. (22:8)

Do you not see that God has committed in your service everything in the heavens and the earth, and has showered you with His blessings-obvious and hidden? Yet, some people argue about God without knowledge, without guidance, and without the enlightening scripture. (31:20)

When their messengers went to them with clear proofs, they rejoiced in the knowledge they had inherited, and the very things they ridiculed were the cause of their fall. (40:83)

But the human being tends to believe only what he sees in front of him. (75:5)[43]

In contrast to Einstein's recognition that unblemished religion and science are essential to increase our understanding of reality, Freud viewed religion as anti-intellectual and contrary to reason. Author of *Deadly Dr. Freud*, Dr. Paul Scagnelli[44] commented about the enduring impact of Freud's writings on on-going pervasive maneuvers to debunk religion and promote a Theophobic environment in academia. Dr. Scagnelli said,

> ...This evil flower [hatred towards God] blossomed fully in his lengthy attacks against God and religion in his books *The Future of an Illusion* and *Civilization and its Discontents*. Undoubtedly, these books have persuaded hundreds of thousands of intellectuals around the world to develop disbelief in God and contempt for religion while emulating Freud's stance of intellectual and moral superiority.[45]

The stance of intellectual and moral superiority coupled with a rejection of religion is an identification badge worn by many contemporary college students and their teachers. Except for church-affiliated schools, many Religious Studies Departments are the least funded, their courses and seminars are the least attended, and their mission and purpose on college campuses are routinely held suspect by an ever-growing body of individuals enamored with a sense of intellectual elitism.

Human Beings: A Special Creation

As an overarching explanation of life by chance, the Theory of Evolution is highly suspect if not entirely discarded by many credible recognized scientists. Regarding the notion that humans evolved from apes, an ever-growing number of scientists are confirming that such a scenario is false. The difference in the number and type of nucleotides in the DNA structures of apes and humans is so great that an ape-to-human link is impossible. On the website, *Creation*, several experts clarify the difference between conjecture and facts regarding this matter. A member of the New York Academy of Sciences and an officer of the Archaeological Institute of America, Dr. I.L. Cohen,[46] noted:

> 'Survival of the fittest' and 'natural selection'—No matter what phraseology one generates, the basic fact remains the same: any physical change of any size, shape or form is strictly the result of purposeful alignment of billions of nucleotides (in the DNA). Nature or species do not have the capacity to rearrange them nor to add to them. Consequently, no leap can occur from one species to another. The only way we know for a DNA to be altered is through a meaningful intervention from an outside source of intelligence—one who knows what it is doing, such as our genetic engineers are now performing in the laboratories.[47]

Dr. Michael Denton,[48] a molecular biologist, observed that:

> In all organisms the roles of DNA, mRNA and protein are identical. The meaning of the genetic code is also virtually identical in all cells. The size, structure and component design of the protein synthetic machinery is practically the same in all cells. In terms of the basic biochemical design, therefore no living system can be thought of as being primitive or ancestral with respect to any other system, nor is there the slightest empirical hint of an evolutionary sequence among all the incredibly diverse cells on earth. For those who hoped

that molecular biology might bridge the gulf between chemistry and biochemistry, the revelation was profoundly disappointing.[49]

Denton pointed out that the composition of a single cell does not reflect its own work, but reflects the handiwork of an external Grand Designer:

> The complexity of the simplest known type of cell is so great that it is impossible to accept that such an object could have been thrown together by some kind of freakish, vastly improbable event. Such an occurrence would be indistinguishable from a miracle…It is astonishing to think that this remarkable piece of machinery, which possesses the ultimate capacity to construct every living thing that *ever* existed on earth…can construct all of its own components in a matter of minutes and weigh less than 10-16 grams. It is of the order of several thousand million times smaller than the smallest piece of functional machinery ever constructed by man.[50]

Other experts and scientists have chimed in to present clear evidence against human evolution. John Reader[51] comments:

> The entire hominid (a so-called 'ape-man' fossil) collection known today would barely cover a billiard table… Ever since Darwin… preconceptions have led evidence by the nose in the study of fossil man.[52]

Degreed with a Ph.D. in Mathematics and a Masters of Science in Physics, Wolfgang Smith[53] stated:

> …now that the actual physical structure of what might be termed the biochemical mainstays of life [DNA] has come into view, scientists are finding — frequently to their dismay — that the evolutionist thesis has become more stringently unthinkable than ever before… on the molecular level, these separations, and this hierarchic order stand out with a mathematical precision which once and for all silences dissent. On the fundamental level it becomes a rigorously demonstrable fact that there are no transitional types, and that the so-called missing links are indeed non-existent.[54]

In his book, *The Bone Peddlers*, published 22 years ago, William R. Fix[55] noted that:

> The fossil record pertaining to man is still so sparsely known that those who insist on positive declarations can do nothing more than jump from one hazardous surmise to another and hope that the next dramatic discovery does not make them utter fools... As we have seen, there are numerous scientists and popularizers today who have the temerity to tell us that there is 'no doubt' how man originated. If only they had the evidence...[56]

Some people assume that components of the human body that seem to them to serve no purpose must be residuals from evolutionary predecessors. The assumption is incorrect.

> The existence of human organs whose function is unknown does not imply that they are vestiges of organs inherited from earl evolutionary ancestors. As medical knowledge has increased, at least some of the functions of all organs have been discovered. For example, the human appendix was once considered a useless remnant from our evolutionary past. Today it is known that the appendix plays a role in antibody production and protects part of the intestine from infections. Its removal also increases a person's susceptibility to leukemia, Hodgkin's disease, cancer of the colon, and cancer of the ovaries. Indeed, the absence of true vestigial organs implies that evolution never happened.[57]

In spite of clear DNA chromosomal evidence that humans did not and could not have evolved from apes, so-called fact-finding arguments about the evolutionary origin of humans continue. The scientific *proof* that debunks the myth of ape-man evolution has *not* been presented in the nation's media and schools. Depictions of humans evolving from apes and claims of the discovery of human bones nearly identical to ape bones are still depicted in some textbooks and in the media. (the latest depiction I saw on television was on August 23, 2003) For example, in his *Edmonton Sun* newspaper article, Ted Byfield [58] reported that:

> If parents check the science textbooks used in Canadian schools they'll see some familiar illustrations, familiar because much the

same art appeared in their textbook. There's the "evolution of man" illustration, starting with an ape-like creature on the left, then progressing to the slightly more erect figure with arms stretching to the ground, then to a less hairy individual, finally to a modern human.... This fall there has appeared a scientifically authoritative book casting grave doubt on the whole basis of these confident illustrations. Dr. Jonathan Wells, a molecular and cell biologist from the University of California at Berkeley who is a senior fellow of the Discovery Institute, in his Icons of Evolution does more than cast doubt.... He takes 10 so-called "proofs" of evolution offered in current textbooks and shows where not one of them is in fact a proof of anything, and several are actually frauds. The speckled moths were actually pasted on the trees, not found there. And while there may be rare instances of species that seem part ape, part human, there is no evidence the one came from the other.[59]

As recent as November, 2004, a team of scientists trumpeted the ape-human link in an article in *Science* magazine. The scientists even had the audacity to claim that humans are among the "living great apes."

A nearly 13 million-year-old ape discovered in Spain is the last probable common ancestor to all living humans and great apes, a research team says in Friday's issue of *Science* magazine. Living great apes include humans, chimps, gorillas and orangutans. The group is thought to have split from the lesser apes, such as gibbons and siamangs, about 14 million to 16 million years ago.[60]

In his *National Review Online* article, "*Darwin in the Classroom,*" John G. West, Jr.[61] wrote,

Thanks to the book *Icons of Evolution* by biologist Jonathan Wells, more people know about how biology textbooks perpetuate discredited "icons" of evolution that many biologists no longer accept as good science. Embryo drawings purporting to prove Darwin's theory of common ancestry continue to appear in many textbooks despite the embarrassing fact that they have been exposed as fakes originally concocted by 19th-century German Darwinist Ernst Haeckel. Text books likewise continue to showcase microevolution in peppered moths as evidence for Darwin's mechanism of natural selection even though the underlying research is now questioned by many biologists.

When not offering students bogus science, the textbooks ignore real and often heated scientific disagreements over evolutionary theory. Few students ever learn, for example, about vigorous debates generated by the Cambrian Explosion, a huge burst in the complexity of living things more than 500 million years ago that seems to outstrip the known capacity of natural selection to produce biological change.

Commenting about the popular yet defunct version of the origin of human life portrayed in the media,

The media's bias in favor of evolution is nothing new. Many local papers regularly carry articles touting claims of evolutionists, offering "proof" for the age of the earth, new monkey skeletons, etc., all without challenge or opportunity for rebuttal. People are left with the impression that every scientist is an evolutionist, and that no thinking mind would ever challenge it. News broadcasts, science-oriented television programs, journals, and magazines present evolution as fact...using the theory as if it were their gospel truth. Yet rarely if ever do these same media outlets report on the truckloads of evidence that clearly disprove evolution and offer support for intelligent design. They ignore and censor the findings of geologists, zoologists, chemists, physicists, mathematicians, doctors, archeologists—people all across the scientific spectrum—who have rejected Darwinism and put their faith in an Intelligent Designer.[62]

Authors of the website, *The Myth of Evolution,*[63] point out:

The human body (or the body of any other creature) cannot live without most internal organs, such as the heart, the lungs, the liver, et cetera. Remove any of these organs, and the specimen dies. This implies that the entire body was created at one point in time.... The cells of living creatures are enormously complex. Every part must be present in order for the cell to survive. All the parts have different 'jobs'. It is not illogical to state that if you remove any one part, the cell cannot survive. This obviously implies that the parts (i.e., the cell membrane, the nucleus, the ribosome, etc.) had to have come into being at the same time.[64]

The vast majority of artists' conceptions are based more on imagination than on evidence. Artists must create something between an ape and a man; the older the specimen is said to be, the more apelike they make it.[65]

The website includes a summary of claims by scientists to have discovered the missing link only to have later recanted or downgraded their discoveries.

Stories claiming that primitive, ape-like men have been found are overstated. Piltdown man was an acknowledged hoax. The fragmentary evidence that constituted Nebraska man was a pig's tooth. The discoverer of Java man later acknowledged that it was a large gibbon and that he had withheld evidence to that effect. The 'evidence' concerning Peking man has disappeared. Louis and Mary Leakey, the discoverers of Zinjanthropus (previously referred to as Australopithecus) later admitted that they were probably apes. Ramapithecus man consists merely of a handful of teeth and jaw fragments; his teeth are very similar to those of the gelada baboon living today. For about 100 years the world was led to believe that Neanderthal man was stooped and ape-like. Recent studies show that this individual was crippled with arthritis and probably had rickets. Neanderthal man, Heidelberg man, and Cro-Magnon man are similar to humans living today. Artists' depictions, especially of the fleshy portions of the body, are quite imaginative and are not supported by evidence. Furthermore, the dating techniques are highly questionable. …Natural selection cannot produce new genes; it only selects among preexisting characteristics. …No known mutation has ever produced a form of life having both greater complexity and greater viability than its ancestors.[66]

The simplest form of life consists of 600 different protein molecules. The mathematical probability that just one molecule could form by the chance arrangement of the proper amino acids is far less than 1 in 10^{527} (10 to the 527th power). The magnitude of the number 10^{527} can begin to be appreciated by realizing that the visible universe is about 10^{28} inches in diameter.[67]

Luther D. Sunderland, M.D., Ph.D. [68] notes that:

> Now, after over 120 years of the most extensive and painstaking geological exploration of every continent and ocean bottom, the picture is infinitely more vivid and complete than it was in 1859. Formations have been discovered containing millions of fossils and our museums are filled with over 100-million fossils of 250,000 different species. The availability of this profusion of hard scientific data should permit objective investigators to determine if Darwin was on the right track. What is the picture which the fossils have given us? ...The gaps between major groups of organisms have been growing even wider and more undeniable. They can no longer be ignored or rationalized away with appeals to imperfection of the fossil record.[69]

The *scientific* journey to the reality of a created universe continues to be questioned and denied, but *facts are facts*. People have a right to read, see, and hear all sides of an argument. They have a right to know the *facts* and draw their own conclusions. In this era, the presentation of the Theory of Evolution coupled with the notion that humans evolved from primate apes is an example of the suppression of information and distortion of facts. Isn't this behavior prevalent in societies where control of information is seen as essential to controlling the people and shaping their beliefs? In current times, people who request to be educated and informed about a confirmed, valid, *scientific* alternative (e.g., Intelligent Design Theory) to the Theory of Evolution have been traditionally labeled by some as closed-minded, anti-science, uneducated, or unintelligent. Conversely, people who cling to the Theory of Evolution have been characterized as irreligious, and atheists. Albert Einstein said, "Science without religion is lame and religion without science is blind." Unaware of the nature of Satanic Hands, millions of people are misled and influenced by lame science and blind religion.

In the Quran and other authentic scriptures, humans are given *proven facts* about who created us, how we were created, and what transpired prior to our entry into this world.

From the Quran:

We created the human being from aged mud, like the potter's clay. .Your Lord said to the angels, "I am creating a human being from aged mud, like the potter's clay. "Once I perfect him, and blow into him from My spirit, you shall fall prostrate before him." (15:26, 28-29)

We then said, "O Adam, this is an enemy of you and your wife. Do not let him evict you from Paradise, lest you become miserable. "You are guaranteed never to hunger therein, nor go unsheltered. "Nor will you thirst therein, nor suffer from any heat." But the devil whispered to him, saying, "O Adam, let me show you the tree of eternity and unending kingship." They ate from it, whereupon their bodies became visible to them, and they tried to cover themselves with the leaves of Paradise. Adam thus disobeyed his Lord, and fell. Subsequently, his Lord chose him, redeemed him, and guided him. He said, "Go down therefrom, all of you. You are enemies of one another. When guidance comes to you from Me, anyone who follows My guidance will not go astray, nor suffer any misery. (20:117-123)

We created the human being from a certain kind of mud. (23:12)

Your Lord said to the angels, "I am creating a human being from clay." (38:7)

God] Creator of the human beings. (55:3)[70]

Church-State Separation: A Nation Under God or A Nation Supplanting God

Open rhetorical challenges to the Divine authority of God, authentic religion, and the moral ethos in society occur more frequently. Some political aspirants present themselves as freedom-loving and law-abiding upholders of the rule of law but endorse and promote unprincipled immoral conduct now deemed as "an alternative lifestyle" and "a woman's right to choose." When such persons are challenged to reflect on the moral implications of their endorsement of such behavior, the individuals decry those others are attempting to push their standards of morality and religious beliefs on them. The individuals also argue that religion should not interfere in the private lives of individuals. By making such statements, Theophobes engender fear in individuals who are hoodwinked into believing that their inalienable rights and constitutional freedoms are being threatened. Reacting out of fear, naïve individuals supplant morality in the name of what they have been led to believe is the preservation of freedom. *It is the preservation of free doom.* Some individuals see themselves as "above the law" and get support from like-minded individuals. The idea of being "above the law" means that an individual is not regarded as culpable by select groups and interests for violating certain moral and legal laws. The individual should not be penalized or sanctioned. The violations are simply dismissed as of no account.

Whether open or clandestine, efforts to separate true religious values from governance and daily public life have been very costly to society. Eric Fromm's comments about the schism between the so-called sacred and secular realms of life are even more relevant today than when he first published his book, *The Art of Loving.* Fromm[71] wrote:

> The disintegration of the love of God has reached the same proportions as the disintegration of man. This fact is a blatant contradiction to the idea that we are witnessing a religious renaissance in this epoch.... Daily life is strictly separated from religious values It is devoted to the striving for material comforts, and for success on the personality market. The principles on which our secular efforts are built are those of indifference and egotism (the latter often labeled as "individualism or individual initiative.")...Life has no goal except the one to move, no principle except the one of fair exchange, no satisfaction except the one to consume.... What can the concept of God mean under these circumstances? It is transformed from its original meaning into one fitting the alienated culture of success.[72]

The Preamble to the Constitution of the United States of America reflects spiritual principles. The founding fathers stated that "all men (and women) are endowed by their Creator with certain unalienable rights that among these are life, liberty, and the pursuit of happiness…." Our Creator bestows these rights upon us. Thus, one cannot separate a righteous government from a government that acknowledges Divine Providence. The inspiration to establish a government free of the abuses of corrupt distorted religion was partly born out of a reaction to the tyrannical control of King George and the corrupt Church of England over the lives of English citizens. In the eighteenth century, individuals had to declare allegiance to the King and the Church of England. Freedom of religion was the linchpin upon which the United States of America emerged as a nation.

The United States was the first and only nation that placed the phrase, "In God We Trust," on its currency. Indeed, there can be no separation between church and state if church simply means belief in God or Divine Providence. In fact, our founding fathers understood that belief in God and the concept of "church" *are not the same*. The concept of "church" resonates with ideas of organized assemblies, man-made dogmas and doctrines, church hierarchies, sects or denominations, and theocratic rule over others. Individuals, who seek to erase *authentic* religion from everyday life, define church and belief in God as one and the same. Claiming to maintain separation of church and state, they attempt to create and muster *legal justification* to remove all phrases, symbols, and laws from our public systems that mirror belief in God and Divine law. In my opinion, no sane person would advocate such action. Yet, there are advocates of such actions within and outside of our legal system.

Characteristics of individuals who relentlessly attempt to escape from God (i.e., Theophobes) include anxieties, low self-esteem hidden by layers of pretense and feelings of superiority, and a *neurotic* pursuit of prestige and possession. Paradoxically, generalized insecurity is heavily promoted in the marketplace to all consumers. Well within their right to freedom of speech, advertisers constantly bombard consumers with messages that they need to purchase and consume something. Advertisers tell potential buyers that if they do not purchase certain items, services, and products, they will miss out on bargains of a lifetime, the products will enhance individuals' self-images and others will envy them, the products will set them apart from others, the products will make them happy, and so on. Some services and products are even given labels and names denoting social status, peace of mind, and an exaggerated sense of permanence and trustworthiness. Many people are primed to purchase their overall psychological security instead of secure it from honest efforts to heed Divine guidance.

A study cited in the journal, *Psychology and Marketing* showed that self-doubt and material excess are more prevalent among individuals who are primed to feel that society is normless and that values are arbitrary (i.e., relative). Authors Robert Arkin and L. Chang [73] said:

> ...those provoked to feel doubt about who they are or about the meaning of existence in society, will invest themselves more in things.... And, if they eventually acquire all those "things," will they find happiness? No...[74]

Many people who have chronic self-doubt and lack a sense of life's purpose find comfort in the belief that they can do and have whatever they desire. The absence of moral accountability coupled with the notion that all values are arbitrary enables them to consume without limit, have fun, and just live. Such persons do not like to be reminded that there is a Supreme Being or that life has a purpose beyond just living.

From the Quran:

We have committed to Hell multitudes of jinns and humans. They have minds with which they do not understand, eyes with which they do not see, and ears with which they do not hear. They are like animals; no, they are far worse—they are totally unaware. (7:179)

Do you think that most of them hear, or understand? They are just like animals; no, they are far worse. (25:44)[75]

The Pursuit of Happiness: A Quality of the Soul

"Life, liberty, and the pursuit of happiness" are rights identified in the Preamble of the U.S. Constitution, and echoed in other free societies. *Happiness is a quality of the soul.* Happy souls seek repose in spiritual truth. Happy souls are healthy souls that nurture productive minds. Societies that accommodated Hislamic practices but failed to counter overt and covert efforts to distort and suppress the true worship of God experienced a steady surge of mental and social problems among its members. In responding to the problems, solutions were sought and offered but none emphasized the necessity to regain spiritual balance and health. Some individuals recovered from their problems. But, the societies drifted into a morass of victims and victimizers. With an ever-growing number of unhappy individuals, productivity decreased while disdain for social order increased. Individuals became more gullible to dogmas and ideologies that promoted illusions of strength and recovery. Unhappy themselves, political figures argued about whose plans and programs could save the society. The rest of the story is history. History lesson: The lack of a correct spiritual anchor in a society leads to legions of perplexed unhappy souls. Life and liberty may be initially present in a society. But, in the absence of opportunities to attain true spiritual happiness, life becomes devoid of inner meaning. Liberty moves closer to licentiousness.

Regardless of the form it takes, Hislam prevents individuals from attaining true happiness and prevents societies from attaining prosperity and social harmony. Members of each community and society seem to have a collective soul. *A preponderance of unhappy unproductive souls and minds in any society is a threat to a society's security.*

From the Quran:

The people of the Gospel shall rule in accordance with God's revelations therein. Those who do not rule in accordance with God's revelations are the wicked. Then we revealed to you this scripture, truthfully, confirming previous scriptures, and superseding them. You shall rule among them in accordance with God's revelations, and do not follow their wishes if they differ from the truth that came to you. For each of you, we have decreed laws and different rites. Had God willed, He could have made you one congregation. But He thus puts you to the test through the revelations He has given each of you. You shall compete in righteousness. To God is your final destiny—all of you—then He will inform you of everything you had disputed. (5:47-48)

Your Lord never annihilates any community unjustly, while its people are righteous. (11:117)

Shifts (of angels) take turns, staying with each one of you - they are in front of you and behind you. They stay with you, and guard you in accordance with God's commands. Thus, God does not change the condition of any people unless they themselves make the decision to change. If God wills any hardship for any people, no force can stop it. For they have none beside Him as Lord and Master. (13:11)

God cites the example of a community that used to be secure and prosperous, with provisions coming to it from everywhere. But then, it turned unappreciative of God's blessings. Consequently, God caused them to taste the hardships of starvation and insecurity. Such is the requital for what they did. (16:112)[76]

Individuals lacking a properly oriented moral compass cannot contribute to the improvement of the *quality* of life in a society. Where Hislam flourishes and goes unchallenged, a gradual numbing of an archetypical awareness of spiritual truth occurs. Along the path, sincere seekers learn how Theophobes and individuals numbed by Hislam promote spiritually toxic beliefs and social behavior. The toxins discussed in this chapter include: misguided religionists attempts to spread distortions of religion, free doom, Theophobia, spiritual threats to national prosperity, Satanic Hands, homosexuality, adultery and premarital sex, abortion, gambling, consumption of intoxicants, academia's denial of authentic religion, denial of the special creation of human beings, the myth of human evolution, distortion of the principle of separation of Church and

State, and misinformation about the human pursuit of happiness. These concerns are even more critical to personal spiritual security. The issues are as important to our national security as having the ability to identify a physical enemy. The security of a community is no greater than the extent that community members heed God's commands.

Imagine a group of travelers walking on a trail wrought with fire hazards. The travelers are initially keen to the smell and presence of smoke. In time, individuals on the path toss aside the fire prevention plan and instructions they were given to put out fires. Some individuals distribute revised manuals that state that precautions to prevent fires are no longer necessary beyond a point that the party had already passed. Despite seeing scattered thin clouds of smoke billowing around them, the travelers proceed forward. A small group continues to review the original fire plan. Sensing danger, the vigilant travelers go in a direction away from the smoke. The travelers who remain on the route attempt to ready themselves by reading distorted manuals and making up rules as they go along. They purposely violate fire safety rules and convince each other that they are safe. Soon enough, tragedy strikes. The larger party gets caught and consumed in a downwind that blows fire and smoke directly in their path. The group that heeds the proven directions is not harmed.

This is not just a story or tale to be dismissed. The allegorical story reflects a reality that is repeated whenever a community ignores Divine guidance, embraces tenets of Hislam, and promotes Theophobic philosophies and behavior. Submitters in any society first seek spiritual peace and attempt to share the key to happiness with their fellows. Regardless of the actions of others, genuine seekers hold fast to the proven truth from God.

From the Quran:

Any community that believes will surely be rewarded for believing. For example, the people of Jonah: when they believed, we relieved the humiliating retribution they had been suffering in this world, and we made them prosperous. (10:98)

We never annihilated a believing community in the past. Are these people believers? (21:6)

Many a community rebelled against the commands of its Lord and against His messengers. Consequently, we held them strictly accountable, and requited them a terrible requital. (65:8)[77]

Notes

1. Khalifa, *Quran*, 6:116, 12:106, 19:73, and 103:1-3.

2. Ibid, 22:45 and 40:82-83.

3. The term, *Theophobe*, is not in the dictionary nor is it in psychiatric manuals delineating mental disorders. It is highly unlikely that many mental health professionals will adopt the term or one like it in the near future. Some of them have attempted to divest mental health of any references to God or authentic religion. Despite its insightful concepts, classical Freudian theory is, by design, a Theophobic theory of personality development.

4. Khalifa, *Quran*, Quran: The Final Testament, 2:6-7, 6:110, and 39:45.

5. Ibid, 43:78, 47:9, 28; 74:49-51, and 85:8.

6. Ibid, 8:73 and 23:71.

7. Ibid, 5:47-48, 22:41, and 38:26

8. Ibid, 17:16, 34:33, and 43:23.

9. Ibid, 40:33-35, 7:127, 8:54, 28:5, 4:97, and 60:5.

10. Ibid, 7:4, 98,165; 13:31, 16:45,112; 17:16, 22:45, 25:37, 28:58, 29:40, and 46:27.

11. Ibid, 11:52, 34:36, and 67:21.

12. Ibid, 11:117, 13:11, and 18:59.

13. The removal of any references to God in external social life 'mirrors' the removal of God-consciousness from mental life. One could easily conclude that individuals who steadfastly promote this world view have a pathological need to "erase" any hint of God from their 'reality.' They are truly deaf, dumb, and blind. (*Quran*: 2: 6-7)

14. Ron Branson, *Legal injustice/corrupt courts/bad judges*, <http://www.geocities.com/silentdestiny36/legalinjustice.html>

15. Khalifa, *Quran*, 7:80.

16. Teams of scientists were endeavoring to confirm accounts that the two ancient cities were destroyed by volcanoes. The scientists also discovered significant widespread meteorite deposits. A tape documentary about this scientific expedition, entitled "Ancient Apocalypse", is available from the Discovery Channel website, http://www.discoverychannel.com/. The documentary was presented on the Discovery Channel cable TV network.

17. "Did A Shower of Meteorites Destroy Sodom and Gomorrah,?" *The Jerusalem Report*, May 15, 1997.

[18] The Jerusalem Report, 12.

[19] Timo Niroma, *The late Third Millennium BC (2100-2400 BC): asteroid/ comet impacts, meteor showers, floods, drop of temperature, drying around the Mediterranean?* <http://personal.eunet.fi/pp/tilmari/tilmari2.htm#sodom>

[20] When you add the chapter and verse numbers of verses 8:32 and 11:82, the sum is a multiple of 19. 8 + 32 + 11 + 82 = 133 (19 x 7). When you combine the chapter number and the verse number for each of these verses to form two different numbers, this sum is a multiple of 19. 832 + 1,182 = 2,014 (19 x 106). The number of verses from 8:32 to 11: 82, including verse 11:82, is 361, a multiple of 19 (19 x 19). Verses 8:32 and 11:82 also contain a key word "shower" (hijaarat), proof that the devastation on Sodom and Gomorrah was a shower from the sky above (8:32) consisting of hard rocks (11:82). These specific multiples are Code-based proof that homosexuality is a sin and, if maintained, results in disastrous consequences. In modern times, the HIV-AIDS virus is one such consequence.

[21] Khalifa, *Quran*, 7:81, 8:32, 11:78-79, 82-83; and 57:4.

[22] The anchorman of the weekly cable news program, *Fox News Sunday*, presented this finding in their broadcast on May 30, 2004.

[23] Cnn, com. "Massachusetts court rules ban on gay marriage unconstitutional" http://www.cnn.com/2003/LAW/11/18/samesex.marriage.ruling/

[24] Verse 11:83 tells us that God designated the shower of rocks (meteorites) to strike transgressors. When you write the date that the marriages were performed (5-17-2004) as one number, and add the number 1,183 (verse 11:83), this sum is a multiple of 19. 5,172,004 + 1,183 = 5,173,187 (19 x 272,273). The integers in the court date sum to 19. 5 + 1+ 7 + 2 = 0 + 0 + 4 = 19. When you add 780 (verse 7:80), 242,004 (Massachusetts court ruling, 2-4-2004), and 1,182 (verse 11:82), the sum is 7,802,420,041,182 (19 x 410,653,686,378). These additional Code-based multiples coupled with cited *Quran* verses are further proof that homosexuality is a sin.

[25] Khalifa, *Quran*, 49:13, 51:49, and 92:3.

[26] John Colapinto, *As Nature Made Him: The Boy Who Was Raised As A Girl*, (Harper & Collins, 2000). For a summary of this true story, visit http://www.utexas.edu/courses/bio301d/Topics/Gay/BoyGirl.htm. There are numerous case studies similar to this one that disprove the notion that gender identity is primarily acquired through learning. An individual does not 'learn' to be a male or a female.

[27] Khalifa, *Quran*, Quran: The Final Testament, 7:135 and 4:48.

[28] Ibid, 5:5 and 25:68.

[29] Roy Maynard, World Magazine http://www.roevwade.org/court.html

[30] Ibid, 1.

[31] There are numerous Pro-Life websites that provide detailed facts about these two Supreme Court cases. One may wonder whether the Supreme Court Judges were aware of the disinformation forwarded by lawyers who claimed to represent the intentions of Ms. Cano and Ms. McCorvey. The lawyers obviously sought to secure legal sanction of abortions.

[32] Dr. Nathanson's admission that he knowingly gave false information to generate greater favor for legal abortions has been cited in numerous articles and books. This citation can be found on the following website: <http:/roevwade.org/illegalmyths.htlm>.

[33] The "Born Alive Infant Protection Act." that outlaws this barbaric immoral so-called "medical procedure" became the 'law of the land' in August 2002. The ban against partial birth abortions is being contested, and is scheduled to be revisited by the Supreme Court.

[34] Elenor Schoen, *"Abortion-Breast Cancer Link Must Not be Ignored,"* In Seattle Post-Intelligencer, (October 26, 2002), http://seattlepi.nwsource.com/opinion/92913_soapbox26.shtml>

[35] Ibid,1.

[36] Douglass Kennedy, Ph.D., *"Lies and more Lies."* Television lecture-presentation, Phoenix, Az., 18 January 2004. Dr. Kennedy presented information about the British Academy of Royal Medical Colleges studies on the abortion-cancer link. He also repeated the health statistic that ABC is epidemic among women in the United States.

[37] Schoen, *Abortion-Breast Cancer*, 1.

[38] Association of American Physicians and Surgeons, Inc., "Politics Trumps Science in Abortion B Breast Cancer Link," In *Medical Journal: Political Correctness Prevents Women From Learning About Abortion Risks*, Washington, D.C., 14 August 2003.

[39] Khalifa, *Quran*, 6:123, 10:21, and 35:43.

[40] Ibid, 2:228, 13:8, and 17:31.

[41] Ibid, 2:219, 4:43 (partial), and 5:90.

[42] Kevin Harris, *Collected Quotes from Albert Einstein*, <http:// rescomp.stanford.edu/~cheshire/EinsteinQuotes.html> (19 August 2003).

[43] Khalifa, *Quran*, Quran: The Final Testament, 22:8, 31:20, 40:83, and 75:5.

44 Paul Scagnelli, Ph.D., *Deadly Dr. Freud*, (Durham, N.C.: Pinewood Publishing Company, 1994).

45 Ibid, 495.

46 I. L. Cohen, *Darwin Was Wrong—A Study in Probabilities*, (Greenvale, N.Y.: New Research Publications, Inc., 1984).

47 Ibid, 209.

48 Michael Denton, *Evolution: a theory in crisis*. (Adler & Adler Publishers, 1997)

49 Ibid, 250.

50 Ibid, 264 and 338.

51 John Reader, "Whatever Happened to Zinjanthropus?" *New Scientist*, March 26, 1981.

52 Ibid, 802-805.

53 Wolfgang Smith, *Teilardism and the New Religion* (Tan Books and Publishers, Inc., 1988).

54 Ibid, 8.

55 William R. Fix, *The Bone Peddlers* (New York: Macmillan, 1984)

56 Ibid, 150.

57 *"Creation: why thinking people are increasingly rejecting evolution on scientific grounds,"* <http://perspectives.freeservers.com/creation.html> (18 August 2003).

58 Ted Byfield, *"Another Jolt For Evolution Theory,"* Posted on Science Prabhupada Hare Khrisna News Network, <http://science.krishna.org/Articles/2000/10/00169.html,> (20 August 2003).

59 Ibid, 1.

60 *"Ancient animal could be human-ape ancestor."* In on-line edition of U.S.A. Today, <http://www.usatoday.com/news/science/2004-11-19-human-ancestor_x.htm > (19 November 2004)

61 John G. West Jr., "Darwin in the Classroom," *In the National Review*, (December 17, 2002). (20 August 2003). John G. West, Jr., Darwin in the Classroom," *In the National Review Online*, (December 17, 2002), <http://www.discovery.org/scripts/viewDB> (20 August 2003).

62 Absolute Truth Ministries, *Evidence that the Media is Distorting the Facts to Keep You in the Dark*, <http://www.absolutetruth.net/id/page4.html> (20 August 2003).

[63] *Myth of Evolution.*, <http://biserica.org/Publicatii/1992/NoI/ XXV_index.html> (8 August 2003).

[64] Ibid, 1, 2.

[65] Ibid, 3.

[66] Ibid, 3.

[67] Ibid, 3.

[68] Luther D. Sunderland, *Darwin's Enigma: Fossils and Other Problems*, (San Diego: Master Books, 4th edition, 1988).

[69] Ibid, 9.

[70] Khalifa, *Quran*, 15:26, 28-29; 20:117-123, 23:12, 38:7, and 55:3.

[71] Eric Fromm, *The Art of Loving*, (New York: Harper & Row Publishers, 1956).

[72] Ibid, 104-105.

[73] R. Arkin and L. Chang, Materialism as an attempt to cope with uncertainty, *Journal of Psychology and Marketing*, 2002, Volume 19, number 5.

[74] Ibid.

[75] Khalifa, *Quran*, 7:179 and 25:44.

[76] Ibid, 5:47-48, 11:117, 13:11, and 16:112.

[77] Ibid, 10:98, 21:6, and 65:8.

Eight

A Conclusion Begins

By God's Grace, in 1972, my sojourn on the path through Hislam via distorted corrupt Christianity and corrupt Islam ended, and my *conscientious* turn towards true Submission began. *True Submission is the Islam described in all authentic scriptures.* With every conclusion, there is a beginning. Graduations from school are called commencements rather than conclusions for a reason. *Learning the proven truth about submission to God alone signals the greatest commencement or beginning in life.*

After any major disaster, debris is removed, and paths are cleared so rebuilding can begin. When in Paradise, our first parents succumbed to Satan's suggestion that they should doubt God's command to them. So did the rest of us. We were in the genes of our first parents. Like those who have walked this life's path before us, we are given an opportunity to reaffirm our submission to our Lord alone. One of the greatest disasters in this life is the emergence of Hislam. Some of us eventually learn the right lessons from this disaster. Some of us willingly contribute to the disaster. Do not listen to external and internal voices that tell you that you are lost, hopeless, or forsaken by God. Now is the time to ask yourself whether you are learning the right lessons, or whether you want to be a willing contributor to this disaster.

Proof eclipses faith alone. Once proofs are brought forward, faith in the sincere evolves into certainty according to God's Plan. With the unveiling of religious truth via the unassailable Miraculous Mathematical Code, accumulated debris spread by Hislam is being removed from the path. Nevertheless, Satanic Hands shall continue to scatter debris disguised as appealing, satisfying, and spiritually uplifting messages along the path. Defenders of Hislam are expressing their free-will decision to oppose God's guidance and corrupt the meaning of the worship of

God. However, it is far more difficult for them to present "fake flowers" as real roses to sincere seekers.

With the discovery of the miraculous Mathematical Code, God's message to humanity has been restored to its pristine purity and world religious leaders are warned to discard false teachings and practices. The Messenger of the Covenant also confirmed existing scriptures and consolidated existing scriptures into the one Divine message to worship God alone. *The conclusion of the Messenger of the Covenant's mission has ushered in the end of Hislam.* Sincere seekers are found in the remotest huts, hamlets, and the largest cities in the world. As has always been the case, sincere seekers need only return to the right path by worshipping God alone. This law of God will never change.

From the Quran:

Absolutely, God's allies have nothing to fear, nor will they grieve. They are those who believe and lead a righteous life. For them, joy and happiness in this world, as well as in the Hereafter. This is God's unchangeable law. Such is the greatest triumph. (10:62-64)

False claimants will continue to declare that they are on the right path and write their own rules and travelers manuals.

From the Quran:

Your Lord is fully aware of those who stray off His path, and He is fully aware of those who are guided. (6:117)

God points out the paths, including the wrong ones. If He willed, He could have guided all of you. (16:9)[1]

For some people, the journey to God seems to be a haunting confusing task, if not a futile one. Regardless of a sincere seeker's traditional religion or lack of religion, no force on earth can prevent the person from being guided to God's truth. Conversely, no force on earth can guide anyone who steadfastly rejects God's proofs. Guidance is solely in God's control.

If a person wants to be one of the best surgeons, the person must study hard in medical school and learn the most up-to-date information about the human body, human biology, medicine, and surgical procedures. If a person wants the best knowledge and guidance to advance spiritually, the person should avail him or herself of intuitive and written guidance that God has revealed to humans. Echoes of divine guidance permeate the writings of all guided thinkers. Signs of the Supreme Architect are in us and around us. Our job is to seek and heed The Architect's guidance.

From the Quran:

Say, "Everyone works in accordance with his belief, and your Lord knows best which ones are guided in the right path." (17:84)

The return to the right path is seldom a straight line. It is straight in the sense that it is in the right direction. All of us tread on some dead ends and sharp curves during our life journeys. Only God knows each person's innermost decision to return or not return to the path of Submission. Despite a person's mistakes, failings, and misdeeds, a repentant sincere person is guided by God to the true path. In God's system, no one is forced to tread on a spiritual path to his or her disliking. A sincere seeker does not knowingly befriend someone who disbelieves in God and persists in remaining on dead-end paths. In their personal lives, sincere seekers associate with fellow seekers and submitters, regardless of faith.

From the Quran:

The believers never ally themselves with the disbelievers, instead of the believers. Whoever does this is exiled from God. Exempted are those who are forced to do this to avoid persecution. God alerts you that you shall reverence Him alone. To God is the ultimate destiny. (3:28)

You shall force yourself to be with those who worship their Lord day and night, seeking Him alone. Do not turn your eyes away from them, seeking the vanities of this world. Nor shall you obey one whose heart we rendered oblivious to our message; one who pursues his own desires, and whose priorities are confused. (18:28)[2]

A person's country, community of origin, wealth, education, intellect, possessions, family size, social status, profession, popularity, reputation, work ethic, social conscientiousness, religious affiliation, and sense of personal piety have no exchange value and are not substitutes for wholeheartedly embracing and heeding God's guidance.

After reading this book, some people may feel stunned, angry, afraid, confused, hopeless, empty, and even doomed. To some extent, I have experienced fear, confusion, and even anger from time to time, when additional facts about the distortion of the true worship of God would trickle into my awareness. As the facts became clearer, I once exclaimed, "What in the world is going on!...It seems like everything that I thought was solid truth about the worship of God is a lie!" Unlike me, some of you may be becoming aware of *all* these distortions *all at once for the first time*. Have no fear. Once a person stands upright along this journey and starts to look at Hislam for what it is, the person either falls prostrate (metaphorically) and glorifies God for being guided to the right path or falls apart (regardless of a person's self-confidence) by denying the truth about Hislam. As I previously said, I fell prostrate to God when I came to terms with distortions of Christianity and later came to terms with distortions in Islam. After the initial shock waves, I experienced hope and relief. The light of hope and relief is more than a flicker. The light produces an overwhelming sense of inner peace and connection to the Divine.

From the Quran:

Those who proclaim: "Our Lord is God," then lead a righteous life, the angels descend upon them: "You shall have no fear, nor shall you grieve. Rejoice in the good news that Paradise has been reserved for you. (41:30)[3]

Do not let initial uncomfortable thoughts and feelings about *proven* truth seduce you into remaining on the vast spiritual obstacle course. Satan and his "travel guides" attempt to heighten any fears a person has about disconnecting from Hislam. They are in the business of sabotaging souls. With the advent of proven truth, Hislam's heyday on the path is coming to an end, and *the Hislamists know it*. Their agenda has been focused on you not knowing about Hislam. God guides each person exactly onto a spiritual path that the person seeks. Not me, you, or anyone else can change or guide another soul.

From the Quran:

We passed the scripture from generation to generation, and we allowed whomever we chose from among our servants to receive it. Subsequently, some of them wronged their souls, others upheld it only part of the time, while others were eager to work righteousness in accordance with God's will; this is the greatest triumph.(35:32)

Successful indeed is the one who redeems his soul. (87:14)[4]

To be sure, irate readers who do not believe in God or think that there are no guidelines from God will distort material in this book. This reaction always occurs when Hislam is exposed to the light. Once taken out of context and distorted, the material becomes fuel used to inflame misguided passions of individuals who blindly practice Hislam. What you do with the information in this book is not for me to know. If I fail to share what I have come to know about the worship of God alone, I will have to answer for it. God is Most Gracious and Most Merciful. God alone forgives the sins of a sincere repentant. There is only one sin that is unforgivable if maintained until one's death. The sin is idolatry, any departure from the worship of God alone. This is God's system. As clarified in *proven* scriptures, the worship of God is indivisible. The worship is rendered to the one absolute God Who has no equals or entities that share in His Being.

From the Quran:

Say, "We believe in God, and in what was sent down to us, and in what was sent down to Abraham, Ismail, Isaac, Jacob, and the Patriarchs; and in what was given to Moses and Jesus, and all the prophets from their Lord. We make no distinction among any of them. To Him alone we are submitters." If they believe as you do, then they are guided. But if they turn away, then they are in opposition. God will spare you their opposition; He is the Hearer, the Omniscient. Such is God's system, and whose system is better than God's? "Him alone we worship." (2: 136-138)

If they fall in sin or wrong their souls, they remember God and ask forgiveness for their sins - and who forgives the sins except God - and they do not persist in sins, knowingly. (3:135)

God does not forgive idolatry, but He forgives lesser offenses for whomever He wills. Anyone who sets up idols beside God has forged a horrendous offense. (4:48)[5]

Submission to God Alone: A Lifelong Opportunity

An individual can make a commitment to submit to God alone at anytime and any place. God is the Supreme Witness, and hears and knows all things. *No one is spiritually doomed who sincerely searches for the most important answers to our spiritual purpose in this life.* When appropriate and, if necessary, make your voice heard in order to strengthen and grow your soul. The Truth about the worship of God is not confined to the Quran. Submitters have lived in this world before the revelation of the Quran and many living today have not heard of the Quran. Because it is proven to be fully intact and the final Divine revelation to humanity, the Quran is my scriptural traveler's manual on this life path. The Quran is my reference to determine the soundness of what I read in other scriptures. It is my ultimate gauge to evaluate any philosophy of life and any proposed principles of healthy psychological development. Anyone who sincerely wants the right answers, God will guide the person to the Truth, in whatever form, according to His Plan for the person.

From the Quran:

God never burdens a soul beyond its means: to its credit is what it earns, and against it is what it commits. "Our Lord do not condemn us if we forget or make mistakes. Our Lord, and protect us from blaspheming against You, like those before us have done. Our Lord, protect us from sinning until it becomes too late for us to repent. Pardon us and forgive us. You are our Lord and Master. Grant us victory over the disbelieving people."(2:286) [6]

Like other authentic prayers for Divine guidance, the first chapter of the Quran, *Al-Fatihah – The Key*, lays out the journey away from Hislam to submission to God alone.

> *In the name of God, Most Gracious, Most MercifuL*
>
> *Praise be to God, Lord of the universe.*
>
> *Most Gracious, Most Merciful.*
>
> *Master of the Day of Judgment.*
>
> **You alone we worship. You alone we ask for help.**
>
> **Guide us in the right path; the path of those whom You blessed;**
>
> *Not of those who have deserved wrath, nor of the strayers. (1:1-7)*

You may wonder to yourself, "What's next for me?" It may be reflection, introspection, contemplation, and correction in the light of *proven* truth. It may not be any of this. If your intention is to pursue the right path,

Pray to God alone for divine guidance.

Observe your thoughts and beliefs including any resistance to Submission.

Consider every step you take away from Hislam as not only possible but your chosen destiny.

Continue to cultivate your spiritual yearning to please God alone.

No one on earth can grow your soul for you. That is your mandate in this world, a Divine mandate to tread the right path and grow your soul to the best of your ability. The sojourner described in the beginning of this book kept reading the traveler's manual, followed God's guidance, and severed connections with Hislam. The sojourner regained true sanity; no more doubts about the purpose of life, no more existential fears and anxieties, no more lying to him or herself, no more fleeting attempts to find happiness. *Happiness is submission to God alone.*[7] With a spiritual yearning replenished with revealed Proof, the sojourner returned to the right path that we started out on. This is God's promise to sincere spiritual seekers of every era, religion, ethnicity, and creed.

Excerpts from the mathematically coded Traveler's Manual:

*"God is my Lord and your Lord; you shall worship Him alone. This is the **right path**." (3:51)*

*He initiated you from one person, and **decided your path**, as well as your final destiny. We thus clarify the revelations for people who understand. (6:98)*

This is My path - a straight one. You shall follow it, and do not follow any other paths, lest they divert you from His path. *These are His commandments to you, that you may be saved. (6:153)*

Say, "My Lord has guided me *in a straight path* - *the perfect religion of Abraham, monotheism. He never was an idol worshiper." (6:161)*

*God invites to the abode of peace, and guides whomever He wills in **a straight path**. (10:25)*

*Therefore, **continue on the path you have been enjoined to follow**, together with those who repented with you, and do not transgress. He is Seer of everything you do. (11:112)*

***God points out the paths, including the wrong ones**. If He willed, He could have guided all of you. (16:9)*

Say, "Everyone works in accordance with his belief, and ***your Lord knows best which ones are guided in the right path**."* (17:84)

*They have been guided to the good words; **they have been guided in the path of the Most Praised**. (22:24)*

Those who are blessed with knowledge will recognize the truth from your Lord, and then believe in it, and their hearts will readily accept it. Most assuredly, **God guides the believers in the right path.** (22:54)

*As for those who strive in our cause, **we will surely guide them in our paths**. Most assuredly, God is with the pious. (29:69)*

*And follow the **best path that is pointed out for you by your Lord**, before the retribution overtakes you suddenly when you least expect it. (39:55)*

This is a reminder; whoever wills, let him choose **the path to his Lord**. (73:19)

*We created the human from a liquid mixture, from two parents, in order to test him. Thus, we made him a hearer and a seer. **We showed him the two paths**, then, he is either appreciative, or unappreciative. (76:2-3)*[8]

A Conclusion Begins

Notes

1. Khalifa, *Quran*, 0:62-64; 6:117, and 16:9.
2. Ibid, 17:84, 3:28, and 18:28.
3. Ibid, 41:30.
4. Ibid, 35:32 and 87:14.
5. Ibid, 2:136-138; 3:129, 135 and 4:48.
6. Ibid, 2:286.
7. The highest yearning in *healthy* human beings is the yearning to be connected to the Divine, be happy, content, and at peace. This state of being is called Islam in the Arabic language. Undoubtedly, similar words are found to describe this state in all languages.
8. Khalifa, *Quran*, 3:51, 6:98, 153. 161; 10:25, 11:112, 16:9, 17:84, 22:24, 54; 39:55, 73:19, and 76: 2-3.

Appendix

These appendices and appendix excerpts are from the Authorized English Translation of the Quran written by Dr. Rashad Khalifa. This material is reprinted with permission of the family of Dr. Khalifa.

In the name of God, Most Gracious, Most Merciful

The following is excepted from QURAN: The Final Testament, Dr. Khalifa's Authorized English Translation of the Quran, Appendix 1 [Simple facts only]

"One of the Great Miracles" [74:35]

The Quran is characterized by a unique phenomenon never found in any human authored book. Every element of the Quran is mathematically composed - the suras, the verses, the words, the number of certain letters, the number of words from the same root, the number and variety of divine names, the unique spelling of certain words, the absence or deliberate alteration of certain letters within certain words, and many other elements of the Quran besides its content. There are two major facets of the Quran's mathematical system: (1) The mathematical literary composition, and (2) The mathematical structure involving the numbers of suras and verses. Because of this comprehensive mathematical coding, the slightest distortion of the Quran's text or physical arrangement is immediately exposed.

<u>SIMPLE TO UNDERSTAND AND IMPOSSIBLE TO IMITATE</u>

For the first time in history we have a scripture with built-in proof of divine authorship - a superhuman mathematical composition.

Any reader of this book can easily verify the Quran's mathematical miracle. The word "God" (Allah) is written in bold capital letters

Appendix

throughout the text. The cumulative frequency of occurrence of the word "God" is noted at the bottom of each page in the left hand corner. The number in the right hand corner is the cumulative total of the numbers for verses containing the word "God." The last page of the text, Page 372, shows that the total occurrence of the word "God" is 2698, or 19x142. The total sum of verse numbers for all verses containing the word "God" is 118123, also a multiple of 19 (118123 = 19x6217).

Nineteen is the common denominator throughout the Quran's mathematical system.

This phenomenon alone suffices as incontrovertible proof that the Quran is God's message to the world. No human being(s) could have kept track of 2698 occurrences of the word "God," and the numbers of verses where they occur. This is especially impossible in view of (1) the age of ignorance during which the Quran was revealed, and (2) the fact that the suras and verses were widely separated in time and place of revelation. The chronological order of revelation was vastly different from the final format (Appendix 23). However, the Quran's mathematical system is not limited to the word "God;" it is extremely vast, extremely intricate, and totally comprehensive.

THE SIMPLE FACTS

Like the Quran itself, the Quran's mathematical coding ranges from the very simple, to the very complex. The Simple Facts are those observations that can be ascertained without using any tools. The complex facts require the assistance of a calculator or a computer. The following facts do not require any tools to be verified, but please remember they all refer to the original Arabic text:

1. The first verse (1:1), known as "Basmalah," consists of 19 letters.
2. The Quran consists of 114 suras, which is ....19 x 6.

3. The total number of verses in the Quran is 6346, or ....19 x 334. [6234 numbered verses & 112 un-numbered verses (Basmalahs) 6234+112 = 6346] Note that 6+3+4+6 =.......19.
4. The Basmalah occurs 114 times, despite its conspicuous absence from Sura 9 (it occurs twice in Sura 27) & 114= 19x6.
5. From the missing Basmalah of Sura 9 to the extra Basmalah of Sura 27, there are precisely ....19 suras.
6. It follows that the total of the sura numbers from 9 to 27 (9+10+11+12+...+26+27) is 342, or ....19 x 18.
7. This total (342) also equals the number of words between the two Basmalahs of Sura 27, and 342 = ...19 x 18.
8. The famous first revelation (96:1-5) consists of ....19 words.
9. This 19-worded first revelation consists of 76 letters .19 x 4.
10. Sura 96, first in the chronological sequence, consists of ....19 verses.
11. This first chronological sura is placed atop the last..19 suras.
12. Sura 96 consists of 304 Arabic letters, and 304 equals .19 x 16.
13. The last revelation (Sura 110) consists of ....19 words.
14. The first verse of the last revelation (110:1) consists of ....19 letters.
15. 14 different Arabic letters, form 14 different sets of "Quranic Initials" (such as A.L.M. of 2:1), and prefix 29 suras. These numbers add up to 14+14+29 = 57 = ...19 x 3.
16. The total of the 29 sura numbers where the Quranic Initials occur is 2+3+7+...+50+68 = 822, and 822+14 (14 sets of initials) equals 836, or .... 19 x 44.
17. Between the first initialed sura (Sura 2) and the last initialed sura (Sura 68) there are 38 un-initialed suras 19 x 2.
18. Between the first and last initialed sura there are ....19 sets of alternating "initialed" and "un-initialed" suras.
19. The Quran mentions 30 different numbers: 1, 2, 3, 4, 5, 6, 7, 8, 9, 10, 11, 12, 19, 20, 30, 40, 50, 60, 70, 80, 99, 100, 200, 300, 1000, 2000, 3000, 5000, 50,000, & 100,000. The sum of these numbers is 162,146; which equals 19x8534.

Appendix

This is a condensed summary of the Simple Facts.

The following is Appendix 7 from QURAN: The Final Testament, Dr. Khalifa's Authorized English Translation of the Quran

Why Were We Created?

We are in this world because we committed a horrendous crime, and this life is our chance to redeem ourselves, denounce our crime, and rejoin God's kingdom.

It all began a few billion years ago when "a feud arose in the Heavenly Society" (38:69). One of the high-ranking creatures, Satan, entertained supercilious thoughts that his God-given powers qualified him to be a god besides God. He thus challenged God's absolute authority. Not only was Satan's idea blasphemous, it was wrong - only God, and no one else, possesses the qualifications and ability to be a god. Consequent to Satan's blasphemy, a division occurred in the Heavenly Society, and all constituents of God's kingdom became classified into four categories:

1. **Angels:** Creatures who upheld God's absolute authority.
2. **Animals**: Creatures who rebelled but then accepted God's invitation to repent.
3. **Jinns**: Creatures who agreed with Satan; that he is capable of being a "god."
4. **Humans**: Creatures who did not make up their minds; they failed to make a firm stand with God's absolute authority.

The Most Merciful

The angels expected God to banish the creatures who did not uphold His absolute authority (2:30). But God is Most Merciful; He decided to give us a chance to denounce our mistake, and informed the angels that He knew what they did not know (2:30). God knew that some creatures deserved a chance to be redeemed.

If you claim the ability to fly a plane, the best way to test your claim is to give you a plane and ask you to fly it. This is precisely what God decided to do in response to Satan's claim. God created seven vast universes, then informed the angels that He was appointing Satan as a god on the tiny mote called "Earth" (2:30). The Quranic accounts related to appointing Satan as a temporary "god" (36:60) confirm the previous scripture.

God's plan called for creating death (67:1-2), then bringing the humans and jinns into this world. Thus, they start over without any biases, and exercise full freedom to uphold God's absolute authority or Satan's polytheistic theory. To make this crucial decision, every human being receives a message from God advocating His absolute authority, as well as a message from Satan pushing his polytheistic principles.

To give us a head start, the Most Merciful gathered all the human beings before Him, prior to sending us to this world, and we bore witness that He alone is our Lord and Master (7:172). Thus, upholding God's absolute authority is a natural instinct that is an integral part of every human being.

After putting the rebels to death, the souls of humans and jinns were placed in a special depository. God then created the appropriate bodies to house the souls of jinns and humans during the test period. The first jinn body was made from fire, and Satan was assigned to that body (15:27). The first human body was created from earthly material, clay (15:26), and God assigned the first human soul to that body. The divine plan called for the angels to serve the humans on earth - guard them, drive the wind and rain for them, distribute provisions, etc. This fact is stated in the Quran allegorically: "Your Lord said to the angels, `Fall prostrate before Adam.'" Satan of course refused to have anything to do with serving the human race (2:34, 7:11, 17:61, 18:50, and 20:116).

> You, Lucifer, said in your heart: "I will scale the heavens. I will set up my throne. Above the stars of God. I will take my seat. on the Mount of Congregation, in the recesses of the North. I will ascend above the tops of the clouds; I will be like the Most High!" [Isaiah 14:13-15]
>
> The devil then took Jesus up a very high mountain and displayed before him all the kingdoms of the world in their magnificence, promising: "All these will I bestow on you if you prostrate yourself in homage before me." At this, Jesus said to him, "Away with you, Satan! Scripture has it: You shall worship the Lord your God; Him ALONE shall you adore.'" [Matthew 4:8-10] & [Luke 4:5-8]

While Adam's body remained on earth, the real person, the soul, was admitted into Heaven in the outermost universe. God gave Adam certain commandments, represented by the forbidden tree, and Satan was appointed as Adam's companion to deliver to Adam his satanic message. The rest is history.

Every time a human being is born, a human person is assigned to the new baby from the depository of souls. God assigns the souls in accordance with His knowledge (28:68). Every soul deserves to be assigned to a certain body, and live under certain circumstances. God alone knows which souls are good and which souls are evil. Our children are assigned to our homes in accordance with God's plan.

An independent jinn soul is also assigned to the new human being to represent Satan's point of view. While the physical body of any jinn is reproduced from the parent jinns, the jinn soul is that of an independent individual. Jinns are descendants of Satan (7:27, 18:50). The assigned jinn remains with the human being from birth to death, and serves as the main witness on the Day of Judgment (50:23). A continuous debate takes place in our heads between the human soul and the jinn soul until both of them are convinced of one point of view.

The Original Sin

Contrary to common belief, the "Original Sin" was not Adam's violation of God's law when he ate from the forbidden tree. The original sin was our failure to uphold God's absolute authority during the Great Feud. If the human person convinces his or her jinn companion to denounce that original sin, and uphold God's absolute authority, both creatures are redeemed to God's eternal kingdom on the Day of Judgment. But if the jinn companion convinces the human being to uphold Satan's idolatrous views, then both creatures are exiled forever from God's kingdom.

To promote his point of view, Satan and his representatives advocate the idolization of such powerless creatures as Muhammad, Jesus, Mary, and the saints. Since we are here due to our polytheistic tendencies, most of us are easy prey for Satan.

Satan's incompetence as a "god" has already been proven by the prevalence of chaos, disease, accidents, misery, and war throughout his dominion (36:66).

On the other hand, the human beings who denounce Satan, uphold God's absolute authority, and refrain from idolizing powerless and dead creatures like Jesus and Muhammad, are restored to God's protection - they enjoy a perfect life here in this world and forever.

Because our life in this world is a series of tests designed to expose our polytheistic ideas, idol worship is the only unforgivable offense (4:48, 116).

The world is divinely designed to manifest our decision to uphold either God's absolute authority, or Satan's idolatrous views (67:1-2). The day and the night change constantly to test our willingness to uphold God's laws by observing the Dawn Prayer and fasting during the hottest and longest days. Only those who are totally certain about God's absolute authority are redeemed (26:89).

Appendix

The following is excepted from QURAN: The Final Testament, Dr. Khalifa's Authorized English Translation of the Quran, Appendix 1 [Simple facts only]

WHY 19!!

As pointed out later in this Appendix, all God's scriptures, not only the Quran, were mathematically coded with the number "19." Even the universe at large bears this divine mark. The number 19 can be looked upon as

Alphabet Letters		
Hebrew	**Arabic**	**Letter Value**
V	W	6
A	A	1
H	H	8
D	D	4

the Almighty Creator's signature on everything He created (see Appendix 38). The number "19" possesses unique mathematical properties beyond the scope of this Appendix. For example:

[1] It is a prime number [divisible only by itself and the number 1].

[2] It encompasses the first numeral (1) and the last numeral (9), as if to proclaim God's attribute in 57:3 as the "Alpha and the Omega."

[3] It [numerals] looks the same in all languages of the world. Both components, 1 and 9, are the only numerals that look the same in all languages.

[4] It possesses many peculiar mathematical properties. For example, 19 is the sum of the first powers of 9 and 10, and the difference between the second powers of 9 and 10. We now understand that the

> The Lord our God is One!
> Therefore, you shall worship the Lord your God
> with all your heart,
> and all your soul,
> and all your mind, and with all your strength.
>
> (Deuteronomy 6:4-5; Mark 12:29; Quran 12:163, 17:22-23)

universal coding of God's creations with the number 19 rests in the fact that it is the gematrical value of the word "ONE" in all the scriptural languages- Aramaic, Hebrew, and Arabic. [See "Alphabet Letters" table] The number 19, therefore, proclaims the First Commandment in all the scriptures: that there is only ONE God.

As shown in Table 7 [table 7 omitted in this excerpt from Appendix 1], the Aramaic, Hebrew, and Arabic alphabets used to double as numerals in accordance with a universally established system. The Hebrew word for "ONE" is "VAHD" (pronounced V-AHAD). In Arabic, the word for "ONE" is "WAHD" (pronounced WAAHED).

The Word "Quran"

The [specific] word "Quran" occurs in the Quran 58 times, with one of them in 10:15, referring to "another Quran." This particular occurrence, therefore, must be excluded. Thus, the frequency of occurrence of this "Quran" in the Quran is 57, or 19 x 3.

Two other grammatical forms of the word "Quran" occur in 12 verses. These include the word "Quranun" and the word "Quranahu." One of these occurrences, in 13:31 refers to "another Quran" that cause the mountains to crumble. Another occurrence, in 41:44, refers to "a non-Arabic Quran." These two occurrences, therefore, are excluded.

[This excerpt from Appendix 1 does not include the list of chapters and verses where the word "Quran," occurs with in all of its grammatical forms. The list is in the original Appendix 1]

The following is Appendix 38 from QURAN: The Final Testament, Dr. Khalifa's Authorized English Translation of the Quran

19: The Creator's Signature

The scriptures are not the only mathematically composed creations of GOD where the number 19 is a common denominator. It is profound

Appendix

indeed that Galilee made his famous statement : "Mathematics is the language with which God created the universe." A plethora of scientific findings have now shown that the number 19 represents GOD's Signature upon certain creations. This divine stamp appears throughout the universe in much the same manner as the signature of Michelangelo and Picasso identify their works. for example:

1. The sun, the moon, and earth become aligned in the same relative positions once every 19 years (see ENCYCLOPAEDIA JUDAICA under "calendar")

2. Haley's comet, a profound heavenly phenomenon, visits our solar system every 76 years, 19x4.

3. GOD's Stamp on you and me is manifested in the fact that the human body contains 209 bones, 19x11

4. LANGMAN' S MEDICAL EMBRYOLOGY, by T.W. Sadler, is used as a text book in most of the Medical Schools in the U.S.A. On page 88 of the Fifth edition, we read the following statement: "In general the length of pregnancy for the full term fetus is considered to be 280 days or 40 weeks after onset of the last menstruation, or more accurately, 266 days or 38 weeks after fertilization. " The numbers 266 and 38 are both multiples of 19.

The following is excerpted from Appendix 2 from QURAN: The Final Testament, Dr. Khalifa's Authorized English Translation of the Quran

How to Distinguish God's Messenger from a Fake Messenger

The Quran provides straightforward criteria to distinguish the true messengers of God Thus, the truthfulness of God's messenger invariably prevails, while the falsehood of a fake messenger invariably, sooner or later, is exposed.

[1] God's messenger advocates the worship of God ALONE, and the abolition of all forms of idol worship.

[2] God's messenger never asks for a wage for himself.

[3] God's messenger is given divine, incontrovertible proof of his messengership. Anyone who claims to be God's messenger and does not meet the three minimum criteria listed above is a false claimant.

> The most important difference between God's messenger and a fake messenger is that God's messenger is supported by God, while the fake messenger is not:
>
> * God's messenger is supported by God's invisible soldiers (3:124-126, 9:26 & 40, 33:9, 37:171-173, 48:4 & 7, 74:31).
>
> * God's messenger is supported by God's treasury (63:7-8).
>
> * God's messenger, as well as the believers, are guaranteed victory and dignity, in this world and forever (40:51 & 58:21).

Index

A
Aaron 34
Abortion 177, 178, 182, 187, 188, 189, 190, 191, 208, 213
Abortion Breast Cancer syndrome 190
Abortion is Murder 187-193
Abraham 27, 28, 29, 30, 104, 152
Adam and Eve 10, 138
Adler, Alfred 45, 46, 53
Adultery 186, 187, 208
AIDS 129, 186, 212
Alcoholism 193
Alfandari, Mordeci 66, 100
Al-Fatihah 112, 113, 223
American Civil Liberties Union 181, 187
American Psychiatric Association 181
American Psychological Association 181
American Society of Breast Surgeons 191
Amora' im Rabbis 42
Amsel, Avrohom 47, 62
Antichrist 68, 100
Anti-Semitism 33, 34
Ape-man evolution myth 197, 198
Arabic language 110, 226
Arabic names adopted 104, 106
Arabism, worship of Arab culture 111
Archaeological Institute of America 196
Arkin, Robert 206, 215

Association of American Physicians and Surgeons 190, 213
Authority 7, 30, 50, 55, 87, 140, 181

B
Baha'I 136, 139, 145, 147
Baha'ullah 145
Bakan, David 49, 51, 53, 62, 63
Basmalah 123, 230, 231
BBC World Service 140, 141, 142, 147
Bernfield, Susan 53
Bible 6, 20, 29, 55, 69, 71-78, 80, 83, 88, 93, 97, 100-103, 114, 133, 150
Bible Codes 73-78, 100-101
Biechler, James E 157, 159
Big Bang Law 46
Birthday celebrations 82
Blood of Christ 86
Born Alive Infant Protection Act 188, 213
Breast cancer 189-191, 213
Breur, Josef 45
British Academy of Royal Medical Colleges 190, 213
Brunton, Paul 48, 62
Buddhism 96, 136, 139-114
Byfield, Ted 198, 214

C
Cancer 122, 134, 189-191, 198
Cano, Sandra 187, 213
Canon Law Society of America 157
Carlson, Royce 84, 101

Case law 55, 178, 182
Catholic 65-66, 71, 75, 79, 86, 93-94, 96, 155, 157-158
Celibacy 154-159
Chang, L. 206, 215
Christ 33, 37
Christ, meaning of 70
Christian 73-75, 8-83, 85-88, 96-97, 101, 103, 110, 119, 148, 156-157
Christian Muslim, See Christian submitter 98-99
Christianity iii, v, vi, 11, 13, 17, 31, 36, 44, 55, 65-67, 71, 78, 81, 94-98, 111, 130, 135, 137, 139, 152, 159
Christmas 78-82
Christmas tree 80
Church of England 108, 205
Church-State Separation 203-206
Claude, bishop of Turin 96
Clergy 107-109, 118, 121, 127, 131, 134, 149-153, 155-158
Clerics 149, 152-153, 158-159
Code x, 15-24, 26, 54,
Code, Bible 73-78, 100-101
Cohen, I.L. 196, 214
Communism 173
Computer 17-18, 76, 114
Confession of Faith 112
Constantine, Emperor 92-95, 130-131
Cornerstone Association 82-83
Council of Trent 156
Covenant 19, 23, 26, 44, 49-52, 94, 219
Cross 85, 89, 94-96, 102, 130

D

Daily Prayers. See Salat
Daling, Janet 189
Dan, Joseph 15, 25
Darwin 197, 199-200, 202, 214-115
Dasyd Ministry 93, 102
Day of Judgement 121, 134
Dead Sea 179-180
Denton, Michael 196-197, 214
Depression 184
Devices for living 41, 61
Devil 6-7, 20, 38-39, 51-52, 68, 87-88, 129, 136, 154, 156, 193, 203, 234 See also Satan
Diana, goddess 131
Discrimination 144, 147, 183
Distortion iv, vii-viii, 4, 5, 7, 10-11, 13, 19-21, 23
DNA 196-198
Doe vs. Bolton 187
Dogs 121-123, 134
Doubt v, x, 7, 10, 17, 20-21, 24
Dreyfus trial 34
Drosnin, Michael 75-76, 100
Drug abuse 40, 51, 193

E

Earth 9, 17-18, 233
Easter 83-88
Eastern Orthodox 65, 92
Egypt 34-35, 133
Einstein, Albert 46, 61, 194-195, 202, 213
Ephesus 121
Equidistant Letter Sequence (ELS) 76-77
Ethnicity 27, 183, 224
Exodus 34-36, 38

F
Fasting 112
Fat'was 109, 151
Final Testament 22
Food dish, liken to spiritual sustenance 5
Free Doom 166-167, 170, 204, 208,
Free will 7
Freedman, Benjamin 32, 60
Freedom 163, 166, 203, 204
Freud, Sigmund 45-54, 168, 185, 211
Fromm, Eric 53, 62, 204, 215

G
Gambling 177
Gemara 42, 61
Gender identity 183, 184, 212
Gospel of Barnabas 88, 102
Gospels 36
Graf, Max 45-46
Grosswirth, Raymond 155, 157
Guilds and societies 153
Guilt 44, 47, 51, 52, 54
Guru Nanak Dev 143-144

H
Hadith , 106, 109, 114-120, 121, 125
Hagar 29-30
Hajj 116
Halloween 85
Happiness 205-207
Heaven, See also Hereafter
Hebrew Bible 76
Hebrews 27-28, 31-32, 34-36, 42, 58, 70
Hereafter 136, 141, 143, 169, 172-173, 186, 218

Herzl, Theodore 34
Hexagram 57-58
Hicks, John 71, 100
Hijab 117
Hillicker, Carl 79, 84,
Hinduism 136, 139, 140, 144-145
Hislop, Alexander 16, 25,
Hitler 171
HIV 129, 186, 212
Holy Spirit 103, 104 154,
Homophobia, clarified 180 182,
Homosexuality 177-178,180-183, 185-186, 208. 212
Horney, Karen 53
Human Beings 104, 109, 152, 196, 203, 208,
Human evolution 197, 208

I
Idolatry 3, 6, 11, 23, 53, 80, 84, 136, 138, 144, 164, 165
Infidels 111,
Ingermanson, Randall 77,
Initials, Quranic 124, 231,
Intellectuals 162,194-195,
Intelligent Design 46, 200, 202,
Intoxicants 193, 208,
Irrelativity 46, 61
Isaac 28-30, 67, 132,
Ishmael 28-30
Islam iii-,ix, 11-14, 17, 19-21, 26-27, 31, 44, 55, 100-101, 103-104-114, 137, 139,144-145, 151,
Israel ,15, 28, 30-31, 33, 35-37,
Istanbul, Turkey 130, 131

J
Jacob 28, 30, 31, 67, 132, 222,
Jenkins, Mark 79, 80-82, 101,

Index

Jeremiah 67, 80,
Jesus 28, 33, 36-38, 54, 59, 65-74, 78-83, 85, 91-99

Jewish 27-34, 105, 114, 132
Jewish calendar 37
Jewish identity 32, 56
Jewish Muslim, See Jewish submitter
Jewish prayers 15
Jewish Submitters 58, 59
John Hopkins University 18
Joshua 85
Judah the Pious 15
Judaism iii, ix, 11, 13, 17, 27, 28, 63, 88, 92, 110-111, 130, 135
Judges 178, 213
Jung, Carl 53

K
Kabaah 116,
Kertzer, Morris 38, 43, 58, 61, 63
Khalifa, Rashad vi, 19-21, 25-26, 126, 128, 229, 232, 236-238
Khazars 33-34, 60
King George 205
Klein, Dennis B. 48, 62
Kushner, Harold 40, 61

L
Lanfranchi, Angelo 187
Lao Tse 14
Latif, Iqbal 109, 133
Law of irreligiosity 168, 170
Lent 84
Lewis, Bernard 108, 133
Lilienthal, Alfred 31, 33, 60
Luqman 165-166
Luther, Martin 66

M
Mahomett II 131
Maimonides 38
Malcolm X (Malik Shabazz) 107
Malec, Karen 190
Martin, William 32, 60
Mary 68, 70-72, 78, 90, 131
Massachusetts State Supreme Court 182
McCorvey, Norma 187, 213
Men's Dress 119
Menorah Ministries 37, 60
Mental health 46-47, 53
Messenger of the Covenant 22 see also Rashad Khalifa 218
Messiah 36-38, 42, 68, 70-72, 74, 90, 95
Meteorites 179-180, 2
Middle East 31, 33, 110, 115, 119, 179
Midrash 55
Ministers, lie about Trinity 88-89
Miracles 69, 72-74
Mishnah 42
Missing link 197, 201
Moon 85, 92, 114
Mosaic Law 51-52
Moses 22, 34-36, 38-39, 44, 53, 55, 59, 152-53
Muhammad 22, 28, 104, 112, 117, 120, 121, 125,-126, 132
Muslim 104-107, 110-119, 123-128
Muslim fundamentalists 20

N
Names, changed and distorted 34
Nathanson, Bernard 188, 213
National Abortion Rights Action League 188

National Association of Social Workers 181
National Cancer Institute 189, 191
National Prosperity 172, 208
National Security 161, 162, 209
Nazareth 65
New Testament 38, 41, 61, 75, 85, 93
New Tyrants 163, 166, 170
Nicene councils 156,
Niemela, Richard 33, 60
9/11 Commission Report 19
Norm troopers 4, 126-127, 162
Nucleotides 196

O
Obligatory Charity 15, 50, 70, 115
Old Testament 31-32, 36, 41, 75
Oppression 70, 127-173
Orthodox 66, 92
See also Catholic
Osman 131
Ottoman Empire 131

P
Paisley, Ian 156, 157
Paraclete 103, 104
Paul 48, 90, 94, 195
Pedophilia 157, 159
People of the Book 28
Periklutos 103
Pharoah 151, 169, 171
Pilgrimage 107, 116
Pledge of Allegiance 178
Pornography 186
Prejudice 29, 78, 181, 182, 183
Premarital Sex 177, 186, 208
Prevailing moral orthodoxy 167
Professional religionists 162. See also Clergy

Prohibition of marriage 156
Prohibitions, bogus 105
Prophet 22, 24, 27, 28, 30, 35-38, 43, 45, 49, 54-57
Psychiatry 168
Psychoanalytic Theory 45-47, 53
Psychological security 206
Psychology 168,, 206, 214

Q
Quran 68-74, 78-79, 83, 86, 87, 90-91, 93-94, 92, 104-132
Quran, tampering with 120-123

R
Rab 72
Rabbi Judah 15-7
Rabbis 33, 38, 42-43
Ramadan fast 114, 115
Rationalization of apostasy 49
Reader, John 197, 214
Reincarnation 140-141, 143
Religious Studies Departments 195
Responsa 55
Resurrection 35, 41, 81, 82, 86
Rig Vedas 140
Roe vs. Wade 187
Roman Empire 65-66, 92
Rugh, Andrea 118, 133
Russia 33-34, 60

S
Sabbath 92-94, 102
Sabbatianism 49
Sabbatians 52
Sacred travelers' manual xiii, 1-3, 6
Saheeh 120, 124-125
Saint Nicholas see Santa Claus
Salat 106, 113-114, 137

Index

Santa Claus 80-82
Satan xiv, 4-5, 6, 8, 10-11, 14, 22 23, 24, 38, 50, 51, 69, 73-74, 89, 90, 91, 111, 136, 139,176-177, 182
Satanic Hands 182, 191, 202, 208, 217,
Saturday 92-93
Scagnelli, Paul 195, 214
Scheinnerman, Rabbi 58
Schoen, Elenor 189, 213
Scientific inquiry 46, 194
Sects 3, 5, 11
Semiramis 80, 85
Semite 31-33,
Separation of church and state 177, 205
Sexuality Information and Education Council of the United States 181
Shahada 112
Shari'ah 111, 120,
Sheimer, Michael 77
Shiite 106
Shinto 136, 139, 141
Siddhartha Gautama 140
Sikhism 143, 144
Silicone chip 18
Sinai, Mount 38
Smith, Wolfgang 197, 214
Social contract 50-51
Social problems 161, 167, 207
Sodom and Gomorrah 178-180, 182, 2110
Solstice 79
Son of God 66, 68, 69, 72-74, 78-79, 87-89, 94, 96
Southall, Timothy & Kimberly 84
Spiritual Seeker 1-26
Spiritual yearning 10
Spring equinox 83-84

Star of David 57-58, 63, 130
Submission 4-5, 14, 23, 26, 28, 31, 35, 38, 50, 54, 58
Submitter Christians 73, 98
Submitter Jews 35, 94
Submitter Muslims 131
Sun worship 79
Sunday 92-93, 102
Sunderland, Luther D. 202, 215
Sunna 109, 120, 121, 125
Sunni 106
Superego 47, 50
Supreme Architect 219
Supreme Court 178, 182, 187-189

T

Tai Chi 143, 147
Talmage, Frank 15
Talmud 33-34, 42-42, 48, 58
Taoism 136, 139, 142
Templeton, Charles 97, 102
Terrorism 10
Theology 162
Theophobes 167-170, 204-205
Theory of Evolution 196, 202
Thief's hand, not severed 127
Tikkun olum 39
Torah 41-43, 47, 48, 59, 62. 74, 152
Torrey, E. Fuller 45, 46,48, 62
Trinity 65-66, 68-69, 71, 91-92
Twerski, Abraham 40, 61

U

Ulama, clergy in distorted Islam 108
United States 157, 181, 188, 190, 204-205,
Universe 7, 16
Veiling 114-115
Vicarious atonement 86-88

W

Wells, Jonathan 199
West, John G. Jr. 199
William of Paris 156
William, R 198
Winter equinox 79, 83

Y

Yajur 140
Yin and Yang 143
Yoke of the Law 50

Z

Zakat 15, 50, 70, 106, 115, 116, 171
Zevi, Sabbatai 52
Zoroastrian 83

www.ingramcontent.com/pod-product-compliance
Lightning Source LLC
Chambersburg PA
CBHW071959110526
44592CB00012B/1143